UKRAINIAN NATIONALISM IN THE POST-STALIN ERA

STUDIES IN CONTEMPORARY HISTORY

Volume 4

UKRAINIAN NATIONALISM IN THE POST-STALIN ERA

Myth, Symbols and Ideology
in Soviet Nationalities Policy

KENNETH C. FARMER
Marquette University, Milwaukee, Wisconsin

1980

MARTINUS NIJHOFF PUBLISHERS
THE HAGUE / BOSTON / LONDON

Distributors:

for the United States and Canada

Kluwer Boston, Inc.
160 Old Derby Street
Hingham, MA 024043
USA

for all other countries

Kluwer Academic Publishers Group
Distribution Center
P.O. Box 322
3300 AH Dordrecht
The Netherlands

Library of Congress Cataloging in Publication Data   CIP

Farmer, Kenneth C.

  Ukrainian Nationalism in the Post-Stalin Era.

  (Studies in Contemporary History = 4)
  Bibliography: p.
  Includes index.
  1. Ukraine—politics and government—1917-
  2. Nationalism—Ukraine. 3. Russia—ethnic relations.
  i. Title. ii. Series.
  DK508.8.F34   320.5'4'094771   80-36865

ISBN-13: 978-94-009-8909-2   e-ISBN-13: 978-94-009-8907-8
DOI: 10.1007/978-94-009-8907-8

Cover design: Martin Mol

GLENDOWER: I can call spirits from the vasty deep.

HOTSPUR: Why, so can I, or so can any man;
But will they come when you do call
for them?

Shakespeare
Henry IV

PREFACE

It is a truism that, with only a few notable exceptions,
Western scholars only belatedly turned their attention to
the phenomenon of minority nationalism in the USSR. In the
last two decades, however, the topic has increasingly
occupied the attention of specialists on the Soviet Union,
not only because its depths and implications have not yet
been adequately plumbed, but also because it is clearly a
potentially explosive problem for the Soviet system itself.

The problem that minority nationalism poses is perceived
rather differently at the "top" of Soviet society than at
the "bottom." The elite views - or at least rationalizes -
the problem through the lens of Marxism-Leninism, which
explains nationalist sentiment as a part of the "superstructure," a temporary phenomenon that will disappear in
the course of building communism. That it has not done so
is a primary source of concern for the Soviet leadership,
who do not seem to understand it and do not wish to accept
its reality. This is based on a fallacious conceptualization of ethnic nationalism as determined wholly by
external, or objective, factors and therefore subject to
corrective measures. In terms of origins, it is believed
to be the result of past oppression and discrimination; it
is thus seen as a negative attitudinal set the essence of
which lies in tangible, rather than psychological, factors.

Below the level of the leadership, however, ethnic
nationalism reflects entrenched identifications and meanings
which lend continuity and authenticity to human existence.
The nationality *problem* is experienced as discrimination
against national languages and cultures, and the domination
of cultural and political life by Russians Minority nation-

alism thus has both a psychological and a substantive base,
and regime policies (and their unintended side-effects)
reinforce it rather than hasten its demise.

The Ukraine - because of its size and certain historical
realities - is a barometer of minority nationalist discontent in the Soviet Union. The Soviet regime appears to be
particularly interested in specifically Ukrainian loyalty
to the Soviet idea. For this reason, the study of minority
nationalism and nationalities policy in the Soviet Union
must always begin with the study of Ukrainian nationalism.

This study has a two-fold purpose: to provide a history
of Ukrainian nationalism in the period 1957-1972 - from
Khrushchev's consolidation of power to the demise of Petro
Shelest - and simultaneously, to develop and employ a con-
ceptual framework useful for the study of a subject such as
nationalism which is fraught with subjectivities, and in the
context of a notoriously data-scarce society. This framework is symbolic politics, and the study of the manipulation
of the myths and symbols which inform ideological discourse.

In the transliteration of Russian and Ukrainian words
and proper names, I have employed a modified Library of Congress system, omitting diacritical marks. For the names of
individuals, I have employed Russian spellings for the names
of Russians, and Ukrainian spellings for Ukrainians. I have
departed from this convention for those names which through
usage have acquired a standard English spelling: Dzyuba,
Podgorny, Hrushevsky, etc. With the exception of the city
and *oblast* of Kiev and the *oblast* of Crimea, I have made it
a point to employ the Ukrainian spellings of Ukrainian
place-names, which seems only proper. Where the Ukrainian
spelling differs markedly from the Russian, the Russian
version appears in parentheses upon the first appearance of
the place-name in the text.

Any scholarly effort is in the final analysis a collective endeavor. While reserving responsibility entirely to
myself for its shortcomings, I am endebted to numerous
individuals and institutions for aid and advice in the

course of this study. Professor John A. Armstrong, who
guided the dissertation out of which this study grew, not
only provided the initial stimulus, but an abiding example
of scholarly integrity and straightforwardness. Professors
Murray Edelman, Ellen Seidensticker, Melvin Croan, and
Michael B. Petrovich, all of the University of Wisconsin,
Madison, and Professor Mary McAuley of the University of
Essex, were generous with their time and kind with their
moral support. Portions of this work were read at various
times by Dr. Walter Dushnyck, and Professors Yaroslav
Bilinsky, Stephan Horak, and John Kress; I am grateful to
them for their comments and criticisms without, to be sure,
implicating them in the final product.

The University of Wisconsin Graduate School provided
travel funds. I am also indebted to the Center for Slavic
and East European Studies at the Ohio State University for
taking time to help me locate materials. Finally, the
Research Department of Radio Liberty in Munich, West
Germany, was patient and generous during my stay there,
and provided access to materials without which this study
could not have been done.

I wish gratefully to acknowledge the contribution in
terms of their time and knowledge of the following indi-
viduals: John Basarab, Ilia Belau, Mariia Belau, Albert
Boiter, Keith Bush, Peter Dornan, Christian Duevel, Natalia
Gorbanevskaia, Mykola Hoffman, Olga Kannabykh, Suzanne
Kilner-Frank, Israel Kleyner, Ivan Koshelivets, Anatoly
Levitin-Krasnov, Borys Lewytzkyj, Viktor Nekrasov, Leonid
Plyushch, Rewenna Rebet, Fatima Salkazanova, and Tatiana
Zhytnykova-Plyushch.

Major portions of Chapter 4 of this book were published
as "Language and Linguistic Nationalism in the Ukraine," in
Nationalities Papers, Vol. VI, No. 2(Fall, 1978). Portions
of Chapter 5 were published in two installments as "Ukrainian Dissent: Symbolic Politics and Sociodemographic Aspects,"
in *The Ukrainian Quarterly*, Vol. XXXIV, Nos. 1 and 2(Spring
and Summer, 1978). I am grateful to the editors of these

journals for permission to use these materials here.

My wife, Jill, assisted me in many ways in all phases of the research and writing of this study; a stern critic, she has also been - and remains - an unfailing source of encouragement and support.

Milwaukee, May 1980

CONTENTS

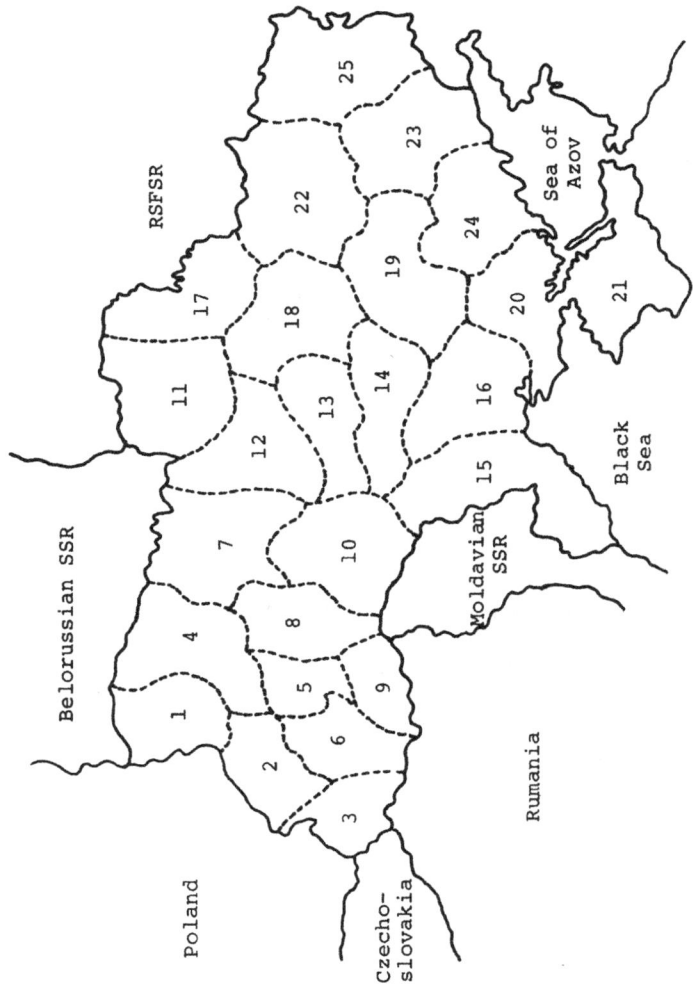

OBLASTS OF THE UKRAINIAN SSR

1. Volyn
2. L'viv
3. Zakarpattia
4. Rivne
5. Ternopil'
6. Ivano-Frankivs'k
7. Zhytomyr
8. Khmel'nyts'kyi
9. Chernivtsi
10. Vinnytsia
11. Chernihiv
12. Kiev
13. Cherkasy
14. Kirovohrad
15. Odesa
16. Mykolaiiv
17. Sumy
18. Poltava
19. Dnipropetrovs'k
20. Kherson
21. Crimea
22. Kharkiv
23. Donets'k
24. Zaporizhzhia
25. Voroshilovhrad

Poland

Belorussian SSR

RSFSR

Czecho-
slovakia

Rumania

Moldavian
SSR

Black
Sea

Sea of
Azov

I
INTRODUCTION: APPROACH AND CONCEPTUALIZATION

The Soviet Union, a multinational state consisting of 131
distinct ethnic and linguistic groups, claims that its
nationalities problem is "solved,"[1] and offers itself as a
model for multiethnic societies of the developing world.[2]
Yet the evidence is overwhelming that the CPSU leadership
has for the last decade and a half faced a national and
ethnic challenge of grave and growing proportions. The
increasingly visible resurgence of self-assertiveness on
the part of the USSR's non-Russian nationalities has its
modern roots in the rehabilitation of deported nationalities and the denunciation of Stalin's repression of minority nationalities following Khrushchev's Secret Speech at
the 20th Party Congress in February, 1956; in the real and
symbolic concessions to national sentiment made in bids for
support in the non-Russian republics by the contenders for
Stalin's succession; and in the general atmosphere of liberalization that accompanied Khrushchev's "thaw." But
while these and other less dramatic developments were
certainly triggering events, the factors underlying and
exacerbating this new ethnic nationalist challenge - the
emergence of what Teresa Rakowska-Harmstone has called a
"new type of nationalism" to distinguish it from the

[1]From the Theses of the CC CPSU for the 50th Anniversary of the
Revolution. Quoted in *Partinaia zhizn'*, No. 12(1977), p. 25.

[2]V. Shcherbitsky, "Mezhdunarodnoe znachenie natsional'nikh otnoshenii
v SSSR," *Kommunist*, No. 17(1974), pp. 14-25.

"traditional" nationalism of now extinct elites[3] - are themselves the products of policies of social transformation, which doctrine had held would create the conditions for a new, unified society.

It should be noted in proper perspective that in comparison with historical patterns of conflict within multinational states (e.g., the Hapsburg Empire, Czechoslovakia and Poland in the interwar period, Russia before 1917, etc.), the Soviet Union has on balance been reasonably successful in its handling of its nationality problem. According to Hans Kohn, this is because, unlike the examples mentioned and others, Lenin and subsequent Soviet leaders have not attempted to regard the Soviet Union as a "nation-state": "Soviet Communism," Kohn urges, "tried to preserve a political and economic unity above the various ethnic, religious or racial groups, a way later followed by Yugoslavia and India."[4]

Another commentator on the nationality problems of the Soviet Union sees their sources in conditions diametrically opposed to those supposed by Kohn. "The Soviet Union today," Richard Pipes asserts, "is in effect an empire run like a nationally homogeneous state, suffering all the consequences of that contradiction."[5]

Soviet "success" in managing a multinational state is reflected primarily in its having so far prevented a successful secessionary move, violent or otherwise, on the part of any of its constituent republics. This measure of the successful management of a multiethnic federation,

---

[3]Teresa Rakowska-Harmstone, "The Dialectics of Nationalism in the USSR," *Problems of Communism*, XXIII, No. 3(may-June, 1974), p. 2.

[4]Hans Kohn, "Soviet Communism and Nationalism: Three Stages of a Historical Development," in Edward Allworth, ed., *Soviet Nationality Problems* (New York: Columbia University Press, 1971), p. 42.

[5]Richard Pipes, "Introduction: The Nationality Problem," in Zev Katz, Rosemarie Rogers and Frederic Harned, eds., *Handbook of Major Soviet nationalities* (New York: The Free Press, 1975), p. 4.

however, should not prematurely be regarded as a "solution" because it sidesteps the question of whether the Soviet leadership will be able successfully to deal with the tensions that are at the root of the problem. Suppression of manifestations of the problem by force or administrative measures may or may not in the long run prove to have "solved" the problem.

In spite of repeated claims to have solved the problem, remarks by members of the Soviet elite confirm that it is nonetheless a matter of grave concern: the Soviet Press constantly attacks "remnants of nationalism," emphasizing the urgency of their eradication. A high-ranking member of the CPSU Politburo has identified ethnic conflict as a principal obstruction to the building of Communism in the USSR.[6] Calls "resolutely to oppose remnants of bourgeois nationalism" appear regularly in Republican and All-Union Central Committee theses and resolutions.[7] Brezhnev, in his address marking the 50th anniversary of Soviet federalism, noted the persistence of "national survivals" and, with a subtle but significant change in emphasis, attributed them not only to "nationalistic prejudices and exaggerated or distorted national feelings," but also to "objective problems that arise in a multinational state which seeks to establish the most correct balance between the interests of each nation...and the common interests of the Soviet people as a whole."[8]

[6]Mikhail Suslov, "Obshchestvennie nauki - boevoi otriad Partii v stroitel'stve kommunizma," *Kommunist*, No. 1(1972), pp. 18-30.

[7]Recent examples include "K 100-letiiu so dnia rozdeniia Vladimira Il'icha Lenina: Tezisy Tsentral'nogo Komiteta Kommunisticheskoi Partii Sovetskogo Soiuza," *Pravda*, December 23, 1969, pp. 1-4; and the Theses in Preparation for the 50th Anniversary of the USSR, *Partinaiia zhizn'*, No. 5(1972), p. 12.

[8]Leonid Brezhnev, "O 50-letii Soiuza Sovetskikh Sotsialisticheskikh Respublikh: doklad General'nogo Sekretara TsK KPSS Tovarishcha L.I. Brezhneva," *Kommunist*, No. 18(1972), p. 13.

UKRAINIAN NATIONALISM

In historical terms, Ukrainian nationalism developed late
in the modern age, in the middle 19th century at the
earliest with the poet Taras Shevchenko (1814-1861), and
later under the influence of intellectual leaders of the
movement - Mykola Kostomarov (1817-1885), Ivan Franko
(1856-1916), and the historian Mykhailo Hrushevsky (1866-
1934).

The mobilized strata of the Ukrainian population at the
beginning of the century had been for the most part
denationalized - Russified in culture, language and outlook. Nationality, at the time of the Revolution, coincided to a great degree with social class; the landowners
and rulers were Russians or Poles, and the middle class was
largely Jewish. For this reason, Ukrainian nationalism in
the 20th century developed as a rival to communism, the
latter being for the most part a city-based movement.[9]

In the confusion of the Revolution and Civil War,
Ukrainian nationalists managed to maintain a series of weak
Ukrainian governments. On January 22, 1918, the Ukrainian
Central *Rada* (Council, or *Soviet*) proclaimed the Ukraine
independent. The *Rada* soon clashed with the German
occupying forces over grain requisition, however, and was
ousted, to be replaced by a quasi-monarchical regime under
het'man Paul Skoropadsky. Skoropadsky was forced to
resign when the Germans withdrew, to be replaced by the
"Directory" - led by Simon Petlura and composed of former
members of the *Rada* - which established the Ukrainian
People's Republic (UNR).

The UNR lasted two years, but by 1920 the nationalist
government had been forced into exile in Poland, and the
Bolsheviks had effectively established Soviet rule in the
East Ukraine. In 1922, the Ukraine signed a treaty with

[9]John A. Armstrong, *Ukrainian Nationalism, 1939-1945* (New York:
Columbia University Press, 1955), p. 10.

Russia, Belorussia and Transcaucasia, forming the USSR.
From June, 1919, until World War II, Poland retained control of all of the West Ukraine.[10]

The culture and outlook of West Ukrainians differ from
those of East Ukrainians by virtue of the former's long
historical association with the West. In terms of
religion, the West Ukrainians are largely Uniates (recognizing the authority of Rome but observing the Byzantine-
Slavonic rite), while the East Ukrainians are, like the
Russians, Orthodox. Spared the Russification the East
Ukrainians endured under the Russian Empire, the West
Ukrainians have retained a stronger sense of ethnic self-
identity. The third wave of Ukrainian nationalist activity
was represented by the Organization of Ukrainian Nationalists (OUN), founded in 1929 in the West Ukraine to struggle against Polish rule.

The OUN adhered to an integral nationalist ideology,
strongly influenced by rising Central European fascism.
This ideology deified the nation to the point of racism,
stressed the primacy of "will" over reason, and adhered
to the *Fuhrerprinzip*.[11] The goal of the OUN was an independent Ukraine in Hitler's new territorial reorganization
of Europe.

In 1939-40, the OUN split into two factions: a moderate
faction led by Andrew Mel'nyk and a militant faction under
Stepan Bandera. The OUN became active in the East Ukraine
after the Nazi invasion of June, 1941. OUN hopes for

---

[10]The West Ukraine comprises seven *oblasts* annexed by the Soviet Union
between 1939 and 1949. Five of these - L'viv (L'vov), Ternopil'
(Ternopol), Ivano-Frankivs'k (Ivano-Frankovsk), Zakarpatia, and
Chernivtsi (Chernovtsy) - had never been under Russian rule before
1939. The remaining two - Rovno and Volyn - had been Russian in the
period 1793-1918. Chernivtsi (formerly Northern Bukovina) belonged
to Rumania until World War II. Zakarpatia (Ruthenia) was under Hungarian control until World War I, then belonged to Czechoslovakia. The
remaining areas, making up Eastern Galicia, were under Austrian or
Polish rule for centuries.

[11]Armstrong, *op. cit.*, pp. 37-39.

German aid in establishing an independent Ukraine did not
bear fruit, however; the Nazis intended to subdue the
Ukraine, not turn it into an independent state, even on the
model of the *Ustashi* sattelite-state of Croatia. The OUN,
now in conflict both with the Nazis and the Soviets,
created a military arm, the Ukrainian Insurrectionary Army
(UPA), which engaged in armed struggle with the Germans,
and then with the Soviets until finally routed in the early
1950s.[12]

It is with the fourth wave of Ukrainian nationalist opposition that we are concerned. With the exception of a
handful of small clandestine groups, the nationalist dissent movement in the Ukraine in the 1960s and early 1970s
was an *ad hoc*, largely unorganized protest on the part of
intellectuals against the Russification of Ukrainian
language and culture. These protests were openly expressed
by young intellectuals wholly educated under Soviet rule,
many of them Marxist-Leninists and integrated into the
system.

Unlike the earlier waves of Ukrainian nationalism,
Ukrainian nationalist protest in this period has not been
characterized by separatism and anti-communism, although
these have been present from time to time. Also in contrast to earlier waves, terrorism and armed insurrection
have not been dominant tactics; the Ukrainian nationalist
intelligentsia has attempted to exhaust all legal forums
and channels of protest, before resorting to civil disobedience and *samvydav* (in Russian, *samizdat*: clandestinely
reproduced and circulated manuscripts).

Finally, the ideology of Ukrainian nationalism espoused
by the nationalist intelligentsia during this period
differs from that of earlier waves in being less virulent,
less exclusivist. The principal demands have been for the
recognition of national diversity for its own sake, for the

---

[12]The origins of the UPA are complicated; as a major force, however, it
unquestionably arose from the Bandera faction of the OUN.

right to national expression, and for the preservation of
the Ukrainian language and culture - especially against
Russification - as the unique Ukrainian national moral
patrimony.

   Scholars vary in their interpretations of the origins
and significance of modern Ukrainian nationalism. Our
preferred interpretation is that it represents a reactive
cultural revival and the reassertion of national identity
and communalism on the part of representative groups that
are convinced that group values and identity are threatened
with engulfment by those of another group - in particular,
a group whose disproportionate influence, privilege, and
even presence, are perceived as illegitimate. The
reactive nature of modern Ukrainian nationalism is the
nexus between the revival of nationalism in multiethnic
communist societies and the more familiar nationalism of
the Third World.

WESTERN SCHOLARLY WRITING ON THE SOVIET
NATIONALITY PROBLEM AND THE UKRAINE

Most Western scholars concerned with the nationality question in the Soviet Union agree that since the period immediately following World War II, when Baltic and Ukrainian
nationalist groups fought openly against the imposition of
Soviet control, the issue has been less one of the territorial extent and form of Soviet government, than of
specific regime *policies* in the cultural sphere and in
the selection, promotion and distribution of elites.
Loyalty to the Soviet system, as distinct from loyalty to
its Russian leaders, seems not to be the issue, and most
national elites probably believe that greater autonomy and
freedom are incompatible, not with the system, but rather
with Russian hegemony within the system.[13]

[13]Brian Silver,"Ethnic Identity Change among Soviet Nationalities: A
Statistical Analysis," PhD Thesis, Department of Political Science,
University of Wisconsin-Madison, 1972, pp. 2-3.

Ethnic nationalism, however, is a worldwide phenomenon, and diffusion may account in part for its upsurge in the USSR. Vernon Aspaturian has advanced the proposition that in modern times, meaning since World War II, feedback back into the Soviet Union of the revival of nationalism that has resulted from decolonization and the national liberation movement (itself at least formally sponsored by the Soviet government and Party) poses a serious threat to Soviet unity. Eastern European communist states enjoy at least formal sovereignty, and the USSR espouses national independence for Third World states. If Czechoslovakia and Cuba can be communist and independent, republican elites might well ask, why not the Ukraine and Georgia?[14]

Another scholar who has stressed the diffusion of ideas as a shaper of Ukrainian national sentiment has been Ivan L. Rudnytsky. Rudnytsky emphasizes historical factors, particularly the Ukraine's association with Poland and the West, in explaining national differences between the Ukrainians and the Russians.[15] In a more recent article, Rudnytsky again argues that contemporary Ukrainian national identity depends upon historical tradition; he urges that the annexation of the West Ukraine, whose cultural and religious ties have been with the West (primarily Poland), helped to bring about a "psychological mutation" of the East Ukrainians, and that the nationalist ferment of the 1960s in the Ukraine cannot be adequately explained without taking this factor into account.[16] While "psychological mutation" may be too strong a term, there can be little doubt that East Ukrainians have been strongly

---

[14]Vernon V. Aspaturian, "Nationality Inputs in Soviet Foreign Policy: The USSR as an Arrested Universal State," in Aspaturian, ed., *Process and Power in Soviet Foreign Policy* (Boston: Little, Brown and Co., 1971), pp. 449-50.

[15]Ivan L. Rudnytsky, "The Role of the Ukraine in Modern History," *Slavic Review*, XXII, No. 2(June, 1963), pp. 199-216.

[16]Ivan L. Rudnytsky, "The Soviet Ukraine in Historical Perspective," *Canadian Slavonic Papers*, XIV, No. 2(Summer, 1972), pp. 235-50.

affected by West Ukrainian attitudes.[17]

The impact of the diffusion of ideas from abroad on Soviet internal developments has received very little attention in the literature on Soviet nationalities problems, and in the literature on Soviet domestic politics in general; a notable exception is the study of Ukrainian involvement in the 1968 Czechoslovak crisis by Gray Hodnett and Peter Potichnyj.[18] Because of the diffusion of ideas across national borders, it cannot be argued with certainty that ethnic problems or manifestations of nationalism occur as a result of social evolution, or are characteristic of particular stages of social evolution. While there are established regularities, to be sure, national and ethnic tensions occur in multiethnic societies at nearly all stages of development, suggesting that nationalist self-assertion may be characteristic of an age, rather than of a stage in social evolution. Diffusion, therefore, must be considered an important potential causal factor in explaining the resurgence of nationalism in the Soviet Union, along with the factors of modernization and social mobilization that will be considered below.

Ithiel de Sola Pool has noted that communications theory explains developments in Soviet society primarily by such diffusion of ideas from abroad. Rather than arguing that similar stages in the evolution of industrial societies lead to similar developments or, what is much the same thing, arguing for convergence, communications theorists tend to see the Soviet Union as an "imitative society." During the Stalin era, the regime took drastic measures to hinder or curtail such diffusion. However, the explosion

---

[17]For a discussion of this, see Yaroslav Bilinsky, "The Incorporation of Western Ukraine and its Impact on Politics and Society in Soviet Ukraine," in Roman Szporluk, ed., *The Influence of East Europe and the Soviet West on the USSR* (New York: Praeger, 1976).

[18]Gray Hodnett and Peter J. Potichnyj, *The Ukraine and the Czechoslovak Crisis* (Canberra: Australian National University, 1970).

of communications in the past twenty years, Pool argues, has rendered the Soviet frontiers so permeable that no major international trend fails to reach the Soviet Union and become an issue there too.[19] International radio has been an important vehicle of diffusion of Western ideas directly into the USSR in the post-war era. The most important factors, however, have probably been cultural exchange, printed media, face-to-face contact - particularly expanded contacts with Eastern Europeans - and general liberalization, rather than changes in the nature of communications itself.

Western scholars concerned with the nature and causes of national discontent in the Ukraine vary as well in their assessment of its essential features and future development. Yaroslav Bilinsky wrote in 1964 that the Ukraine had "matured" in the 1960s "into a sociologically balanced nation," possessing all the requisites of nationhood, and capable of self rule despite Russian policies aimed at short-circuiting Ukrainian cultural and political autonomy.[20] Bilinsky speculates that in the short run, the highest Ukrainian elites will prove themselves loyal to the Soviet regime in order to protect their political careers, but he suspects that in the *long* run, "the rise of native cadres to responsible positions in Moscow and within the Republic itself will strengthen a form of Ukrainian Titoism."[21] Bilinsky sees the long-run resolution of the problem as contingent on the overall stability of the regime: the Ukrainians will find a *modus vivendi* with the regime if the humiliating excesses of the Stalin era are

[19]Ithiel de Sola Pool, "Communication in Totalitarian Societies," in Pool *et. al.*, eds., *Handbook of Communications* (Chicago: Rand McNally College Press, 1973), pp. 462-511.

[20]Yaroslav Bilinsky, *The Second Soviet Republic: The Ukraine after World War II* (New Brunswick, N.J: Rutgers University Press, 1964), P. 83

[21]*Ibid.*, pp. 306-7.

not repeated and the regime remains stable. Should the
system disintegrate from the center, however, local Ukrainian elites will attend to the interests of Kiev rather than
to those of Moscow.[22]

John A. Armstrong classifies the Ukrainians as "younger
brothers" of the Russians, low in social mobilization, and
relatively close to the Russians ethnically, culturally,
and linguistically. Armstrong considers the Ukrainians,
along with the Belorussians, to be scheduled by the Soviet
regime for immediate, complete Russification.[23] Armstrong
takes the view that the principal group nurturing a separate Ukrainian identity is the peasantry, and the success
of the regime in assimilating them to Russian identity will
depend on the implementation of policies aimed at improving
their social and economic position in the society.[24]

We subscribe completely to Professor Armstrong's interpretation. While it is true, however, that traditional
Ukrainian identity and linguistic attachment resides in the
peasantry, some scholars make a distinction between "traditional" and modern nationalism. The "old, romantic,
peasant style and anti-Semitic nationalism of the Ukraine
of the past," writes Tibor Szamuely, "has been replaced by
the modern, ideological nationalism of an industrialized,
urbanized and literate society."[25] Similarly, Teresa
Rakowska-Harmstone notes that while rural elements display

---

[22]*Ibid.*, p. 310. More recently, Bilinsky is more pessimistic about the
possibility of the emergence of "consociational oligarchy" in the USSR.
See "Politics, Purge and Dissent in the Ukraine since the Fall of
Shelest," in Ihor Kamenetsky, ed., *Nationalism and Human Rights:
Processes of Modernization in the USSR* (Littleton, Colo: Libraries
Unlimited, Inc., 1977), p. 178.

[23]John A. Armstrong, "The Ethnic Scene in the Soviet Union: The View of
the Dictatorship," in Erich Goldhagen, ed., *Ethnic Minorities in the
Soviet Union* (New York: Praeger, 1968), pp. 14-21.

[24]*Ibid.*, pp. 14-15, 18, 32.

[25]Tibor Szamuely, "The Resurgence of Ukrainian Nationalism," *The
Reporter*, May 30, 1968, pp. 16-17.

more "nationalist prejudices" than do city dwellers, the
new "modern" nationalism is a characteristic of the urban
intelligentsia and professional people. This "new nationalism," Rakowska-Harmstone argues,

> results from a dual process involving (1)
> a change in content as a result of super-
> imposition of new conflicts on top of old
> differences, and (2) a shift in the main
> locus of nationalistic impulses, to the
> new national elites.[26]

It will be useful at this point to reconcile concept-
ually these two apparently opposing viewpoints on the
social base of Ukrainian nationalism. We take the view
here that the nationalist *challenge* to the Soviet regime
in the period under study is a distinctly urban phenomenon, but that it is based, as Armstrong has noted, on a
peasant reservoir of national distinctiveness. Some important distinctions must be made to clarify this.

It is true, to begin with, that the core Ukrainian culture that is idealized and defended by the urban intelligentsia consists, in addition to the language, of essentially rural values and traditions. This is so because in
recent times - since the early 19th century - there has
been no distinctly Ukrainian urban culture. The Ukraine
was colonized, industrialized and modernized by Russians,
and social mobilization and urbanization has *meant* Russification for those Ukrainians who have become mobilized; it
was to counter this virtually atuomatic side-effect of
modernization that campaigns of "Ukrainization" were undertaken in the 1920s and 1930s, before halted by Stalin. The
"nationalist" resistance of the countryside to Russification and assimilation is best characterized as the same
resistance of traditional societies to modernization and

---

[26]Rakowska-Harmstone, *op. cit.*, p. 11. Also see Armstrong's similar
comments on an article by Arutunian in "Societal Manipulation in a
Multiethnic Polity," *World Politics*, XXVIII, No. 3(April, 1976),
pp. 440-49. Armstrong has always argued that the urban intelligentsia
in the Ukraine in all periods has been the articulate force.

the encroachment of the "hostile and alien" city on the
peasant "little tradition" that has been observed around
the world. Rural Ukrainian peasants are "Ukrainian" without having to assert it; presumably they do not question
it or think much about it, and pressures to Russify are
minimal in areas where there are comparatively few Russians, literacy is low, and access to mass media is limited. An "assertion" of Ukrainian identity implies some
pressure to deprive individuals of that identity, or the
presence of marked contrasts. It is in the cities, among
mobilized Ukrainians, that these pressures and contrasts
are most marked.

Mobilized Ukrainians who seek a return to a sense of
Ukrainian identity for whatever reason (reasons may include
resentment of Russian privilege or of regional economic
disadvantage, or reasons growing out of a romantic predi-
lection) can only turn to the rural tradition to find a
uniquely *Ukrainian* heritage to assert vis-a-vis Russian
culture and language. It is only in this sense, we maintain, that modern Ukrainian national assertiveness has
rural roots. The assertiveness is a product of social
mobilization, with its attendant exposure to Russians, to
the diffusion of ideas from other parts of the world, and
to a sense of "dual" identity or "identity lost" resulting
from consciousness of assimilation. Not to make an analytical distinction between the rural sources of the national
tradition and the urban sources of nationalist discontent,
is to lump together under the same rubric (i.e., Ukrainian
nationalism) two phenomena that grow out of different
causes, and may have different consequences.

The nexus between rural traditions and the resurgence of
nationalism may also be misleading when it is noted that
many of the Ukrainian nationalist dissenters, though urbanized, have come from rural families. It is possible,
though probably not demonstrable in the Soviet case, that
first generation mobilized individuals are more likely to
exhibit nationalist sentiments because of their dual

14

socialization. Research among immigrants in America and elsewhere, however, tends to substantiate the thesis that first generation immigrants (and by close analogy, the reasoning goes here, newly mobilized Ukrainians) embrace the new culture and suppress the old when this is the path of upward mobility and advantage. The underlying assumption is that it is the immediate life situation of the individual, rather than his demographic background, that is most relevant in explaining his attitudes and behavior. Thus, in this conceptualization, mobilization and urbanization are the necessary, but not as yet sufficient, conditions for ethnic national assertiveness in the Soviet Union.

In a statistical analysis of ethnic identity change among minority nationalities in the Soviet Union, Brian Silver has attempted to assess the effects of social and geographical mobility, exposure to Russians, and religion on the Russification of minority nationalities. Silver employs attachment to the group name and language as operational measures of ethnic loyalty. Silver's overall conclusion is that Sovietization has hardly affected the maintenance of nationality differences in the basic ethnic mix of the USSR "from a crude demographic standpoint."[27] Among those factors that militate in favor of Russification, Silver finds, are urbanization, residence outside the official national territory, and the presence of Russians in the urban population of the national territory. Silver attributes the low level of Russification of ruralities to the high ethnic homogeneity in rural areas, low rural levels of education, and the more consistent provision of native-language schools in these areas.[28] Differential rates of social mobilization and change in levels of communal mobilization, Silver concludes, tend to foster

[27]Silver, *op. cit.*, p. 8.

[28]*Ibid.*, pp. 87-90.

awareness of "relative deprivation" among less advantaged groups in the Soviet Union, and therefore contribute to ethnic conflict.[29] In addition and significantly, Party *policies* - the delineation of national boundaries on an ethnic and linguistic basis, the development of national literary languages, and the use of ethnic labels in official documents such as passports - foster the maintenance of ethnic identity.[30]

By focussing on the individual's reporting of his native language and ethnic identity (in the All-Union census of 1959), Silver is purposely restricting his focus to a narrow range of values or symbols that are by definition ethnic or national. These indicators are both operational and sufficient for his purposes. He deliberately avoids treating ethnic identity in the sense of "collective identity" as used by Lucian Pye,[31] or as a collective self-identification in the sense that Daniel Glazer writes of ethnic identity.[32] Silver is aware of the limitations of his indicators, and cautions against the assumption that urbanization and social mobilization lead on from simple linguistic identification to actual loss of ethnic identity.[33] This loss of ethnic identity has not occurred in the United States, where the "melting pot" ideal has a longer history than in the Soviet Union, and where such structural factors as autonomous governments and official recognition of minority languages are absent. Research on

---

[29]*Ibid.*, p. 5.

[30]*Ibid.*, pp. 9-10.

[31]Lucian W. Pye, "Identity and the Political Culture," in Leonard Binder *et. al.*, eds., *Crises and Sequences in Political Development* (Princeton: Princeton University Press, 1971), pp. 101-34.

[32]Daniel Glazer, "Dynamics of Ethnic Identification," *American Sociological Review*, XXIII, No. 1(February, 1958), p. 32.

[33]Silver, *op. cit.*, pp. 8-9.

the persistence of ethnic identity in the United States
indicates that ethnic identities may persist long after
most distinct cultural patterns, including language, have
disappeared. Erich Rosenthal has made a distinction between "cultural" and "structural" assimilation: culturally
assimilated groups are those that are almost completely
acculturated, but continue to prefer contacts with members
of their own groups; "structural" assimilation would require entrance into primary group relations with members of
the host or core culture.[34]

Karl Deutsch has cited six balances important in determ-
ining the rate of assimilation: the similarity of communication habits; the teaching-learning balance; the balance of material rewards and punishments; the balance of
values and desires; and the balance of symbols and barriers.[35] The rate of assimilation, for Deutsch, must be
faster than the rate of mobilization of an ethnic group if
that ethnic group is to become part of a homogeneous
nation-state. A favorable balance must be achieved in the
direction of assimilation. Deutsch's model, based on his
theory of modernization,[36] can be used to explain the
growth of nations in many cases, but it has little to say
about areas where the maintenance of distinct ethnic identity vis-a-vis state-national identity is at stake. An

---

[34]Erich Rosenthal, "Acculturation without Assimilation: The Jewish
Community of Chicago, Illinois," *American Journal of Sociology*,
LXVI, No. 4(November, 1960). On ethnic identity maintenance in the
United States, also see Nathan Glazer and Daniel P. Moynihan, *Beyond
the Melting Pot: The Negroes, Puerto Ricans, Jews, Italians and Irish
of New York City*, 2nd ed. (Cambridge: M.I.T. Press, 1970); Michael
Parenti, "Ethnic Politics and the Persistence of Ethnic Identity,"
American Political Science Review, LXI (September, 1967), pp. 717-26;
Vladimir C. Nahirny and Joshua A. Fishman, "American Immigrant Groups:
Ethnic Identification and the Problem of Generations," *The Socio-
logical Review*, XIII (November, 1965), PP. 311-26.

[35]Karl W. Deutsch, *Nationalism and Social Communication* (cambridge:
M.I.T. Press, 1966), pp. 156-62.

[36]Karl W. Deutsch, "Social Mobilization and Political Development,"
American Political Science Review, LV, No. 3(1961), pp. 493-514.

explanation of this omission may be that the psychological
and perceptual aspects of ethnic identity have not been
adequately taken into account.

The Western scholarly studies reviewed here in fact
point implicitly to the thesis that the essential nature of
ethnic identification is of necessity psychological. As
Milton Gordon, who treats ethnicity in the conventional
manner as consisting of race, language, religion and national origin, points out, the link between all these components - the common aspect of ethnicity - is a shared
sense of "peoplehood" that ethnic and national groups en-
gender for their members: ethnicity in the final analysis
is a "subjective sense of belonging to a particular
group."[37] Ethnic and national groups distinguish themselves from other groups through a shared belief in a claim
to having common ancestral roots in a distinctive society
which is, or was at one time, sovereign and self-sustain-
ing.

Even more emphatic in elaborating the psychological
basis of ethnic identification is Walker Connor, who defines a nation as a "self-differentiating ethnic group":

> The essence of the nation is not tangible.
> It is psychological, a matter of attitude
> rather than of fact.... Because the essence
> of the nation is a matter of attitude, the
> tangible manifestations of cultural dis-
> tinctiveness are significant only to the de-
> gree that they contribute to the *sense* of
> uniqueness.[38]

It is our thesis that to achieve a proper understanding
of the sources, nature and possible consequences of the
conflict between universalism and ethnic particularism, and

[37]Milton Gordon, *Assimilation in American Life: The Role of Race,
Religion and National Origins* (New York: Oxford University Press,
1964), pp. 23-30.

[38]Walker Connor, "Nation-Building or Nation-Destroying?" *World
Politics*, XXIV, No. 3(April, 1972), p. 337.

18

of the inter-relationships between jurisdictional and
ethnic particularism, in the Soviet Union and in communist
societies in general, the psychological aspect must be
grappled with. We propose to approach this through a study
of the *content* of the various myths and ideologies of
national identity, and through a study of the *utility* of
these myths and ideologies for their adherents. If the
story of the relationship between communism and ethnic
nationalism is, as Andrew C. Janos has suggested, one of
strain, conflict and adaptation,[39] this relationship
should be studied in both its subjective and objective
aspects, its attitudinal as well as behavioral consequences explored, and the utility, both psychological and
pragmatic, of the substantive premises of both universalist
and particularist myths for the groups and individuals
involved, carefully examined. To undertake this task,
Janos suggests, will require methods of investigation that

> would include a careful analysis of sym-
> bolic systems with respect to esoteric
> and exoteric forms of communication, the
> examination of elaborate signalling de-
> vices (such as political trials and the
> messages they convey to both the elite and
> the masses), and the calculation of costs
> involved in a particular policy to separate
> symbolic and "real" responses to the chal-
> lenges of the environment.[40]

[39]Andrew C. Janos, "Ethnicity, Communism and Political Change in
Eastern Europe," *World Politics*, XXIII, No. 3(1973), pp. 493-521.

[40]*Ibid.*, p. 520. Edward Allworth makes a similar appeal: "There is
value in subordinating our perhaps too quantified representation of
this fascinating question to a greater concern with genuine human factors, if the approach is to realize its greatest potential. Giving
attention to expressions of behavior, not always on a mass scale, will
deepen and humanize the question, and will move the scholar much further toward discovering the residence of nationality itself (not
always as romantic abstraction but as living energy)." Allworth,
"Restating the Soviet Nationalities Question," in Allworth, ed.,
Soviet Nationality Problems (New York: Columbia University Press,
1971), p. 12. Allworth is arguing, and we subscribe to the argument,
that qualitative approaches should *supplement*, not replace, more
rigorous quantitative treatments.

In the spirit of Janos's suggestions, the purpose of
this study is to examine Ukrainian nationalism in the period
1957-1972 from the standpoint of the unintended effects as
well as deliberate manipulation of myths and symbols of the
nation and of internationalism. We are in fact pursuing a
dual purpose: a substantive one of examining the phenomenon
of modern Ukrainian nationalism, and a theoretical one of
contributing to our knowledge of the role of myths and symbols in political conflict - in particular, in the context
of a society in which political communications are severely
restricted.

We seek insight into the following broad questions:

1. What is the substantive content of the competing myths
and meaning-sets associated with nationalism and proletarian internationalism in the Ukrainian and Soviet context?

2. How have the proponents of each myth attempted to inject elements of the respective myths into the official
ideology so as to legitimate policies favorable to their
interests, and how successful have these efforts been?

3. How have symbols of the national and proletarian
internationalist myths been employed in Soviet cultural
and linguistic policy to legitimate the expansion or contraction of the expression of national identity?

4. How have Ukrainian nationalist dissenters employed
symbolic action to circumvent closed communication channels
and the proscription of the articulation of nationalist demands in the Soviet Union, and what symbolic devices has
the regime at its disposal to discredit the demands of the
dissenters?

5. What are the political uses of the mythology and symbolism of nationalism and internationalism in the struggle
for political power and mobility of elites, and can conflict
with its sources in nationalism *per se* be separated from
conflict arising out of federalism and regionalism, and the
natural desire of republican elites to further their regions' interests, and to protect their decisional autonomy

from the center, apart from ethnic, cultural and linguistic
assertiveness?

A better approach to the study of the national attitudes
and orientations of a culture may perhaps be survey research, but this is impossible in the Soviet Union.[41] The
study of myths and symbols of nationalism and internationalism can unfortunately tell us little about the extent to
which such orientations are prevalent in the population.
Our purpose is rather to examine with this approach the
types of attitudes that do exist, the mechanisms through
which they are expressed, and the secondary uses to which
symbols - which are the overt expressions of such attitudes - are put.

Taking the long historical view, the Soviet nationality
problem can fruitfully be regarded as part of the still un-
resolved dialectical conflict between the two great ideas
of the 19th century: nationalism and socialism. Despite
the assurance of Soviet spokesmen that the problem has been
"solved," we have noted, it has not been; nor is the smug
assurance of many in the West that the Soviet experiment is
doomed to failure any the less premature.

It is the theme of this study that both nationalism and
communist universalism are mythic structures that, in the
Soviet context at least, undergo constant evolution and
adaptation to one another and to the exigencies of everyday
politics. Although they are conflicting myths, it is wrong
to conceive of their interaction as a Manichaean struggle
between two monolithic and inelastic conceptions of the
world, or that a workable *modus vivendi* is not possible.

Western social scientists have long recognized that the
CPSU is itself not monolithic, and that there is conflict
and sometimes overt "legitimate opposition" over matters

---

[41]Although secondary analysis of the slowly growing body of Soviet
"concrete" sociological studies may potentially serve as a surrogate
for survey research in the USSR. See John A. Armstrong, "New Prospects
for Analyzing the Evolution of Ukrainian Society," *The Ukrainian
Quarterly*, XXIX, No. 1(Spring, 1973), pp. 357 ff.

of policy,[42] although the general pattern is that such conflict is muted, not public, and concealed behind an elaborate facade of unanimity. When conflict spills into the
public media, yet is recognized - or intended to be recognized - only by the parties involved, it is veiled and
Aesopian, the type of discourse Gabriel Almond has called
"esoteric language."[43] For the Communist Party openly or
implicitly to admit the existence of factions by permitting
the open debate of policy or doctrine would both violate
the sacrosanct rule of "democratic centralism" and cast
doubt upon the myth that the Party is and always has been
the sole source of wisdom, firmly in control of historical
events. For these reasons, the leadership has always been
loath to admit that the society could be divided against
itself. At the same time, however, it is essential that
impending changes in doctrine or policy, as well as personal stances in policy disputes, be communicated to sub-
elites, due, in Myron Rush's words, to

> ... the need of sub-elites to know the
> distribution of power within the elite
> circle and the corresponding need of an-
> tagonists among the top leaders to secure
> support from these lower political echelons.[44]

Western students of Soviet politics have long relied on
exegesis of "esoteric" and "veiled" discourse to detect impending policy or personnel changes, searching communications for clues that may reside in the "subtext": insin-
uation, textual nuance, shadings of emphasis, and modifica-
tions of standard terminology and formulas. This is a

---

[42]See, e.g., H. Gordon Skilling and Franklyn Griffiths, *Interest Groups in Soviet Politics* (Princeton: Princeton University Press, 1971).

[43]Gabriel A. Almond, *The Appeals of Communism* (Princeton: Princeton University Press, 1954), pp. 66-79.

[44]Myron Rush, *The Rise of Khrushchev* (Washington, D.C: Public Affairs Press, 1956), pp. 88-89. Deciphering esoteric communications, it goes without saying, is an essential skill for the *Soviet* politician or bureaucrat as well.

variant of the method highly developed by the Paris School
of Diplomatics, the Ecole des Chartes, called *explication
de texte*, to study medieval and classical texts containing
specific policy disputes disguised as theological debates.[45]

Conflict, open and veiled, takes place not only over the
implementation of immediate policies and minor nuances of
doctrine, but over the fundamental mythological themes that
underlie the formal ideology and form the foundation of the
regime's legitimacy. Such a conflict over mythological
premises informs Soviet discussion and treatment of the
nationality question since the 20th Party Congress; its
dimensions are a dramatic illustration of what Ernst Cassirer has termed "the power of mythical thought."[46]

Our task requires an analytical framework for the study
of meaning and the transmission of meaning under the
censorship conditions of an authoritarian society. The
purpose of our analytical framework is not to construct a
formal model of communications in the Soviet Union, but
rather to provide a theoretical framework that is intern-
ally consistent, useful, and grounded in accepted scholarship. While we contribute some new definitions and dynamic
propositions, we have for the most part relied on existing
scholarship in the fields of communications theory and symbolic interaction theory. The remainder of this chapter
comprises a formal explication of this framework.

---

[45]William E. Griffith, "Communist Esoteric Communication: Explication
de Texte," in *Handbook of Communications*, pp. 512-20. Other treatments
of methods of analyzing Soviet esoteric communications include Sidney
I. Ploss, *Conflict and Decision-Making in Soviet Russia: A Case Study
of Agricultural Policy, 1953-1963* (Princeton: Princeton University
Press, 1965); Robert Conquest, *Power and Policy in the USSR* (New York:
Harper and Row, 1961, 1967), esp. Chapter 3, "Questions of Evidence;"
Franz Borkenau, "Getting at the Facts Behind the Soviet Facade,"
Commentary, No. 17(April, 1954), pp. 393-400, and others.

[46]Ernst Cassirer, *The Myth of the State* (New Haven: Yale University
Press, 1968), p. 8.

AN ANALYTICAL FRAMEWORK

Communications and Communications Systems

Communications theorists distinguish between "information" and redundancy. Information, in this technical sense, in- heres in a communication between sender and receiver to the extent that something not possessed in common is transmit- ted. Information is novel, surprising; the remainder is re- dundant. What the sender and receiver possess in common is redundant, then, and consitutes a structure of *meaning*. Information is that which is not known or expected, and when transmitted and received, it alters meaning. Redun- dancy in communications serves the positive functions of a) insuring accurate reception, and b) reinforcing meaning.

In an ideal-type, open communications system, there would be no redundancy, because there would be no "noise" and no cognitive, sociological or governmental barriers to communication. Everything communicated would be informa- tion, and everything transmitted would be received. Such an ideal-type communications system, of course, does not exist. There are three reasons for this. The first is the unavoidable presence of "noise" - the presence in all com- munications channels of "signals" unrelated to the message, or the presence of other messages. The second reason is the cognitive limits of the human mind in separating in- coming messages, absorbing new information, and fitting it in a logical and orderly manner into meaning structures. The third, and for our purposes the most important, reason is the *functionality for various groups in the society of distorting communications*.

Claus Mueller has noted three types of distorted com- munications systems, his classification based at once on the severity and the sources of the distortion:

    1. Arrested communications: this refers to the restricted

capacity of some groups and individuals to engage in political communications because of limited communications
skills.

2. Constrained communications: this results from successful attempts by private and governmental groups to
structure and limit communications so that their interests
will prevail.

3. Directed communications: this refers to conscious
government policy to structure language and communications.[47]

We are characterizing the Soviet Union as a "directed
communications system." *The effect of Soviet directed
communications is to maximize redundancy.* "Revisionism"
and ideological unorthodoxy, influences from the West,
artistic innovation, the opening of unofficial channels of
communications (*samizdat*), and dissent in general, all constitute the introduction into the communications system of
something "novel," of information. The regime reserves
solely to itself the prerogative of introducing information.

The function of coercive censorship is to maintain centralized control over the introduction of information. The
functions of this form of maximization of redundancy are,
in the first instance, to reinforce officially approved
meanings, and secondly, to prevent the emergence of a challenge to the political myths upon which the legitimacy and
interests of the regime rest.

In addition, the regime attempts to manipulate the
sema-siological functions of symbols - e.g., to modify the
transmission of meaning structures - in an effort to erad-
icate all myths at variance with the dominant political
myth.

[47]Claus Mueller, *The Politics of Communication* (London-Oxford-New York: Oxford University Press, 1973), p. 19.

Political Myths

The 20th century has been an unprecedented era for the
production of political myths, largely because it has been
the century of the totalitarian state which, with its centralized monopoly of nearly all channels of communication,
is in a favorable position to construct, alter and dis-
seminate structured communications. The importance of this
lies in the fact that for all states, the basis of legitimacy is a set of myths, reinforced constantly by symbolism. A regime characterized by "directed communications"
is in a better position to shape myths and manipulate symbols than one in which communications are relatively open
and myths are periodically irreverently debunked: an open
marketplace of ideas.

Totalitarianism differs from ordinary dictatorship or
authoritarianism partly in that, increasingly since the
French Revolution, all governments must accommodate the
myth that sovereignty resides with the people. Because
the "will of the people" is always ambiguous, ambivalent,
and subject to influence, this myth is often a source of
power for regimes, rather than a restraint. The relationship between the governors and the governed - the manner in
which this democratic sovereignty is expressed - comprises
the *political myth* prevailing in a given society at a given
time.

Myths, as a general term, are propositions concerning
the fundamental nature of reality, or the "essence" of
reality. They are largely unquestioned bodies of belief,
held by large numbers of people;[48] their truth or false-
hood is of less concern to us than the social and political
functions they often serve.

Myths probably originate as efforts to explain a prob-
lematical reality, in response either to anxiety or simple

[48]Murray Edelman, *Politics as Symbolic Action* (Chicago: Markham
Publishing Co., 1971), p. 14.

curiosity. They can be created and propagated in a short
time, however. They need not be the products of a long
period of "folk" creation, nor are they necessarily the
products of the dim recesses of the psyche; they can be
quite prosaic.

Myths typically become institutionalized, and remain so
beyond the time when the conditions or events they were
originally to explain have become de-mysticized. While
their original function may have been to provide reassurance of order in a seemingly chaotic world, very often they
come to provide a rationale for the exercise of power; thus,
Malinowski defined the function of myth as a device to account for social strain - a rationalization of inequalities
of power and privilege.[49] It is this component of the total
mythic structure of any society - that dealing with the
distribution of power and benefits, the proper locus of
power, and the justification for the exercise of authority - that we are calling the "political myth." The concept of the political myth will be recognized as similar to
Plato's "noble lie," Sorel's notion of "myth," Mosca's
"political formula," Pareto's "derivations," Mannheim's
"ideology," Cassirer's "myth of the state," and other
classic concepts.[50]

Myths typically become dogma only upon reaching the
stage of institutionalization as the moral foundation of a
set of political institutions. When this stage is reached,
dissidence in dogma is tantamount to a threat to the institutions, and the latter defend themselves with whatever
means are at their disposal; they frequently resort to
coercion to this end. Intolerance and dogmatism therefore

---

[49]Bronislaw Malinowski, *Magic, Science and Religion, and other Essays*
(New York, 1948), p. 93. Quoted in Murray Edelman, *The Symbolic Uses
of Politics* (Urbana: University of Illinois Press, 1967), p. 18.

[50]See, for example, Harold D. Lasswell's discussion of the concept of
the political myth, in *Language of Politics* (Cambridge: M.I.T. Press,
1949, 1965), p. 10.

derive not from the myths themselves, but from their political functions; the essential function of political myths
is to create willing obedience. Rulers have therefore
always concentrated their attention on the investiture of
myth.

If an alternative political myth exists, or arises in
a society, there will be a challenge to the legitimacy of
the government. Under such conditions, the challenge will
take one of two forms:

1. An alternative political myth will be offered (this
is a *revolutionary* challenge).

2. It will be claimed that the myth has been corrupted,
and must be restored to its pure version (this is a
reformist challenge).

Ideology - as a coherent body of principles that seeks
to explain social reality in "scientific" terms and to
provide guidelines and imperatives for action - is inclus-
ive of political myths, the latter being assumptions concerning the relationship of men to the state upon which
the ideology is grounded. If, in the Soviet context,
marked policy changes must be rationalized in terms of the
ideology (as they must), organized changes in the ideology
may require alterations of more deeply seated and often
implicit elements of the underlying political myths.
Ideologies are mythical formulations insofar as they are
a set of refined, ordered and rationalized political myths,
bearing a coherent relationship to one another.[51] If a
crucial element of a political myth comes under challenge,
it may threaten the integrity of the entire ideological
structure. The Soviet nationalities *problem*, at root, is
the failure of the ideology to reconcile the tenacious
political myth of "national self-determination" with the
myth of class unity, or proletarian internationalism.

[51]Lee C. McDonald makes a more rigorous distinction: myths, as
"tensive, diaphoric and epiphoric" structures, are always past-oriented
while ideologies, as pseudo-sciences and therefore predictive, are

Symbols

In semantic theory, a "sign" is an event that signifies, or predicts to, another event, or *object*. This relationship arises through the correlation in nature or the man-made environment of the sign and the object. For the relationship to exist, a *subject* must find the object more interesting than the sign, but the sign more easily available.[52]

An event (including a word) used *symbolically* rather than signally, however, is associated not with the object itself, but with an abstracted mental *conception* of the object.[53] A conception can be carried around, permitting individuals to think about and react to the object in its absence. Symbols, thus, are vehicles for the conception of objects.

Symbols make possible not only signification and denotation, but also connotation, in that they are capable of arousing the emotions associated with the conception of the object, in the object's absence.

The denotative and connotative power of symbols derives from the human ability to abstract: what we abstract from reality is a concept, characterized principally by the logic of organization of the elements of the original object or situation. This is also the source of the human ability to generalize and categorize: the elements of a concept are those elements of the object that a specific

always forward-looking. "Myths, Politics and Political Science," *Western Political Quarterly*, XXII, No. 1(March, 1969). While we agree that myths are backward-looking, we prefer to reserve Mannheim's notion of "utopia" for forward-looking ideologies. Ideologies as *doctrines* (such as Marxism-Leninism) purport to explain past and present, as well as future, reality.

[52]Susanne K. Langer, *Philosophy in a New Key* (Cambridge: Harvard University Press, 1974), p. 58.

[53]*Ibid.*, pp. 60-61.

instance of the object has in common with other specific
instances of the same object, or category.

It is a further property of symbols that they can carry
connotations and denotations relatively far removed from
the symbol's elemental denotation. In some cases, they are
able to carry a relatively large burden of meaning - the
"meaning" or *content* of a symbol being defined as the conception and associated connotations. The meaning of a symbol is not inherent in the symbol itself, but is conditioned by experience. Two consequences of this condition
are of crucial importance: symbols can have different
content for different subjects, and the content of symbols
can be altered.

The *semantic space* of a symbol is defined as the logical
limits of meaning; because of universal human experience,
for example, one does not expect to find a wild boar symbolizing "gentleness" in any culture. The degree to which
a symbol has a *wide* or *open* semantic space is the degree to
which the content of the symbol is inherently ambiguous.

Most scholars distinguish between "referential" and
"condensation" symbols. In our usage, referential symbols
are in fact signs. Condensation symbols not only evoke a
conception with associated connotations, but tend to "con-
dense" into a single symbol an elaborate range of similar
conceptions and strong associated emotions.[54]

Many things other than words can serve as condensation
symbols: architecture, customs, great men and women, rit-
uals, and ideas. The important thing is that they connote
an elaborated mythic structure, and are more immediate than
their objects. Often, the conceptions and connotations
which condensation symbols evoke are elements of larger
myths. The importance of symbols to politics derives from
the myths that they evoke, because myths are the basis of
the legitimacy of political systems.

[54]On condensation symbols, see Edward Sapir, "Symbols," *Encyclopedia of the Social Sciences* (New York, 1934), pp. 492-95.

Myths, Symbols and Soviet Nationalities Policy

We are concerned with two major and conflicting political
myths prevalent in Soviet society. The first - the dominant political myth - is the *myth of proletarian internationalism*, which holds that the principal political
entity with which Soviet citizens identify is the class,
not the nation, and that indeed, national characteristics
will become increasingly less important as the society
evolves toward communism. An important sub-category of
this myth, however, is the myth of Russian patrimony of the
former Tsarist empire - the myth that because Russians have
taken responsibility for the Soviet Union, Russians have
the first prerogative of rule, and that the international
culture that will emerge with the building of communism
will in fact be Russian culture. The foremost value of the
myth of proletarian internationalism is the integrity of
the Soviet Union as a political entity, governed from
Moscow.

Opposed to this is the national myth, or as it is termed
in this study, the *myth of national moral patrimony*. We
choose the latter term because the myth is embraced both by
those who oppose the dominant myth from a reformist standpoint - who, e.g., resent the corruption of the pure proletarian internationalist myth by intrusion of the myth of
Russian primacy - and by those who oppose it from a revolutionary standpoint: who reject the myth of proletarian
internationalism altogether as a political organizaing
principle, believing instead that nations are legitimately
governed only by themselves. The essential elements of the
myth of national moral patrimony that we shall study are
those of the *authenticity* of national culture, traditions,
and language, and the functions these serve for *differentiation* of the national group from other groups.

We are guided by the assumptions of a conflict, rather
than an equilibrium, theory of the social process. Myths

serve different purposes for different groups.[55] The myth
of proletarian internationalism functions to bolster the
legitimacy of Russian rule, and presumably will be espoused
by individuals whose careers lead them to identify their
interests with the all-Union rather than with republican
Party organizations. Elements of the national myth serve
the purposes of political elites interested in republican
decisional autonomy, and national cultural elites interested in expanded national expression.

Both groups endeavor to mold the official ideology in
ways that elements of the myth that legitimizes their interests will be reflected, or (from the opposing viewpoint), discredited.

Additionally, because of closed communications channels,
cultural figures will often attempt to articulate their
interests through symbolic behavior or the manipulation of
symbols. Symbol manipulation is perhaps not the only
form that this confrontation takes, but under conditions of
severely restricted communications, it is the most important form. Specific forms of symbol manipulation are discussed below.

The most important form involves conflict over the content, or meaning, of symbols that are entrenched in the
culture, and tend to have a wide semantic space. This
means that efforts are made to detach tenacious symbols
from one myth and attach them to another, i.e., to "co-opt"
them.

We know by definition that a symbol has both an emotional and a substantive mythic content. The emotion is attached to the myth, not to the symbol itself, but the symbol becomes capable of arousing the emotion. The task of

---

[55]The best justification for the use of the conflict approach can be
found in John A. Armstrong, *The European Administrative Elite* (Princeton: Princeton University Press, 1973), pp. 8-9. For a different
approach, see Pierre L. van den Berghe, "Dialectic and Functionalism:
Toward a Theoretical Synthesis," *American Sociological Review*, No. 28
(October, 1963), pp. 695-705. Our analytical framework makes no assumptions of a system-maintenance function.

32

detaching a symbol from one mythic structure and attaching
it to another means, essentially, that the emotion must be
transferred from one object to another. Should co-optation
misfire, it may in fact strengthen the original mythic content of the symbol. The most effective long-range strategy
for symbol co-optation, of course, is early political
socialization through education. The regime, however,
through the propaganda apparatus, conducts a continuous
re-socialization campaign of symbol co-optation.

The specific mechanism by which symbols are co-opted is
metaphoric transfer.[56] If certain elements of the symbol
under attack can be identified with similar elements of
another symbol, the content of one can be transferred to
the other by association. Symbols of nationalism, for
example, are frequently associated with entrenched symbols
that evoke fear and unease, such as fascism, imperialist
subversion, Maoism and Zionism. The creative use of metaphor is the most important and most frequently used mode of
symbol manipulation.

Other less important stylistic devices include:

1. *Synechdoche*: the use of a part to describe a whole,
   or vice-versa; this will emphasize certain elements
   of a symbol's content over others.

2. *Oxymoron*: the combination of contradictory or incongruous words or concepts; this is a mode of metaphoric
   transfer.

3. *Meiosis*: understatement, for humorous or phatic
   effect.

4. *Personification*: treating abstractions as living
   beings with free will; this achieves simplification,
   and also humorous and phatic effect.

5. *Hyperbole*: overstatement or exaggeration; for apoc-
   alyptic or Manichaean evocations.

---

[56]On metaphoric transfer, see Nelson Goodman, *Languages of Art: An
Approach to a Theory of Symbols* (Indianapolis: Hackett Publishing
Company, 1976), pp. 74ff.

Syntactical devices, including antithesis and inversion, can be employed to create the illusion of expanded semantic space of symbols. Literary devices - irony, eulogy, sarcasm - are often employed for semantic purposes as well, and also phatically. Among logical devices, reification and the inversion of cause and effect are employed very frequently; the most important logical device, however, is anachronism -- the projection of the concerns of the present far into the past, and manufacturing mythical versions of the past, for the purpose of lending historical legitimacy to current situations.

We define *symbolic action* as action the effect of which is symbolic, rather than the manifest, instrumental goal of such action. In the Soviet context, this includes civil disobedience and political trials.

Finally, the following less easily classified techniques are employed in the manipulation of symbols and meanings:

1. *Censorship*: the effort to obliterate symbols whose content cannot be changed.

2. *Labelling*: the effort to transfer the connotations of names to the objects to which they are applied.[57]

3. *Typologizing*: since naming means classifying things into groups, the implication of typologies is that everything with the same name has the same properties. Properties can be ascribed to objects, therefore, by carefully assigning them to categories.

4. Attempts to extrapolate from accepted and legitimate tenets of the ideology to extended conclusions or corollaries that favor one or another group.

5. Attempts to associate a sense of threat or reassurance with one or another symbol.

6. Efforts to establish "scientific" credulity for myths.

7. Use of the "dialectic" to escape blatant contradictions or to avoid undesirable but ineluctable conclusions from arguments made for another purpose.

---

[57]On labelling, see Murray Edelman, "The Political Language of the Helping Professions," *Politics and Society*, IV, 3(1974), pp. 295-310.

Before closing this chapter, it will perhaps be well to make some epistomological remarks concerning the research design and sources. The principal sources for this study have been written communications. For the study of the myth of proletarian internationalism, and for the reconstruction of the myth of Russian primacy, we have relied on the legitimate Soviet press, in addition, of course, to substantiated interpretations in Western secondary sources. The sample of the Soviet press includes newspapers, books, Party journals, and academic publications. Soviet printed output is voluminous, and for this reason, a randomly selected sample would perhaps be representative, but not necessarily of literature relating to the problem of Ukrainian nationalism. Rather than attempt to derive a random sample, therefore, sources were collected as follows.

We utilized the very thorough and topically organized file of clippings from the Soviet press maintained by Radio Liberty Research in Munich, West Germany. This enabled us to go directly to press items from a wide range of sources, covering the entire period under study, and to obtain a much more complete sample than a lone researcher could have done. Secondly, we relied on the advice of experienced analysts to draw our attention to important documents that we may have missed. This was supplemented by scanning the entire *Digest of the Soviet Ukrainian Press* for additional items, and to determine whether we had missed any significant trend in Soviet press treatment of the nationalities problem and Ukrainian nationalism.

For the analysis of the myths and symbols of nationalism, we have relied in part on official Soviet publications, but for the most part our sources for this phase of the research have been Ukrainian *samvydav* materials. We were able to gain access to all the Ukrainian *samvydav* that was available in the West by 1976.

We conducted interviews with recent Ukrainian and Russian emigres in Paris and Munich, and in addition, there are

some interviews with Soviet citizens. The total number of
interviews is small; therefore, while they shed light on
occasional topics, interviews have not been used as a systematic inferential data source.

Research of this type, while it is empirical, is pre-
eminently qualitative in nature. We dismissed the idea of
quantitative content analysis early: for many of the symbols we have studied, frequency of appearance is considerably less important than channel and audience, or the mere
fact of their appearance in the first place. Also, textual
analysis - essential to the study of meaning and the manipulation of meaning - is not amenable to quantitative analysis.

The problem of Ukrainian nationalism is a contemporary
and ongoing one. Although the most outspoken dissent has
been silenced since 1972, it is extremely unlikely that the
issue has been finally decided. Grand conclusions and
prognoses, therefore, are inappropriate, and we have con-
fined the scope of the study to middle-range questions and
middle-range conclusions. Neither is the study comparative. Although we believe that our theoretical framework
is applicable to nationality problems in communist societies in general, an exploratory investigation of this
sort on a comparative scale would entail time and linguistic demands beyond the capacity of a lone researcher.

In Chapter 2, we discuss the manipulation of symbols in
the effort to inject elements of each myth into the official
ideology. Chapters 3 and 4 examine culture and linguistic
policy respectively, as major components of the myth of
national moral patrimony, and as the arenas of conflict
over symbols. Chapter 5 is devoted to nationalist dissent
and the regime response. In Chapter 6, we discuss the fall
of Petro Shelest - an event which, in retrospect, marks the
end of the fourth wave of Ukrainian nationalism - briefly
summarize the findings and conclusions, and offer suggestions for future research.

II
IDEOLOGY AND MYTH:
SOVIET NATIONALITIES POLICY

Given our model of the Soviet communications system as set
forth in Chapter 1, we can assume that if an issue is more
or less openly debated in official channels over an extended period, then the central Party leadership either
considers the matter unimportant, or the leadership is
itself divided on the issue, since under these conditions
both sides of the debate are "legitimate" until an official consensus is proclaimed. As we have adequate reason
to believe that the nationalities question is not unimportant to the Soviet leadership, the existence of clearly
drawn - and only thinly veiled - debate indicates that the
leadership is divided over the substance of nationalities
policy and the theories that underlie it.

Soviet nationalities policy is the arena of both open
and veiled struggle between the proponents of greater centralization of political power and greater uniformity of
culture on the one hand, and proponents of wider political,
economic and cultural autonomy for nationalities on the
other. While the Soviet media refer to nationalities
policy in the singular, and imply that it is the fixed
and immobile patrimony of the October Revolution, it is in
fact neither monolithic nor unchanging; there is no solid
consensus among elites as to what the "policy" is or
should be, except at the rarefied level of ideals and plat-
itudes: equality, mutual respect, and some form of "drawing
together" in the more or less remote future. Below this
level, Soviet nationalities policy is characterized by an
ambiguity that both reflects and facilitates the efforts of
diverse groups within the society to mold official ideology

so that group interests can prevail while the overall stability of the system - upon which the same group interests
also depend - will be minimally threatened.

Fluctuations in Soviet nationalities policy - ranging
from oppression and Russification at one extreme to compromise, accommodation and deferral of regime goals on the
other - are thus responses to demands from republican cultural and political elites. What is fundamentally at
question, therefore, are the CPSU's mechanisms of adaptation, on the one hand, and processes of interest aggrega-
tion and articulation under conditions of severely restricted communications, on the other.

The flexible instrument of Soviet nationalities policy
must serve both functions: the ideology is the tie that
divides as well as binds. Given that ideology derives from
the political myth, and that governmental legitimacy in the
Soviet Union rests on the ideology, then, reinterpretation
or reformulation of specific elements of the myth, and
invocation of key elements of the myth, or successful in-
jection of elements of other myths into the ideology, serve
to legitimate demands and initiatives on the part of particular interests, and actions or inactions on the part of
central or republican authorities. Soviet nationalities
policy, therefore, is the *resultant* of efforts on the part
of national elites to reshape the ideology so as to preserve cultural identity or republican political autonomy;
on the part of central authorities, it is the resultant of
similar efforts to limit such demands to a level at which
they do not threaten all-Union interests or Russian
interests, to accommodate (symbolically or substantially)
demands that cannot be limited or suppressed, and to try
to reshape demands - all without violating a vaguely defined but irreducible core of socialist ideology, and preserving above all the leading role of the Communist Party.
We refer to nationalities policy as the *resultant* of these
conflicting pressures to emphasize that the policy that
emerges may not be what anyone or any group particularly

wanted; in vector geometry, a "resultant" is the sum of a
number of vectors, but it rarely coincides with any particular vector that produces it.

We are concerned in this chapter with the evolution of
official nationalities policy since the death of Stalin,
from the viewpoint of mythic inputs: overt efforts to reshape or to interpret the official ideology so as to
legitimize particular interests. This is an incremental
process, and takes place almost entirely within legitimate
channels of communication; we are not concerned in this
chapter with opposition nor with *samvydav* channels, which
represent a more focused effort to replace the official
myth with another, rather than to reshape the interpretation of ideology in order to make it more amenable to the
national myth. We admit that the distinction is arbitrary,
but submit that it is logical in terms of our theoretical
focus on how symbols become a medium of interest articulation under conditions of restricted communication.

We have attempted in this chapter to emphasize wherever
possible Ukrainian input into official nationalities policy.
The discussion that follows, however, relates to official
nationalities policy as it concerns all of the Union Republics. Ukrainian cultural and political elites must define
the Ukraine's relationship to the center and to the USSR as
a whole within the ideological framework of all-Union
nationalities policy. Much of the content of this chapter
thus has general applicability to all-Union nationality
problems and policies.

In order to proceed, it will be necessary to make a distinction, though again an arbitrary one, between "ideology
in flux" and the "official" ideological position. It will
be convenient and not unreasonable to take as the official
position of the Party at a given time those versions of
nationalities policy that are crystallized in the Resolutions of CPSU Congresses. Three Congresses in the period
under study — the 20th (1956), 22nd (1962) and 24th (1971) —
stand out as marking major reformulations of official

nationalities policy.

The organization of the argument in this chapter is
evolutionary: an attempt is made to lend chronological
coherence to our topical concerns. We will focus attention
on three major areas of theoretical contention in the
development of nationalities policy:

1. The nature of the "nation" and the pace of the realization of the "merger" of nations, and the proper dialectical interaction between the processes of "flowering"
and "drawing together."

2. The nature of Soviet federalism as it concerns the
legal, cultural and political rights of the Union Republics,
and the fate of these in the course of "building communism."

3. The pace and character of ethnic and linguistic
assimilation.

THE MYTH OF PROLETARIAN INTERNATIONALISM

The framework for the overt ideological expression of the
myth of proletarian internationalism is the writings of
Marx, Engels, Lenin and Stalin. The central premise of the
classical Marxist theory of the nation is that it is de-
cidedly a historical phenomenon. In the classical Marxist
conception, nations are formed only when the inhabitants of
one territory, speaking one language, are also united by
economic bonds. Internal economic ties and a means of communication weld the various parts of a people into a
nation.

The classical Marxist conception recognized that nations
differ from one another and from other groups and communities in their intangible characteristics, or "psychological
makeup." The Marxist approach to national character differs
from that of the integral nationalist myth, however, in
that, while the conditions under which people live together
from generation to generation do manifest themselves in a
distinctive culture, such a character is not biologically

rooted, has nothing to do with the "landscape" or soil, and
does not, in any idealistic sense, represent the fixed
"essence" of a nation. In short, the "psychological makeup"
of a nation is also historically conditioned.

"Leninist nationality policy" emerged out of the writings
of Lenin and Stalin, and out of the tactical requirements
of the Bolshevik revolution, to become one of the prime
legitimating symbols of Soviet rule in the former Tsarist
empire. Leninist nationality policy, as the original
Leninist component of the myth of proletarian internationalism, can be summarized as encompassing the following five
principles:

1. All nations and languages are equal.

2. Since nationalism is a bourgeois ideology, and the
proletariat has no nation, the proletarian party cannot be
divided on national grounds.

3. The right of nations to secede (the "right of national
self-determination") is to be upheld, but secession must be
in line with the interests of the proletariat, as defined
by the party.

4. Even in a socialist state, concessions may have to be
made to national consciousness; the policy in such cases
must be to promote cultures "national in form, but socialist in content."

5. Under full communism, national distinctions will disappear, and nations will merge.

While Leninist nationality policy is a myth, or, more
precisely, an element of a larger myth, it also functions
as a complex symbol with a highly ambiguous content. It is
one of the prime symbols in the clash between the regime
and its challengers. Central authorities in Moscow urging
internationalism and seeking to legitimate specific
policies, republican political and economic elites striving
for decisonal autonomy, and republican cultural elites
critical of Russification and demanding the right of
national cultural expression, all are able to base their
claims on Leninist nationality policy, because of its

ambiguity, and because of the force of the figure of Lenin
as a legitimizing symbol.

In fact, Lenin's primary concern was less with the re-
conciliation of nationalism with Marxism than with the
accomplishment and institutionalization of Soviet power
throughout the former Tsarist empire. Lenin was preoc-
cupied with the consolidation of power, and for him,
nationalism was a force to be harnessed in the service of
the revolution, and dealt with later. Lenin thus left a
legacy of ambiguity and ambivalence on national issues that
was later to be pressed into service by ideologues and
spokesmen on both sides of the nationalities question, but
by none with so great success as by the spokesment of a
deeper myth, the fundamental myth underlying proletarian
internationalism: the myth of Russian primacy.

In the Soviet conventional wisdom, two deviations have
stood in the way of the implementation of Leninist nationality policy: Great Russian chauvinism, and bourgeois
nationalism. Russian chauvinism represented the ethno-
centric attitudes of Russian communists insensitive to
minority national customs, languages and autonomy.
Bourgeois nationalism referred to excessive aspirations
for autonomy on the part of non-Russian cadres, and local
hostility to Russian domination. Over time, bourgeois
nationalism came to be regarded as the greater sin, and by
the late 1930s, the term Great Russian chauvinism had all
but disappeared from official discussions of nationalities
policy.

Stalin's *de facto* preference for Russification was
evident even at the height of the policy of "Ukrainization"
in the Ukraine. When Oleksandr Shums'kyi, Ukrainian
Commissar of Education, complained to Stalin that
Russian assimilationist pressures were dominant, and that
only intervention from Moscow would alleviate the situation - replacing Russian and Russified Ukrainian cadres
with Ukrainians committed to Ukrainian ways - Stalin's response was less than salutary for Ukrainization: conceding

that Russifying tendencies must be opposed, he nonetheless
insisted that neither could Ukrainization be rushed. Not
only were there insufficient Ukrainian cadres to replace
Russian and Russified leaders, but the interests of Russian minorities in the Ukraine had to be protected, too.
Further, Ukrainization was not to be permitted to play into
the hands of the nationalists by pursuing it too vigorous-
ly. In any event, the Ukrainians were instructed that they
were not to reject Russian influences outright; Russia
provided a revolutionary example that the minority nationalities should emulate.[1]

By 1933-34, the policy of favoring the appointment of
ethnic Ukrainians preferentially to leadership posts had
given way to the promotion of "tried and tested people
educated in the BOlshevik spirit."[2] This spelled the end
of Ukrainization; pressure on urban Jews and Russians to
adopt Ukrainian ways came to an end, and indeed, with those
Ukrainians who had pressed vocally for localism coming
increasingly under suspicion of "bourgeois nationalism,"
there came to be a premium on knowledge of Russian among
Ukrainians.[3]

The old prejudice of the Tsarist regime that Ukrainian
was a vulgar peasant dialect, inferior to Russian, again
began to be publicly articulated. In 1938, a requirement
was adopted that the Russian language be taught throughout
the Ukrainian school system. Where previously writers and
artists had been encouraged to use and develop the Ukrainian language and to exploit Ukrainian folk themes, after
1938 the pressure increased on Ukrainians to avoid such
"nationalist" themes, and to write in Russian.

[1]J.V. Stalin, *Socheneniia* (Moscow: Izdatel'stvo "Politicheskoi Literatury," 1949-1953), Vol. VIII, pp. 149-50.

[2]*Visti Ukrains'koho Tsentral'noho Vykonavs'koho Komiteta* (Kiev),
January 17, 1933.

[3]P.P. Postyshev and S.V. Kossior, *Soviet Ukraine Today* (Moscow: Foreign
Languages Publishing House, 1934), pp. 50-56.

The policy of Russification of the Ukraine continued
after World War II, and for the remainder of Stalin's regime. The myth of Russian primacy began to receive public
articulation after the war. Stalin was convinced of
Ukrainian disloyalty during the war. The Ukraine had borne
the brunt of the Nazi attack and occupation, and the
Ukraine was cut off from Soviet control and support.
During this time, there was a resurgence of Ukrainian
nationalism, and the organization of armed groups to fight
the Soviet regime, despite the indifference and even contempt of the Nazi occupiers. Armed anti-Soviet insurrection on the part of the OUN and UPA was not decisively
quashed until 1950, and OUN cells were still being uncov-
ered in the 1960s.[4]

Stalin's May, 1945 toast to the Russian people[5] evoked a
latent but quite firmly entrenched myth of Russian responsibility for the Soviet family of nations, buttressed by a
not altogether unfounded myth of Russian sacrifices for the
sake of the Union. Russians were conscious that the revolutionary movement of the 19th century was a Russian movement, and that the genius of Soviet Marxism is Russian
Marxism. The Revolution itself was "Russian," and the
Civil War had been fought and won largely by Russian Bolsheviks. It had been Russians who carried socialism, culture and modernization to the backwaters of the Tsarist
empire. In the aftermath of a bloody war against the
fascists, along with the perception of lack of support from
the "nationalist" borderlands, there was ample sentiment to
be tapped by Stalin's toast. The myth that the Revolution
and the Soviet Union were a Russian patrimony unquestionably always existed just below the surface of Leninist
nationality policy; Stalin's encouragement of Russian
nationalism during the war and his attitude exemplified in

[4]See Chapter 5, below.

[5]*Pravda*, May 25, 1945. See translation in Robert V. Daniels, ed.,
A Documentary History of Communism (New York: Vintage, 1962), p. 138.

44

in his toast, brought it to the surface.

It is worth emphasizing that there is a deeper historical dimension to the identification of the USSR with
Russia. The Tsarist imperial philosophy conceived of the
empire as "*Rossiyskaia*." Richard Pipes notes that the Russian empire somewhat followed the French colonial pattern:
in contrast to the British, the French extended the full
rights of French citizenship to their colonies, hoping
thereby to assimilate them.[6] The analogy is apt: the entrenched belief that Algeria was somehow "French" came out
of this pattern of colonialism, and Russian identification
with the former colonies of the Tsars undoubtedly did also.

Crystallization of the myth of Russian patrimony of the
former Tsarist empire began almost at once, with the rewriting of history. The theme of Russian primacy early
became more or less incorporated into Marxist-Leninist
ideology through the doctrine of "friendship of peoples"
(*druzhba narodov*). The "friendship of peoples" doctrine
is a remarkable example of mythmaking through anachronism:
the projection of the concerns of the present into the
distant past.

The friendship of peoples myth projects the "friendship"
of the future Soviet "family of nations" far into the past,
and emphasizes that the resistance of the borderlands to
Russian colonization was resistance not to Russians *per se*,
but to Tsarism. The myth maintains that the minority
peoples of the empire in fact welcomed the Russian colo-
nizers as brothers in the revolutionary struggle.[7]

The myth of the friendship of peoples was crucial in
legitimizing the myth of Russian primacy, because it con-
tradicts and belies the Russian colonial domination of
minority nationalities. With this as background, we can

[6]Richard Pipes, "Introduction: The Nationality Problem," in Zev Katz,
Rosemarie Rogers and Frederic Harned, eds., *Handbook of Major Soviet
Nationaities* (New York: The Free Press, 1975), p. 2.

[7]On the "friendship of peoples" myth, see Lowell Tillett, *The Great
Friendship* (Chapel Hill: University of North Carolina Press, 1969).

formulate the myth of Russian primacy as follows:

1. The Soviet Union is a Russian enterprise. The basis of this is that the former Tsarist empire belonged to Russia, and because Russians took the initiative in forming and defending the Soviet Union.

2. The prerogative of rule thus belongs to Russians, and to Russified members of other ethnic groups.

3. Russian culture and the Russian language are not only superior, but are inviolable.

4. The new culture and language that will coalesce as the eventual result of drawing together and merging (*sblizhenie* and *sliianie*) of nations of the USSR will be Russian language and Russian culture.

The myth of Russian primacy serves to give a specific content to the myth of proletarian internationalism: that Russian culture is to be central to the "socialist content" of national cultures. As early as 1946, in an article condemning the "away from Moscow" slogan of Mykola Khvylovyi (1893-1933), it was made explicit that Ukrainian culture could not develop separately from Russian culture: that Russian culture is superior to, and is to be the model for, national cultures.[8]

We should clarify that the myth of Russian primacy is distinct from Russian *nationalism* - both the neo-Slavophilism of Solzhenitsyn and the integral nationalism of *Veche* and *Slovo natsii*.[9] It is clear that a myth of national identity based on blood is incongruous with the merger of nations through intermarriage, migration and assimilation, which is the goal of Soviet nationalities policy, and an integral part of the myth of proletarian internationalism. Nicholas DeWitt has suggested that as early as the mid-1930s, the official Soviet concept of nationality had

[8] *Bolshevik*, XXI, No. 22(November, 1946), pp. 1-8. Quoted in Yaroslav Bilinsky, *The Second Soviet Republic* (New Brunswick: Rutgers University Press, 1964), pp. 410-11.

[9] See, for example, Dmitry Pospielevsky, "The Resurgence of Russian Nationalism in Samizdat," *Survey*, XIX, No. 1(Winter, 1973), pp. 51-74.

changed from one of "root nationality" based on ethnic descent to one of "self-declared nationality."[10]

In the period of comparative liberalization that followed the death of Stalin, the meaning of the term "nation",
the determinants of ethnic identity, and the pace of "drawing together" became the foci of debate between "cultural
pluralists" and "assimilationists," in an effort to modify
the myth of proletarian internationalism in the direction
of lesser and greater, respectively, de-nationalization
through government policy. It is to the specific content,
the mythical premises, and the reasoning and techniques of
argumentation of this debate that we now turn our attention.

THE MYTH OF PROLETARIAN INTERNATIONALISM
IN FLUX, 1956-1972

The events immediately following Stalin's death in 1953 at
first seemed auspicious for Ukrainian autonomy. On June 13,
1953, CPUk 1st Secretary L.G. Mel'nikov, an ethnic Russian,
was dismissed for appointing Russified East Ukrainians to
high positions in the West Ukraine. His dismissal was accompanied by calls to emphasize the training and development of local cadres to develop programs in "locally mean-
ingful ways.[11] He was replaced by Kirichenko, the first
ethnic Ukrainian to hold the top Party post in the Ukraine.
Khrushchev, who had been Ukrainian Party boss from 1938 to
1949, turned to his former regional Party organization for
support in his own succession struggle, and also as a source
of loyal supporters for leadership positions throughout the
Soviet Union.

For the first time in the Soviet period, the Ukrainians

[10]Nicholas DeWitt, *Education and Professional Employment in the USSR*
(Washington, D.C: National Science Foundation, 1961), p. 354.

[11]*Pravda Ukrainy*, June 13, 1953, p. 1.

were designated as "junior partners" of the Russians. The
"junior" aspect of the partnership was emphasized, since
the Russians remained the "principal bearers of the great
revolutionary ideas of freedom and progress." But, as the
Ukrainians, along with the Belorussians, were part of the
"great Slavic family," they, as distinct from the other
national minorities, were to be regarded as co-leaders in
the Russian enterprise.[12]

While no doubt reassuring to the Ukrainians, particularly
in its contrast to Stalin's ill-concealed contempt, it has
been suggested that the partnership theme also served to
remind the Ukrainians that, as partners, they were also
equally responsible for Soviet programs,[13] and, close as
they are to the Russians in language and culture, slated for
intensive Russification.

The high point in the post-Stalin liberalization of
nationalities policy came with the 20th Party Congress in
February, 1956. Among the crimes for which Khrushchev cas-
tigated Stalin was that of "rude violations of the basic
Leninist principles of the nationality policy of the Soviet
state."[14] Khrushchev referred in this context to the mass
deportations of minorities suspected of collaboration with

[12]*Pravda*, May 30, 1954. Bilinsky reports that as early as 1948, Molotov
reported to the Jubilee Session of the Ukrainian Supreme Soviet that
the Ukrainians were the first to have entered the road to socialism
after the Russians, but this theme remained subdued until 1954;
Bilinsky, *op. cit.*, p. 19. For informed Western discussions of the
hierarchy of Soviet Republics, also see John A. Armstrong, "The Ethnic
Scene in the Soviet Union: The View of the Dictatorship," in Erich
Goldhagen, ed., *Ethnic Minorities in the Soviet Union* (New York:
Praeger, 1968), and Vernon V. Aspaturian, "Nationality Inputs in Soviet
Foreign Policy: The USSR as an Arrested Universal State," in Aspaturian,
ed., *Process and Power in Soviet Foreign Policy* (Boston: Little, Brown
and Co., 1971).

[13]Robert S. Sullivant, "The Ukrainians," *Problems of Communism*, XVI,
No. 5(September-October, 1967), p. 53.

[14]See "Khrushchev's Secret Speech," in Dan N. Jacobs, ed., *The New
Communist Manifesto and Related Documents*, 3rd edition (New York:
Harper and Row, 1965), pp. 147-48.

the Germans, and to Stalin's alleged desire to deport the
Ukrainians to Siberia, too, but for their numbers. The
inronic tone of this portion of the speech clearly implied
that Stalin's suspicions of nationalist plots in the borderlands were an illusion, and this must have gone far in
relegitimizing, and even stimulating, stepped up demands
for greater rights to cultural expression and political
autonomy.

A few months following the Congress, Lenin's "Testament,"
containing documents suppressed in the USSR since 1923, was
published, and included an article that, while it had long
been known in the West, became the entering wedge of a new
theme in the mythical aspects of Soviet nationalities policy. In the article, Lenin criticized Stalin's plan to incorporate the Union Republics as provinces of the Russian
Republic, and urged tact in dealing with minority nationalities; in particular, he warned against the suppression
of non-Russian languages.[15]

As a direct result of the 20th Party Congress and the
publication of the "Testament," a myth of an egalitarian
and benevolent Lenin was fostered, and greater emphasis was
placed on his respect for national cultures - a consideration that had been quite openly tactical in nature - than
a dispassionate reading of Lenin would seem to justify. In
the wake of de-Stalinization, it was the benevolent Lenin
that became the symbol of the legitimacy of the post-Stalin
order as far as nationalities policy was concerned.

Symbolic concessions to national sensitivities, not to
mention the reforms of 1955-1957,[16] inevitably raised the

---

[15]V.I. Lenin, "On the Question of Nationalities, or 'Autonomization,'"
Kommunist, No. 9(1956), pp. 22-26. English translation in *National
Liberation, Socialism and Imperialism: Selected Writings of V.I. Lenin*
(New York: International Publishers, 1968), pp. 165-71.

[16]Federal powers in the fields of finance, planning, judicial administration and light industry management were transferred to the Republics, among other decentralization measures. See E.G. Bloembergen,
"The Union Republics: How Much Autonomy?" *Problems of Communism*, XVI,
No. 5(September-October, 1967), pp. 27-35.

expectations of national political and cultural elites for
further concessions.   These were not forthcoming.   Khrushchev, his power secure, began in 1959 a trend toward administrative recentralization, accompanied by removal of
some of the more outspoken national leaders, and renewed
attacks on the survivals of "bourgeois nationalism."

The Third Party Program

In official nationalities policy and theory, the effort to
repair the breaches in the myth of proletarian internationalism caused by the succession crisis began in August,
1958, with an authoritative article by the Tadzhik scholar
B. Gafurov.   Gafurov's article in effect announced the
forthcoming reversal of the regime's nationalities policy
as it had been defined by the 20th Party Congress.   In
counterpoint to the recent emphasis on the "flowering" or
"flourishing" (*rastsvet*) of national cultures, Gafurov
reintroduced the concepts of "drawing together" (*sblizhenie*)
and "merger" or "fusion" (*sliianie*) of the Soviet nations,
which, in the liberal euphoria of the succession, had almost
disappeared from the media.
    Obstacles to the attainment of unity remained for Gafurov
"nationalist prejudices" and "national narrow-mindedness,"
and in particular, "the tendency to marshal cadres of different nationalities,"[17] reluctance to fulfill plans for
inter-republican deliveries, and in general, emphasis on
the locality at the expense of the Union as a whole.
Repeating familiar themes, Gafurov finds in the field of
ideology that nationalist survivals are manifested most

[17]B. Gafurov, "Uspekhi natsional'noi politiki KPSS i nekotorie voprosy
internatsional'nogo vospitaniia," *Kommunist*, No. 11(August, 1958),
p. 18.   This complaint turns out to be among the most common in accusations of "bourgeois nationalism."   Considering the migration of Russians to the borderlands, and the new-found (if short-lived) power of
native cadres, and not discounting simple nepotism, we urge the power
of a political symbol such as bourgeois nationalism in so mundane an
affair as who gets a job.

50

often in:

> ... idealization of the historical
> past, in an uncritical attitude to-
> ward various national movements, in
> forgetting the principle of *partiinost'*
> in elucidating questions of culture,
> literature, the arts.[18]

Gafurov does not fail to include Russian chauvinism as
an obstacle to unity:

> ... we should keep in mind V.I. Lenin's
> advice that it is above all Russians who
> should combat Great Russian chauvinism,
> and representatives of a given nationality
> who must struggle against local nationalism.[19]

Yaroslav Bilinsky, however, commenting on the same passage
from this article, urges that the apparent fairness of this
passage is qualified by the fact that few Russians criticize Russian chauvinism, and the tenor of the passage suggests that "the struggle against Russian nationalism is not
to be taken seriously, while the struggle against non-Russian nationalism is."[20]

Finally, Gafurov addressed the question of when unity
will finally be achieved:

> The fusion of nations is an altogether
> complex and lengthy process. For its
> achievement, not only the victory of
> socialism throughout the world is necessary,
> but also the transition from the first,
> lower phase of communist formation - soc-
> ialism - to its second and higher phase -
> communism.[21]

---

[18]*Ibid.*, p. 28.

[19]*Ibid.*, p. 23.

[20]Bilinsky, *The Second Soviet Republic*, p. 23.

[21]Gafurov, p. 16.

What is remarkable is that, whether Gafurov's theses
were in the nature of a *ballon d'essai* from higher sources
or his own independent initiative, they were enshrined,
point for point, in the 3rd Program of the CPSU, adopted
at the 22nd Party Congress in October-November, 1961.

The section of the Party Program dealing with nationality policy begins:

> Under socialism the nations flourish
> and their sovereignty grows stronger.[22]

Thus, the concept of *rastsvet* - at least during the period
of socialism - was instituted as an integral part of official nationalities policy: nations were to be allowed to
flourish. But,

> Full scale communist construction con-
> stitutes a new stage in the development
> of national relations in the USSR, in
> which the nations will draw still closer
> together until full unity is achieved.
> The building of the material and tech-
> nological basis of communism leads to
> still greater unity of the Soviet peoples.[23]

Khrushchev specifically endorsed this section of the new
Program in his second major speech to the 22nd Party Congress on October 17, 1961.[24]

The concepts of *rastsvet, sblizhenie* and *sliianie* were
not new in Soviet ideological polemics. The terms had been

[22]"The Program of the Communist Party of the Soviet Union," *Pravda* and
Izvestiia, November 2, 1961, pp. 2-9. Translation in Charlotte Saikow-
sky and Leo Gruliow, eds., *Current Soviet Policies*, IV (New York and
London: Columbia University Press, 1962), p. 26.

[23]*Ibid.*, p. 26.

[24]N.S. Khrushchev, "On the Program of the Communist Party of the Soviet
Union," *Pravda* and *Izvestiia*, October 19, 1961, pp. 1-10. Translation
in *Current Soviet Policies*, IV, pp. 103-104. Note that these early
documents refer to the Soviet peoples - in the plural - a usage that
had changed by the 24th Congress.

52

used by Lenin and Stalin, and the thesis that *sliianie* would
come only with the achievement of communism had been adum-
brated in Lenin's pre-revolutionary writings.[25] *Sliianie*
had not been perceived as much more than a symbolic threat
so long as its realization remained in the distant future.
Neither Gafurov's reintroduction of the terminology, nor
its enshrinement in the Party Program, would have created
significant controversy had it not been for another, in fact
the main, theme of the Program: that the CPSU and the Soviet
Union were in fact now *entering* the period of transition to
communism, and the transition was to be completed, not in
the dim and irrelevant future, but, Khrushchev assured the
22nd Congress, by the year 1980:

> We base ourselves on strictly scientific
> estimates, which indicate that we shall,
> in the main, have built a communist society
> within twenty years.[26]

The implication was clear to everyone concerned with
nationality problems. Khrushchev, in asserting that the
myth of proletarian internationalism was to be transformed
into reality, inaugurated a debate of immediate perceived
practical significance over what the substance of the myth
actually was. That the regime seemed to conceive it in
extreme assimilationist terms was hinted in the Program:
the ominous assertion that "the boundaries between the Union
Republics of the USSR are increasingly losing their former
former significance...."[27] suggested the coming end of

[25]See, e.g., "Critical Remarks on the National Question," *National
Liberation, Socialism and Imperialism*, p. 27.

[26]*Current Soviet Policies*, IV, p. 89.

[27]*Ibid.*, p. 26. Their "former significance," of course, following
Lenin, was the tactical necessity of respecting national sensitivities.
As federalism became less significant, so, clearly, would national
rights and autonomy in all areas, and the program of fusion seemed
explicitly to exclude the Russians from its effects.

federalism.

The Party Program offered no explicit rules on how it was to be implemented, but later debate on the provisions of the proposed new constitution suggest that the abolition of the Union Republics was being given serious consideration.

It seems clear in retrospect that the reversal in official nationalities policy following Khrushchev's consolidation of power was prompted in large part by quite practical considerations. Khrushchev's decentralization of industrial and agricultural management in 1957 left the non-Russian republics in a position of unaccustomed strength. Judging from the numerous press articles denouncing "localism," "nepotism," "preferential treatment," and the like between 1958 and 1962, it appears that the republican elites made heavy use of their new powers in matters of cadre selection.[28]

As the 1961 Party Program's theses were to the point but skeletal, offering no explicit guidance on how it was to be implemented, the Program gave rise to a spate of academic and publicistic writing on the subject of nationalities policy over the following decade, activity which, taken altogether and in retrospect, can be characterized as a more or less esoteric "debate" over which of the two myths will guide the interpretation of official nationalities policy.

The participants in this debate were academics and ideological spokesmen; top Party officials rarely took *public* part, except to affirm resolutions and theses of the Party. The channels of the debate were the official press, the academic press, and Party journals; since all these channels of communication are subject to censorship, the representatives of extreme views were excluded from *open* participation, and sought other, illegal, channels (*samizdat*).

---

[28]See, e.g., I. Kravtsev, "Sblizhenie i rastsvet sotsialisticheskikh natsiei," *Pravda Ukrainy*, January 20, 1962, pp. 3-4. Brezhnev also believed the *sovnarkhozy* encouraged localism: *Pravda*, September 30, 1965.

The operative rule is that views and polemics, if their proponents expect publication, must not contradict the skeletal official policy of the Party as it is enshrined in its theses and resolutions. The task, therefore, and the key to effective articulation of interests, is not to propose bold new themes, but to demonstrate that one or another specific policy proposal follows logically from, or is in some way legitimated by, that much of policy that has become "official."

The fundamental issue at stake in this debate was, of course, the continued existence of Union Republics organized along national lines, with as much a measure of political and cultural autonomy and national characteristics - most especially language - as possible, *versus* the protection of Russian dominance, and its extension, through cultural and linguistic assimilation and political centralization of decision-making. Although certainly many people in the USSR think of these issues and discuss them privately in terms as stark as this, the issue cannot be publicly discussed in the forthright way we have formulated them here, nor can the myths that underlie them be articulated. It is the ambiguity inherent in the official version of nationalities policy that is manipulated in an effort to shape a future policy that will legitimate either increased centralization and Russification, or increased national autonomy.

There are three principal tactics peculiar to this form of ideology-shaping:

1. The most important of these is the evocation of the symbolic authority of Lenin. The potency of the Lenin symbol cannot be overstressed. So long as the regime is not its own legitimation, it must rely on symbols external to itself, and Lenin is the most important of these. The ambiguity of Lenin's legacy provides the proponents of interests with a legitimating symbol for their demands, too. If a sufficiently convincing argument can be made that a policy direction is consistent with "what Lenin actually intended," the proponents of that policy will have gone far

in legitimating it. Very rarely does anyone assert (and then only at the highest levels) that what Lenin said fifty years ago may in fact be irrelevant to the country's problems today.

2. The effort to extrapolate from accepted ideological premises to conclusions that favor one or another policy preference is another device. In this case, we have in mind academic debates over esoteric themes such as what constitutes a "nation," in which the practical implications of resolution of theoretical questions are veiled but real.

3. A third device involves theoretical arguments built around the "dialectic." This device is most often used to *maintain* the ambiguity of official policy, to stalemate discussion, or to camouflage blatant lapses of logic.

The Concept of the Nation

The common element in all Marxist treatments of the nation (*natsiia*) is that it is not a racial or a tribal community, but the product of a definite historical epoch, that of rising capitalism. Nationalities (*natsional'nosti*) and peoples (*narody*), on the other hand, have their origins in precapitalist industrial relations. Engels spoke of the "fusion" or "merger" (*sliianie*) of tribes and clans - as a result of the appearance of private property, classes, trade, etc. - into "peoples," more or less stable ethnographic and historical formations, with their own cultures and written languages. A people or nationality is not merely an alliance of tribes, but a *merger* of them, in which they become fused and lose their individuality and their local governments, their territories merged under a single government.[29]

Lenin, following Engels, stressed the historical nature

[29]Engels, *Origin of the Family, Private Property and the State,* pp. 118, 125.

of the nation, and capitalism as its economic basis. But
in criticizing the historian Mikhailovsky, who had held
national ties to be a generalization of clan ties, Lenin
argued that only the modern period of Russian history -
since the 17th century - is marked by true fusion of the
formerly disunited Russian provinces, lands and municipal-
ities into a single whole. More importantly, Lenin urged,
this fusion was not the result of continuation and generalization of clan ties, but rather it was called forth by
"growing exchange among the provinces...the concentration
of small local markets into one all-Russian market."[30]

The importance of the historical-materialist and economic theory of the origins of nations to the myth of proletarian internationalism cannot be overstated. If clans and
tribes can, on the basis of economic integration, be
"merged" into single nations with the arrival of capitalism,
then further economic integration under socialism can be
expected to lead to the further merger of nations into
larger units with, it is implicit, single, centralized
governments. The awkward formula of national self-determination can then be considered as appropriate only for
capitalist states, and the corollary to national self-
determination, "national communism," as a wholly unscien-
tific deviation.

Until the period shortly following the adoption of the
1961 Party Program, Stalin's definition of the nation, with
its four factors (common language, territory, economy and
psychological makeup) remained unquestioned. In addition,
for Stalin, "merger," while inevitable, is explicitly
reserved for the dim future, the present being a time of
"flowering" of the national cultures that had been oppressed
under Tsarism.[31] Stalin's explicit rejection of immediate

[30]V.I. Lenin, *Sochineniia* (Moscow), Vol. I, pp. 137-38.

[31]J.V. Stalin, *The National QUestion and Leninism* (Moscow: Foreign
Languages Publishing House, 1950), p. 23.

merger, and his insistence on the indispensability of his four defining characteristics, particularly "psychological makeup," make his *theory* of the nation and its development (as distinct from his practice) rather more consistent with the cultural pluralist view than with the assimilationist view.

With the promulgation of the Party Program, and at the height of officially encouraged criticism of Stalin, his definition of the nation was open to modification. The assimilationist thrust in the definition of the nation was to reduce to a minimum the number of defining characteristics of nationhood, and in particular, to minimize the significance of the psychological aspects of national identity and to emphasize the role of "objective factors," - particularly economic and territorial ones. For assimilationists, "national self-consciousness" may exist, but only as a carry-over from pre-socialist nationhood; the self-declared concept of nationality is preferred over the concept of "root" nationality, based on ethnic descent. For assimilationists, any attempt to assert the stability of the psychological makeup of the people of a given nation is to treat the nation as a "naturalistic" community, rather than a "historical" one.

The arguments of the cultural pluralists consistently assign high importance to the psychological aspects of nationhood. M.S. Dzhunusov, among the most prolific and respected of the cultural pluralist nationality specialists, argued fervently, for example, at a conference on Problems of the Drawing Together of Socialist Nations held in Luhans'k (Lugansk) in January, 1966, that the study of nationality problems requires analysis of psychological phenomena "more than does any other subject."[32]

Cultural pluralists tend to project the existence of nations farther back into the past than is strictly

[32]"Konferentsiia po voprosam internatsionalizma," *Pravda Ukrainy*, January 25, 1966. For a report on the substance of the conference, see *Narodna tvorchist ta etnohrafiia*, No. 3(May-June, 1966), pp. 103-105.

58

orthodox and, of course, much farther into the future, and
they tend to deal somewhat more openly with tensions between nations both before and after the revolution. Pre-
dictably, it is only cultural pluralist writers who mention
the dangers of Russian chauvinism. The cultural pluralists,
as indeed they must, concede the necessity and desirability
of integration, but with a marked emphasis on genuine
equality. As Gray Hodnett notes, in the case of some
writers, it is this emphasis on genuine internationalism
that distinguishes the cultural pluralist position from a
form of crypto-nationalism.[33]

Like the assimilationists, the cultural pluralists appeal
to the symbolic authority of Lenin, but more so in criticism
of Russification than in defense of the existence of nations
in their own right, for, as we have seen, while Lenin urged
respect for the rights of national minorities as a tactical
measure, he was unequivocal in his contempt for nationalism
per se, and clearly argued that nations will ultimately
merge under socialism.[34]

Merger, the Nation, and Federalism

Disagreement over policies of denationalization and the
delimitation of the prerogatives of Union Republics is
often cast in the form of theoretical debates over the pace
of the realization of merger. A variety of variations on
the themes of *sblizhenie, rastsvet,* and *sliianie* have
emerged, which are indicative of the positions individuals
take on these issues.

[33]Gray Hodnett, "What's in a Nation?" *Problems of Communism*, XVI,
No. 5(September-October, 1967), p. 8.

[34]Dzyuba, for example, makes the error of confusing Lenin's tactical
emphasis on respecting the feelings of nationalities with a rejection
of merger. See *Internationalism or Russification?* (New York: Monad
Press, 1968), pp. 42-43.

The process of *sblizhenie* - "drawing together" or "rapprochement" - of the various nations is to be the result of the building of a Union-wide economic, political and cultural unit. In its ideal form, the process of *sblizhenie* is envisaged to mean that each culture will be influenced by the others, with the ultimate end-point being the amalgamation of the best of all cultures in a new, single international culture.

Because of the dominance of Russians, however, the term *sliianie* - "merger" - has come to mean, operatively, assimilation into Russian culture. There is, in fact, little empirical evidence that, where one culture is dominant, any such process as *sliianie* is ideally intended to describe actually occurs. The experience of minority and immigrant groups in America suggests that the dominant culture does not "blend" with diverse minority cultures to produce a new one combining the best features of all. Rather, the pattern appears to be complete assimilation into the dominant culture, or maintenance of ethnic ways behind a superficial "acculturation," or, if the dominant culture permits it, cultural pluralism.[35]

The theme of merger was clearly dominant in the period between the 22nd and 24th CPSU Congresses. The academics and publicists who most adamantly argued that merger was around the corner were those who also argued against the psychological interpretation of nationhood and for the abandonment of federal arrangements in the proposed new constitution.[36]

After the fall of Khrushchev, the merger theme fell into the background. This was not due to a victory of the cultural pluralists, for the theme re-emerged in the 1970s.

---

[35]That the American experience is not entirely lost on the Soviet Union was shown in a review of Glazer and Moynihan's *Beyond the Melting Pot* by Sh. Bogina in *Sovetskaia etnografiia*, No. 1(1966), pp. 184-87. See English translation in *Soviet Sociology* (Summer, 1967), pp. 56-60.

[36]Hodnett, *op. cit.*

But uncertainty regarding Brezhnev's position on the subject, reinforced by his reticence on nationalities policy
prior to the 24th Congress and the 50th Anniversary celebrations, surely was cause for caution.

A collective of scholars in L'viv (L'vov) seized upon
the temporary hiatus to carry the polemic with the opponents
of national statehood one step further: not only, they
asserted, must merger await the achievement of communism,
but a further condition for the merger of nations under
communism will be the final "withering away of the state."[37]
This was a reckless assertion, if only because the "withering away of the state" has long been rejected by the CPSU
even as a myth, but the thesis was attacked on its own
grounds in a review in *Komunist Ukrainy*. The reviewer
pointed out that Lenin had argued in his "Summary of a Discussion on Self-Determination"[38] that it is the accelerated
convergence and merger of nations which will itself result
in the disappearance of the state.[39]

The immediate device by which the issue could be tem-
porarily shelved without either side withdrawing from its
position was the "dialectic." In Soviet polemics, the
dialectic is often used as a device for either escaping
the logical conclusions of an argument carried too far, or,
when policy disputes are being discussed in doctrinal
terms, of recognizing a stalemate and ending public discussion.

The proposition that merger is a dialectical process -
i.e., that both "flowering" and "drawing together" take
place simultaneously - was first explicitly discussed in

[37]*Torzhestvo Lenins'kykh pryntsypiv proletars'koho internatsionalizmu*
(L'viv: "Kamenar," 1971), p. 96.

[38]V.I. Lenin, *Sochineniia*, Vol. XXII, p. 302.

[39]H. Emelianenko, "Lenins'ky pryntsypy proletars'koho internatsionalizmu," *Komunist Ukrainy*, No. 11(1971), p. 92. In addition to the fact
that merger will result in a single state structure, the Soviet leadership, for good and obvious reasons, do not like to discuss the "withering away of the state."

1962 by M.S. Dzhunusov. That either process occurs, of
course, has been said many times, but Dzhunusov's article
was significant for suggesting that they occur simultaneously, and for pointing out the implications of this for
the pace of merger - that it will be slower.[40]

Official acknowledgement that the merger theme was no
longer operative came in 1969:

> Under the leadership of the Communist
> Party the multinational Soviet nation
> firmly proceeds toward communism. Each
> Soviet nation and nationality brings its
> own weighty contribution.... In the
> process of creation of communism, they
> reach many-sided flowering and ever-closer
> drawing together. In all spheres of
> material and spiritual life of the Soviet
> people there are multiple lines common
> to all nations. However, the drawing
> together of Soviet nations and their
> internationalist unity should not be re-
> garded as their merger. The removal of
> all national differences is a long pro-
> cess, which cannot be achieved except
> long after the victory of communism in
> the world and its firm establishment.[41]

This excerpt from an otherwise routine article is notable
on several accounts. Besides lending the Party's authority
to the equal weight of flowering and drawing together, and
returning to the pre-1961 position that merger is remote,
it offers "internationalist unity" as a midway point along
the path of drawing together, short of merger. The use of
the word "unity" (*edinstvo*) in describing the Soviet Union
is certainly not new, but its elevation to the status of a
category, or stage of development, is new, and, as we shall
discuss more fully below, is a Brezhnev contribution.

[40]*Istoriia SSSR*, No. 3(1962), p. 43. Cited by Hodnett, p. 11.

[41]"Torzhestvo Leninskoi natsional'noi politiki," (editorial), *Kommunist*,
No. 13(1969), p. 10.

62

Even more remarkable is the reference to the Soviet Union
as a "nation" (*natsiia*). It is accepted usage in the Soviet
media and academic writings to refer to the Soviet "state"
(*gosudarstvo*), "country" (*strana*), Fatherland (*Otchizna*),
motherland (*rodina*), and "people" (*narod*), but a reference
to the Soviet "nation" is rare. We have been unable to locate another instance of this usage.

If the Soviet Union were to be considered a "nation" by
any of the definitions discussed, it would mean that merger
had already been achieved. Since the Party has endorsed
the view that merger will only follow the world-wide victory of communism,[42] it is logical that the Party must also
reject the concept of the Soviet Union as a "nation." The
effort, apparently of assimilationists, to label the Soviet
Union explicitly as a "nation" seems easily to have been
defeated.

If we can assume that high-level disagreement over federalism is what stalled the long-delayed new constitution
(adopted in 1977), and there is evidence that this is the
case,[43] it seems clear that there must be high-level sympathy with the demands of pro-federalist academics. It is
worth noting that none of the Union Republic 1st Secretaries
came to Brezhnev's support when, at the 50th anniversary
celebrations in 1972, he proposed that work on the new
constitution be terminated early and submitted to an "all-
people's referendum," and while Brezhnev's remarks on the

[42]See, e.g., *Pravda*, July 16, 1971, p. 4.

[43]See, for example, the radically contending views of juridical writers
on the proposed new constitution over the years, esp. G. Aleksandrov,
"O razvitii konstitutsii SSSR v svete reshenii XXI s'ezda KPSS,"
Sovetskoe gosudarstvo i pravo, No. 9(1959), 113-15; D.L. Zlatopol'skii,
"Sovetskaia federatsiia na novom etape razvitii natsional'nykh vzaimootnoshenii," *Vestnik Moskovskogo Universiteta*, No. 2(1962), 21-22; B.L.
Manelis, "Sootnoshenie konstitutsionnogo zakonodatel'stva Soiuza SSR
i soiuznykh respublikh," *Obshchestvennye nauki v Uzbekistane*, No. 1
(1965), 24-26. An excellent discussion of the wide range of issues involved in theoretical debates over federalism is Gray Hodnett, "The
Debate over Soviet Federalism," *Soviet Studies*, XVII, No. 4(April, 1967)
pp. 458-81.

new constitution were printed, the printed version omitted
his reference to an "all-people's referendum."[44]

In place of the apparently defeated Soviet "nation,"
there emerged after the 24th Party Congress the formula of
the "New Historical Community of People - the Soviet
People" (*Novaia istoricheskaia obshchnost' liudei - sovetskii narod*). Like many formulas raised to ideological
status by the Party, this is not new, the full phrase
having been used by some writers in the early 1960s.[45] It
did not become ubiquitous, however, until Brezhnev, in his
report to the 24th Congress, elevated it to the status of
a developmental plateau:

> A new historical human community - the
> Soviet people - has emerged in our country
> during the years of socialist construction.[46]

In one sense, the announcement of the achievement of a
new plateau brought a sense of relief: it signified, in
fact, that there was to be no dramatic change. The same
ambiguity of the formula, however, like that of the 1961
Party Program, gave rise to conflicting interpretations
based on concrete institutional and group policy goals.

[44]The discrepancy in the live version of Brezhnev's speech (Radio Moscow, December 21, 1972), and the published version (*Pravda*, December
22, 1972), was brought to my attention by Christian Duevel, Radio
Liberty Central Research Service, Munich, West Germany.

[45]The phrase "historic community of people," but without "Soviet *narod*,"
was first used by Khrushchev at the 22nd Party Congress; see *Current
Soviet Policies IV*, p. 84. The term "Soviet *narod*" itself first appeared in the resolutions of the 18th Congress and Statutes of the
VKP(b); see *KPRS v rezolutsiiakh z'izdiv, konferentsiy i plenumiv TsK*
(Kiev, 1954), Vol. 3, p. 360. The expression "Soviet *liudi*," also
meaning "people" but without the organic connotation, was used in the
first days of the revolution; Lenin's first use of the term is reported
to have been in March, 1919, in his "Appeal to the Red Army," *Sochineniia*, XXIX, p. 213. See V.M. Honchareva, "Radians'kyi narod - nova
istorichna spil'nist' liudei," *Filosofs'ka dumka*, No. 2(1972), 36-45.

[46]*Radians'ka Ukraina*, March 31, 1975, p. 7.

It became another ambiguous symbol to be filled with mythic
content.

To some degree, however, the semantic space of the word
narod in the Russian and Ukrainian languages[47] is restricted. Unlike the term *liudi*, also meaning "people" but in
the discrete sense of a group of individual persons, *narod*
carries a distinct spiritual and organic connotation; the
semantic distinction is similar, if not identical, to that
between *Volk* and *Leute* in German. *Narod* thus implies an
organic tie among people over and above that of mere citizenship. In addition, when used outside the "populist"
context, the word carries a symbolic connotation of empire
inherited from Tsar Nicholas I's ideology of "Official
Nationality," in which *narodnost'* was one of the three
pillars of the regime.

As used in the 19th century, especially by the Slavo-
philes, the term had a romantic frame of reference that derived from German Idealism. While there was, to be sure,
conflict among government ideologists at the time over the
"nationalistic" *versus* the "dynastic" interpretation of
narodnost', there is no doubt that in the popular mind and
in the intellectual mind, the term carried with it a connotation of the supreme metaphysical, even mystical, importance of the Russian people and Russian messianism, and it
certainly served as an ideological justification for Tsarist
policies of Russification.[48]

The word *narod*, therefore, at least in part is a symbol
of the myth of Russian primacy, carrying a heavy load of
historical significance; hence, the importance of Brezhnev's
having raised the formula "Soviet *narod*" to the status of
an ideological shibboleth.

---

[47]Although the Ukrainian word is *narid*, Ukrainian writers writing in
Ukrainian use the Russian word *narod*.

[48]See Nicholas Riasanovsky, *Nicholas I and Official Nationality in
Russia, 1825-1855* (Berkeley: University of California Press, 1969),
p. 124.

For assimilationists, the "new historical community"
formula was conceived as a compromise, or watered down,
version of the more desirable "Soviet nation." If, as we
have seen earlier, for Marxists the nation is a "historical
community," it does not take much dialectical imagination
to make a logical inversion and conclude that a "historical
community" is a sort of "nation." Evidence that this perception exists can be found in the attempts of assimilationist writers to identify the terms *narod* and *natsiia*.
V.I. Kozlov has done the most effective job of this type of
semantic-symbolic manipulation, and it is therefore worth
quoting him at length:

> In the Russian language in the first
> half of the 19th century, the word
> nation (*natsiia*) had predominantly a
> political meaning, but it yielded that
> meaning to the word "people" (*narod*)
> and came to be used for the most part
> in the ethnic sense. The same thing
> occurred with the derived word nation-
> ality (*natsional'nost'*), although in
> the 20th century the meaning of the
> latter has been greatly expanded....
> In particular, there has been a drawing
> together of the term *natsional'nost'*
> with the term *narod*, (the term *Sovet
> natsional'nostei*, for example, now means
> the same as *Sovet narodov*). The term
> *natsional'nost'*, however, in distinction
> to *narod*, is never used in the meaning
> of "race" (*plemia*). At the present
> time, in our literature, the term
> *natsional'nost'* is most often used to
> designate ethnic (national) membership...
> the term in foreign languages closest
> to our own is "ethnic nationality."[49]

So far, while Kozlov has equated *natsional'nost'* with
narod, his views do not as yet represent a significant
departure; Kozlov, a sociologist, is merely describing
current usage. The identification comes later. On page 57,

[49]V.I. Kozlov, *Dinamika chislennosti narodov: metodologiia issledovaniia i osnovnye faktory* (Moscow: "Nauka," 1969), p. 20n.

Kozlov equates the term "ethnic community" (*etnicheskaia obshchnost'*) with *narod*. Then:

> ... in an ethnic community (*etnicheskaia obshchnost'*) as already noted above, while usually related indirectly to economics, *not one* of its basic features - self awareness, language, territory, etc. - fails, as a rule, to undergo substantial changes during the transition from one mode of production to another. Therefore, if we assume that the type of ethnic community is determined all and for the most part by a social-economic formation, then we may characterize the peculiarities of every type basically as merely those same characteristics which are typical of the given formation, i.e., specific industrial relations or social class composition. The terms *plemia, narodnost'*, and *natsiia* are in that case altogether superfluous, since it is more correct to call them all similar "types" of ethnic communities: *narod* of primitive society, *narod* of slave society, and so forth; in the final analysis, they look no more strange than the currently used terms "capitalist nation" and "socialist nation."[50]

In the process of proposing simplified sociological terminology, Kozlov has identified *narod* with ethnic community, and defined capitalist and socialist nations as sub-sets of that category. On this basis, he is prepared to define a *narod*:

> A people (*narod*), or an ethnic community, is a social organism, made up on a definite territory of a group of people who already have or are in some measure evolving various links in a community of language, common features of culture and everyday life, peculiarities of psychic disposition, and, if these are differentiated racially, then considerable cross-breeding among them.[51]

[50]*Ibid.*, p. 58.

[51]*Ibid.*, p. 57.

It will be noted that Kozlov's definition of a *narod* is in all respects identical to Stalin's definition of a nation. The same is true of his definition of an ethnic community, previously identified with *narod*:

> The basic characteristics of an ethnic community are: self-awareness and self-identification, language, territory, peculiarities of culture, a definite form of social-territorial organization or a distinctly expressed striving to create such an organization.[52]

The interpretation of the "new historical community" concept as one that equates *narod* with *natsiia* and all which that entails has been challenged head-on by cultural pluralist academics.[53] Brezhnev himself has more or less explicitly rejected the notion that *narod* is equivalent to "nation." In a speech at the presentation of the Order of the Friendship of Peoples to Kazakhstan, he said:

> In speaking about the new historic community of people, we certainly do not mean that national differences are disappearing in our country, or all the more, that a merging of nations has occurred.[54]

Similarly, in his report to the 24th Congress of the CPSU, at which he advanced the "historic community" thesis,

---

[52]*Ibid.*, p. 57. Kozlov researched and wrote at least two years before the 24 Congress at which Brezhnev elevated the "Soviet *narod*" to ideological status. The explanation, of course, is that Brezhnev himself hardly originated the idea; he borrowed, from among academic disputants, the ideas that served him.

[53]See, for example, I.P. Tsamerian, *Teoreticheskie problemy obrazovaniia i razvitiia sovetskogo mnogonatsional'nogo gosudarstva* (Moscow: "Nauka," 1973). See review by E. Tadevosian in *Izvestiia*, January 23, 1974, p. 3.

[54]Quoted by Tadevosian, *op. cit.*

Brezhnev made it clear that the "drawing together" and
"flowering" of the socialist nations - referring to
"nations" in the plural - were still to be considered as
coexisting tendencies.[55]

Bearing in mind the criterion that high-level pronouncements of this type represent "official" ideology, it seems
clear that the Party does not regard the Soviet *narod* concept as favoring the proposals of the assimilationist
school. At the very least, it was clear at the time of the
24th Congress that there was no "Soviet nation" in the
official view, and that flowering and drawing together were
of equal importance.

For assimilationists, simply calling the Soviet Union a
"nation" is not an end in itself: this is a device for
ascribing the *attributes* of a nation to the Soviet Union,
so as to legitimate further policies of denationalization
and centralization. With the idea of a "Soviet nation"
defeated, the crux of the debate turned on defining the
characteristics of the "Soviet *narod*." The assimilationist
strategy has been simply to define them as those of a
nation, without calling it that. The remarks of Rogachev
and Sverdlin, among the foremost representatives of the
assimilationist school, are typical:

> The new historic community - the
> Soviet people - is a *community of
> a higher order than a nation*. It
> resembles a nation by many essential
> features: community of economy, ter-
> ritory, culture, psychology, con-
> sciousness of belonging to the Soviet
> people, the presence of an all-Union
> language of international discourse, etc.[56]

[55]*Radians'ka Ukraina*, March 31, 1971. English translation in *Digest of the Soviet Ukrainian Press*, May, 1971, p. 16.

[56]P.M. Rogachev and M.A. Sverdlin, "SSSR - otechestvo mnogonatsional'-nogo sovetskogo naroda," *Filosofskie nauki*, No. 2(1973), p. 10.

Cultural pluralists, in addition to explicitly denying
the equation of *narod* and nation, place greater emphasis on
the multinational (*mnogonatsional'naia*) character of the
"new historical community," which is not surprising. But
when discussing the characteristics of the Soviet *narod*,
they place primary emphasis on the *class* nature of the
community. To a certain degree, this is an alternative to
the crypto-ethnic interpretation placed on it by the assimilationists. But it is also a response to another symbol
raised to ideological status by Brezhnev at the 24th Congress: that of "unity" (*edinstvo*). The full symbolic sig-
ficance of the "unity" theme did not become apparent until
the celebration of the 50th anniversary of the formation
of the USSR in 1972, but its significance was evidently
apparent to some scholars before then.

Unity, like the other terms discussed here, is not new
to ideological discourse. Its import in Brezhnev's speech
derived in part from the frequency of usage, but primarily
from the qualifiers he used. Before 1971, it was common
to speak of the "unshakeable" (*neterpimoe*) unity of the
nations of the USSR, a usage directed at foreign commen-
tators who, in the Soviet polemical view, were trying to
exploit the disunity they saw - i.e., minority nationalism.

Brezhnev spoke repeatedly, however, of the "monolithic"
unity of the peoples of the USSR.[57] "Monolithic" has quite
a different connotation. Whereas "unshakeable" refers to
resistance to an external force, "monolithic" implies an
internal cohesion, and is directed at internal threats to
unity.

The thrust of the efforts of cultural pluralists to define "unity" in class terms is to give it a demotic, or
civil, connotation, rather than an ethnic or organic one.

Ukrainian cultural pluralist scholars figured very
prominently in the effort to classify "unity" and the

[57]*Radians'ka Ukraina*, March 31, 1971, pp. 2-8. English translation in
Digest of the Soviet Ukrainian Press, May, 1971, p. 16.

70

Soviet *narod* in class rather than ethnic terms. Exemplary
of this theoretical thrust are the remarks of V.M. Honchareva:

> We know that the term *narod* is used
> in two meanings: 1) as a synonym for
> the term "nation" (for example, in
> such expressions as the "Russian
> nation," the "French nation," the
> "Ukrainian nation," etc. 2) in its
> own meaning to designate the "working
> people." Obviously, the category
> "Soviet *narod*" is not used in the same
> sense as Russian *narod* or French *narod*.
> This term describes the unity of the
> working people of the Soviet Union
> without regard to their national affil-
> iation. The category "Soviet *narod*"
> signifies not so much the uniformity of
> language or ethnic composition, as the
> unity of USSR workers regardless of their
> differences in lifestyle, mentality,
> culture, and so forth. That is, it
> is a unity of an international type.[58]

Whereas assimilationist writers can cite numerous pas-
sages from Lenin in support of either the ultimate or the
immediate merger of nations, we have seen that this option
is not open to cultural pluralists, who are forced to rely
on Lenin's tactical calls for respect for national feelings.
Through a careful exegesis of Lenin's pre-war writings,
however, Honchareva attempts to imply that Lenin regarded
merger to mean a merger of.class interests only, rather
than of ethnic characteristics:

> ... V.I. Lenin preferred the idea of a
> merger of the working classes of all nations
> over the abstract slogan calling for the
> merger of nations.[59]

---

[58]V.M. Honchareva, "Radians'kyi narod - nova istorichna spil'nist'
liudei," *Filosofs'ka dumka*, No. 2(1972), pp. 36-45. Note the juxta-
position of the Ukraine with Russia and France, in effect equating their
status.

[59]*Ibid.*

Honchareva's citation of Lenin to this effect in fact is a passage dealing with Lenin's well-known preference for international proletarian unity over alliances betwen bourgeois states.[60] The fallacy in Honchareva's appeal to the symbolic authority of Lenin is a confusion in levels of analysis.

Writing apparently with the same aim in mind, but approaching the question from the standpoint of republican *versus* Union sovereignty, V.M. Terlets'kyi, the former Chief Editor of *Komunist Ukrainy*,[61] writes:

> Socialist democracy provides for and
> tangibly ensures the equality of
> nationalities in Soviet society....
> In the USSR, the Union state does
> not exist above and beyond the repub-
> lican states. It is a form of Union
> of the republics, a means for jointly
> realizing Union rule - they act as one
> through Union organs in accordance with
> the USSR constitution, as well as
> through their republican organs....[62]

Were it only so! Terlets'kyi is arguing here that the USSR is not a federation at all, but a confederation in which the Union derives its powers from the constituent republics, rather than vice-versa - a view that is patently false in the Soviet case, as well as a velleity.

---

[60]V.I. Lenin, *Sochineniia*, Vol. XX, pp. 19, 378; Vol. XVI, p. 146.

[61]Valentyn M. Terlets'kyi, Chief Editor of *Komunist Ukrainy* since 1969, disappeared without explanation from the editorial board of the journal with the November, 1972 issue, closely following the ouster of Petro Shelest. Under Terlets'kyi, the journal had adopted a relatively progressive line, and on some occasions had published articles critical of Brezhnev's centralist policies. V.F. Sorenko, Terlets'kyi's replacement, is thought to have served as an ideological official in Dnepropetrovsk *ca.* 1969. For a discussion of these and related issues, see Christian Duevel, "A Brezhnev Protege as Chief Editor of *Komunist Ukrainy*?" Radio Liberty Research Paper 343/72, November 29, 1972.

[62]*Radians'ka Ukraina*, May 30, 1971, pp. 3-4.

Terlets'kyi's style, as does that of many liberal publicists, exemplifies the technique of attributing the views
of domestic ideological opponents to the common Cold War
enemy:

> Therefore, the various attempts of anti-
> communist ideologies, including those of
> Ukrainian bourgeois nationalists, to slander
> the Union state consisting of all the
> nations of our homeland and to portray
> the Soviet Ukraine, as well as other Soviet
> republics, as having no rights, are in vain.[63]

The important thing to note is that Terlets'kyi's criticism here is directed as much at individuals such as Sverdlin and Rogachev, as to foreign anti-communists. The technique is similar in principle to that of airing and discussing proscribed views and interpretations under the guise
of criticizing bourgeois ideology. Cultural pluralist
writers who place stress on a "class" rather than an ethnic
interpretation of the "new historic community of people"
rely on this technique frequently. Thus, the cultural
pluralist writer S. Kovalev, after explaining at great
length the class nature of the Soviet *narod*, assures his
readers that there can be no American "people" comparable
to the Soviet *narod* because of the conflict of economic
classes in America.[64] The esoteric reasoning is that, if
the reason that the Americans have not achieved a *narod*-like
community is because of class conflict, then the reason that
the Soviet community *is* a *narod* is because of class unity.
Thus, both "unity" and the "Soviet *narod*" are placed outside an assimilationist framework: the characteristics of
a *narod* that the author wishes to legitimate - namely,
ethnic and cultural diversity - are excluded from the

[63]*Ibid.*

[64]S. Kovalev, "Radians'kyi narod - nova istorychna spil'nist',"
Sil's'ki visti, July 21, 1971, p. 2

criteria for differentiating the two systems.

As we have pointed out, cultural pluralists, while they frequently appeal to the authority of Lenin, more often appeal to the Marxist "classics." The author just cited and others, for example, quote liberally from Marx and Engels' *The German Ideology*, for much is made in that work of the *illusory* community of peoples that characterizes capitalist societies. To argue that there can be no genuine community of peoples where unemployment reigns, billionaires rule, and class antagonism in general is rife is to juxtapose as an ideal society the myth of a Soviet Union where *these* problems do not exist, rather than to juxtapose the Soviet Union to a society where these problems are attributed to the maintenance of cultural and linguistic problems. The thrust of this strand of cultural pluralist argument is that merger, if it is ideologically necessary, need not involve the dissolution of cultural and linguistic externals in order to achieve the type of social justice that the myth envisages.

In his lengthy speech on the occasion of the 50th anniversary of the USSR in December, 1972, Brezhnev explicitly endorsed the dialectical interpretation that flowering and drawing together proceed apace as equal tendencies:

> The further drawing together of the nations and peoples of our country is an objective process. The Party is against speeding it up artificially; there is no need for that, this process is dictated by the entire course of our Soviet life.
>
> At the same time, the Party considers inadmissable any attempts to restrain the process of drawing together of the nations, to create hindrances to it under one pretext or another or artificially to consolidate national isolation, for that would run counter to the general direction of development of our society, to the internationalist ideals and ideology of communism, and to the interests of communist construction.[65]

74

Two things are clear in this authoritative statement.
The first is that the Party will not undertake aggressive
denationalization of the type advocated by the more vociferous assimilationists, nor will the Party relax is hostility to national particularism. Secondly, the thrust of
the pronouncement is that the Party *endorses* drawing together, even though it does not anticipate "speeding it up
artificially." It is not so much a centrist position as a
status quo position, although the brunt of it is against
those who advocate aggressive implementation of *sblizhenie*,
rather than against those who plead for moderation. *Pravda*,
in October and December, 1972 began explicitly insisting in
its editorials that the two trends of the contentious dialectic were of equal rank.[66] Ivan I. Bodiul, Moldavian
Party 1st Secretary, nonetheless amended the formula in his
speech at the 50th anniversary celebrations, referring to
"the path of unflinching drawing together, which has now
become the *leading tendency in the twin processes* of national relations."[67]

We may speculate that Brezhnev foresees that the best
path to retirement with honor lies in maintaining a centrist
position in nationalities policy, particularly in relation
to the doctrinal questions we have discussed. Certainly,
his contribution to the polemic has been in the direction
of moderation: the introduction of the "new historic community" concept to replace the assimilationist "Soviet
nation" idea, and the elevation of "unity" to the status of
of an ideological category, to replace the contentious and
abrasive *sliianie*. Unity and its derivative formulations
(such as "full unity" - *polnoe edinstvo*), while ambiguous
and giving rise to debate in their own right, have a more
softened, less overtly assimilationist connotation, than

[65]*Pravda*, December 22, 1972.

[66]See, for example, *Pravda*, October 12, 1972, p. 1.

[67]*Pravda*, December 23, 1972.

does *sliianie*, which is associated in the minds of the minority nationalities with denationalization and Russification. By introducing a number of new terms and concepts,
Brezhnev has been able to ameliorate the intensity of the
nationalities problem in purely symbolic terms, without
changing the substance of policy. In spite of the stale-
matihg of discussion and the bridling of the assimilationists, there has been little change in policy; indeed,
during the period since the 24th Party Congress, Brezhnev
has effectively curbed the autonomist tendencies of the
Ukrainian party under Shelest, and the most outspoken
nationalist dissidents in the Ukraine have, since 1972,
been all but silenced.

CONCLUSIONS

The crisis of legitimacy in Soviet nationalities policy
lies in a certain lack of uniformity, or inconsistency, in
the adaptation of ideology to the mythic structure of the
society: the ideology simply does not properly address
ethnic processes in the Soviet Union. To illustrate this,
we can divide the various alternative interpretations of
the national question along the dimensions of commitment
to the integrity of the Soviet Union (the vertical axis,
representing degrees of political centralization, with a
highly centralized "Soviet nation" at one extreme, and outright separatism at the other), and the dimension of
assimilation (the horizontal axis, "flowering" of cultures
and languages at one extreme, merger at the other).
What this simple graph illustrates is the disjunction
between myths and ideology. The mythic structure does not
divide conveniently in the way that ideologically expressed
demands do. The most salient dimension from the viewpoint
of the regime is the vertical axis, as can be judged from
the fact that the regime has arrested and imprisoned those
who adopt positions below the horizontal axis. The debate

76

HIGH

*Dimension of political
centralization*

"Assimilationists"   "Cultural Pluralists"

shared myth

HIGH ————————————————————— *LOW*

*Dimension of
cultural
centralization*

"Separatists"
Empty category   "National Communists

LOW

between assimilationists and cultural pluralists, however,
is legitimate, and takes place entirely in legitimate channels of communication. Because what these positions have
in common is high commitment to the integrity of the Soviet
Union, this can be interpreted as the irreducible core of
the myth of proletarian internationalism: the territory of
the Soviet Union must remain a political entity governed
from Moscow.

The political myth on which the nationalists - below the

horizontal axis - base their demands is the myth of national
self-determination: that a nation is legitimately governed
only by itself. This is not parallel to the regime's definition of what constitutes a legitimate ideological position, however, for - as the graph is intended to show -
this is the same myth that underlies the arguments of the
assimilationists. In arguing for a single Soviet nationality - whether achieved through Russification or genuine
"merger" - they implicitly endorse the same myth as do the
nationalists, albeit a radically different method of trans-
forming the myth into political reality.

In terms of concrete policy proposals and demands for
respect for national cultures and languages, the cultural
pluralists are a moderate midpoint between the assimilationists and the nationalists. But in terms of the mythic basis
of the legitimacy of the state, it is the assimilationists
and the nationalists who are united; the cultural pluralists
seek a demotic, rather than an organic, basis of cohesion:
a genuinely multinational and multicultural federation
based on *class* unity. Where the assimilationists and the
nationalists divide, therefore, is not over the mythic basis
for the legitimacy of a state (any state), but over the
specific myth of proletarian internationalism: that the
former Tsarist empire must in one form or another remain a
state, and governed from Moscow.

This disjuncture - the simultaneous existence and legitimacy of two opposing political myths, and conversely, the
casting of opposed political demands based on a single
myth - perpetuates conflict over the *form* of the continued
existence of the Soviet state, simultaneously with conflict
over whether the Soviet state has a right to exist at all.

III

CULTURE AND SYMBOLISM:
THE MYTH OF NATIONAL MORAL PATRIMONY

In the preceding chapter, we have discussed the manipulation
of symbols of the national myth and of proletarian internationalism, as they have been exploited by cultural pluralists and assimilationists in the effort to shape ideology.
We turn our attention in this chapter to specific concrete
elements of the myth of Ukrainian national moral patrimony
as they have been interpreted and exploited by Ukrainian
writers and artists.

We are concerned in this chapter with culture, not in the
anthropological sense, but in the sense of creative pursuits
that are valued over and above their everyday utility.
Specifically, the concern is with the expression of symbols
of national authenticity as opposed to all-Union (or, as
frequently is the case, explicitly Russian) themes in
Ukrainian literature, graphic arts, music, drama and cinema.

SOCIALIST REALISM AND NATIONAL
CULTURAL REVIVAL

One of the most obvious and explicit vehicles for symbolism
and the expression of politically relevant myths in a society is the arts. It is for this reason that totalitarian
societies have placed rigid controls over literature,
graphic arts, and the performing arts.[1]

---

[1] For a brief but informed discussion of state control of the arts in
fascist Italy, Nazi Germany and the Soviet Union, see Igor Golomshtok,
"The Language of Art under Totalitarianism," Radio Liberty Special
Report 404/76, September 8, 1976.

Because our concern is with the "national" as opposed to
the strictly artistic in Ukrainian culture, much of the
liberation from the restrictions of Zhdanovism that followed
the 20th Party Congress is not of central relevance. Two
considerations, however, force us to consider the rebellion
of writers and artists against the confines of "socialist
realism" as relevant to the problem of the assertion of
ethnic identity under conditions of official pressure to
assimilate. The first is that art, of necessity, must draw
upon human experience; while the Soviet experience in the
20th century could certainly have provided rich opportunities for the portrayal of common national moral, ethical,
and spiritual experience, it has in fact been limited to
superficial themes stressing optimism and utopian notions of
virtue. Secondly, where socialist realism has drawn on folk
themes, it has tended to emphasize *Russian* folk themes
rather than the folklore of non-Russian nationalities.

Socialist realism, as it was interpreted during the
Stalin era, is a heroic romanticism, portraying an idealized
future, and picturing an idealized present-day reality.
Mood and naturalistic detail are discouraged, as is conflict
stemming from human weakness or the dimmer recesses of the
psyche. The result is art that is monumental, sometimes
even bombastic, celebrating strength, youth, work, energy
and optimism. It is calculated to uplift, edify, and teach
by example.

Art which must be accessible to and understandable by
"the masses," and which must serve didactic and propagandistic aims, is bound to be leveled to a very low standard,
and this has frustrated Soviet artists of talent. Creative,
experimental and progressive artists, even when their work
is not expressly hostile to the state, have been subject to
extreme censure.

The reason is that works of art and literature, even when
they are manifestly non-political, are concrete manifestations of some myth, and thus they are symbols. A state
concerned with restricting symbolic expression to a single

mythic structure which it believes bolsters its legitimacy
or otherwise serves its ends will therefore seek to control
artistic expression. The task of socialist realism, then,
is to depict reality as already conforming to the myth of
proletarian internationalism. There follows logically from
this the other characteristics of socialist realism: the
independence of its aesthetic ideals from all other artistic
standards, and the heightened relevance of non-aesthetic
categories such as social didacticism.

Ukrainian art and literature at the end of the Stalin
era suffered not only from gray, lifeless, repetitive
themes,[2] but also from the near-complete removal of all
national elements other than those elements of Slavic culture that it shared with Russia. The re-emergence of art
and literature during the thaw was characterized not only
by creative and stylistic experimentation, but also by a
felt need to search for and find some basis of national
authenticity, based on a variously felt and vaguely defined
national myth: cultural and folkloristic themes that are
valued above all because they are uniquely Ukrainian.
Ukrainians, too, felt that the internationalist demands of
socialist realism were an insufficient framework for the
expression of human spirituality. The most explicit statement of this is that of Ievhen Sverstiuk:

> Today, everyone...understands that the
> point is not poetization of a Cathedral
> of all mankind, but above all its quite
> concrete embodiment in oneself, the
> elaboration of one's *own individuality as
> a part of one's own nation*, as a reliable
> foothold for cultural and spiritual life.[3]

[2] See, for example, Ivan Svitlychnyi's criticisms, in *Vitchyzna*, No. 4 (April, 1961), pp. 162-77.

[3] Ievhen Sverstiuk, *Sobor u ryshtovanni* (Baltimore: Smoloskyp, 1970), p. 20.

The Ukrainian cultural revival in the "thaw" period followed developments in the RSFSR, in that there was a revival
of honest literary criticism, a number of significant rehabilitations, and a concern with experimentation and influences from the West. There was, however, an added concern with national elements of art and literature that was
absent from the cultural scene in Moscow.

The revival of distinctly Ukrainian literature can be
said to have begun with the rehabilitation of Volodymyr
Sosiura's patriotic poem "Love the Ukraine." The poem, a
lyrical elegy with predominately landscape imagery, had been
written in 1944 and was tolerated for some years, until it
came under scathing criticism in 1951. The critic was able
to conclude that Sosiura had been "singing of some primor-
dial Ukraine, of the Ukraine in general," rather than of
the *Soviet* Ukraine.[4]

The poem was reappraised in *Kommunist* in 1956, and found
to be innocent of the charges brought against it.[5] Writings
began to appear that expressed or inspired Ukrainian pride.
Criticisms of the Stalinist style in art and literature
appeared both in the RSFSR and in the Ukraine.[6] Ivan Dzyuba
and Ivan Svitlychnyi, later to figure heavily in the Young
Writers Movement and later still as dissidents, were frequent contributors of this style of straightforward criticism, their writings and reviews appearing in the "liberal"

[4]*Pravda*, July 2, 1951, p. 2. The attack in *Pravda* was triggered by the
poem's appearance in *Zvezda* (Leningrad), XXVIII, No. 5(1951), pp. 128-29.
John Kolasky reports having been informed that the author of the attack
in *Pravda* was Kaganovich; *Two Years in Soviet Ukraine* (Toronto: Peter
Martin Associates, Ltd., 1970), p. 260n.

[5]*Kommunist*, No. 12(1956). See commentary by Ivan Burlai, *Vitchyzna*,
No. 1(1958), pp. 176-89, and B. Kyryluk, *Radians'ka Ukraina*, January 5,
1958, p. 2.

[6]For a review of early Soviet criticisms of the Stalinist style, see
A. de Vincenz, "Recent Ukrainian Writing," *Survey*, No. 46(January,
1963), pp. 143-50.

journals *Vitchyzna* and *Dnipro*, as well as in *Literaturna
hazeta*.[7] Maksym Ryls'kyi, an establishment writer of considerable esteem, who was later to defend the Young Writers
and their views, also had an early voice in the advocacy of
art for art's sake.[8]

Accompanying and no doubt in part accounting for the
sudden surge of conscientious literature and literary criticism in this period was the influence of Eastern Europe.[9]
Several eminent Ukrainian cultural figures travelled exten-
sively in Eastern and Western Europe, and were undoubtedly
influenced by the more open and experimental atmosphere
that prevailed there, and brought these influences back
with them. In the aftermath of the Hungarian uprising, and
because of large Ukrainian populations in Poland and Czechoslovakia with ties to the West Ukraine, such influences
were looked upon by the regime with as much alarm as influences from the "bourgeois West." Another source of concern for the regime was the increasing availability in the
Ukraine of works by emigre Ukrainians.

A final development that was both a symptom of and a
contributor to the Ukrainian cultural revival was the rehabilitation of Ukrainian writers and artists of the 1920s
and 1930s who had been purged by Stalin for "nationalist
deviations." The movement began among the younger Ukrainian intelligentsia, who called for rehabilitations under
the slogan "fight the impoverishment of our Ukrainian
heritage!"[10] There was considerable support for this

[7]*Vitchyzna*, No. 4(April, 1961), pp. 162-77; *Dnipro*, No. 4(April, 1962),
pp. 144-52; *Literaturna Ukraina*, December 4, 1962, p. 3, and others.

[8]*Radians'ka kultura*, No. 6(June, 1956), pp. 12-13.

[9]Viktor Nekrasov believes that contacts with Poland, France and Italy
were among the most important stimuli of the Ukrainian cultural
renaissance in the 1950s. Personal interview, Paris, June 27, 1976.

[10]*Literaturna hazeta*, December 20, 1956, p. 2, and January 15, 1957,
p. 3.

sentiment, even among establishment intellectuals who later became indifferent or even hostile to it.

These rehabilitations are important because they were often used by advocates of greater cultural expression to justify engaging in many of the activities for which the rehabilitated individuals had originally been purged. The issues raised in debates over rehabilitations set the agenda for controversy over cultural expression in the years to come: more latitude to seek greater national authenticity in art and literature, demands for more extensive use of national personnel in the performing arts, more latitude for the use of national folk themes, and recognition of the independent roots of Ukrainian culture.

Open calls for rehabilitations began at the 4th Plenum of the Ukrainian Writers' Union in January, 1957. Maksym Ryls'kyi, writing in *Literaturna hazeta* in November, 1957, announced the most interesting of the early rehabilitations, that of Oleksandr Oles'-Kandyba (1878-1944), who had died in the emigration.[11]

The effort to rehabilitate Mykola Khvylovyi (1893-1933) who, in the 1930s under the slogan "away from Moscow" had openly urged that Ukrainian culture model itself on that of Western Europe, was unsuccessful. Khvylovyi was too explicitly nationalistic in the eyes of many establishment intellectuals, and remained, along with other national communists of the early 1920s and 1930s, a symbol of unacceptable nationalism in culture. The debate over Khvylovyi

[11]This was the father of the OUN-Melnyk leader, known as "Ol'zhych," who perished at the hands of the Germans in the same year at Sachsenhausen. The rehabilitation plan adopted in this case was one suggested by Babushkin: that the author's works be edited, and those of a non-nationalist nature be printed; see *Radians'ke literaturnoznavstvo*, No. 1(1958), p. 9. D. Kopytsia opposed the rehabilitation of an undoubted "nationalist" on the grounds that it would be at variance with the principle that the Party alone must guide literary evaluation; see *Literaturna hazeta*, October 10, 1958, p. 2. Similar attempts by West Ukrainian literary students to rehabilitate Bohdan Lepkyi and Andrii Chykovs'kyi, both branded nationalists by Stalin, failed; Viktor Nekrasov, personal interview, Paris, June 27, 1976.

84

also colored the rehabilitation of the dramatist Mykola
Kulish (1892-1942), and that of Les' Kurbas (1887-1942),
the producer and director of the famed *"Berezil"* theater
group in the late 1920s and early 1930s.[12]
· One of the most important rehabilitations for its effect
on setting the tone of demands for national authenticity
was that of Oleksandr Dovzhenko (1894-1956), a Ukrainian
film director and prose writer with an international
reputation.[13] Dovzhenko's early and later films and memoirs
emphasized landscape imagery and themes of love, endurance,
and death. His concern, by his own admission, was with the
"eternal verity" of the Ukrainian land and culture, and he
was anxious to portray the Ukrainian language on the screen
in the vernacular, rather than in stilted, textbook Ukrainian.[14]
More than any other rehabilitated cultural figure, Dovzhenko became a symbol of the revitalization and re-authen-
tication of Ukrainian culture. Typically, he was exploited
both by the regime and by advocates of national expression.
The potency of Dovzhenko as a symbol was also constantly
fed by reference to his international stature.[15]

[12]On the controversy over rehabilitation of Kurbas, see: *Radians'ka
Ukraina*, No. 42(May 23, 1957); *Radians'ka kultura*, No. 37(May 5, 1957);
Vitchyzna, No. 2(February, 1958), pp. 180-83; *Literaturna hazeta*, April
25, 1958; *Vitchyzna*, No. 5(May, 1959), pp. 163-78; *Sovetskaia Ukraina*,
No. 7(July, 1961), pp. 159-70; *Mystetstvo*, No. 2(March-April, 1965).

[13]Dovzhenko had been censured by the Party for his silent films of
Ukrainian life. In 1958, his early silent film *The Earth* was rated at
the Brussels Film Festival as one of the twelve best films of world
cinematography. Because of his world reputation, he was pardoned by
Stalin and allowed to work on Party-commissioned films. He returned to
the Ukraine in 1952 and began work on his last film, *The Poem of the
Sea*. After Stalin's death, he was permitted to publish his memoirs,
"The Enchanted Desna," in Ukrainian in *Dnipro*, No. 4(1956).

[14]O. Dovzhenko, "Notes and Materials on 'The Poem of the Sea',"
Dnipro, No. 6(June 1957), and No. 7(July, 1957).

[15]*Vitchyzna*, for example, reprinted a favorable review of Dovzhenko by
the French historian of cinema Georges Sadoul, which had appeared in
Nasha kultura, a supplement to the Polish Ukrainian language newspaper

Several Ukrainian composers were rehabilitated during
this period, facilitated by a resolution of the CPSU Central
Committee of May 28, 1958, condemning "Zhdanovism" in
music.[16] Music in particular is a rich field for folk and
national themes. Russian composers since Glinka and Tchai-
kovsky have traditionally turned to Russian folksongs for
themes for their compositions, and they still do. Ukrainian composers who turn to Ukrainian folk music for themes,
however, are frequently accused of "bourgeois nationalism,"
and socialist realism in music means, as much as optimism
and emphasis on the upbeat, the avoidance of non-Russian
folk themes.

The period was marked as well by increasing calls for
the right to existence of an independent, authentically
unique Ukrainian culture; these demands are related to the
ideological emphasis discussed in Chapter 2 on the "flowering" of national cultures. These demands were of three
general types, apart from the question of language:
1. for recognition of the mutual (and not merely one-sided)
influence of Russian and Ukrainian culture on each other;
2. for greater exploitation of Ukrainian historical and
cultural themes in the arts; and 3. demands for the training
and utilization of native Ukrainian personnel in the performing arts. These demands remained essentially unchanged
throughout the period under study, and they came from the
same sectors of society: those engaged professionally in
history, literature, philology, art, drama, and cinema.

The common element underlying all of these is the theme
of authenticity, which derives from the myth of the nation
as the repository of moral values. Culture is the examination and depiction - whether for the purpose of criticism or edification - of that which is considered of enduring value in the human experience. These demands arise

Nashe slovo; see *Vitchyzna*, No. 11(November, 1958), pp. 183-85.

[16]*Pravda Ukraina* and *Radians'ka Ukraina*, May 29, 1958.

out of desire for the recognition of the value of the
Ukrainian national patrimony, in part for its intrinsic
worth, and in part in protest against what is perceived as
a claim for the universal validity of the Russian patrimony.

The thesis that Ukrainian culture, and literature in
particular, as well as that of all the other minority
nationalities, developed under the influence of Russian
literature, became increasingly a leading tenet in Soviet
criticism after World War II, and is directly related to
the "friendship of peoples" myth.

The most widely quoted example of this thesis of the
Russian formative influence is the debt that Shevchenko is
said to have owed to the Russian writers Chernyshevsky,
Belinsky, and Dobroliubov,[17] despite the fact that, as John
Kolasky has pointed out, these writers were still children
when Shevchenko published his *Kobzar* in 1847.[18]

An early challenge to the thesis of primary Russian formative influence came in a book by G. Lomidze in 1957.
Lomidze urged literary critics and philologists to pay more
attention to national peculiarities derived from folklore
and national character, rather than to continue seeking
superficial commonalities in language and themes.[19] Lomidze's
ideas were picked up at once in the Ukraine. Borys Buriak,
for example, openly argued that researchers on the "brother-
ly ties" between Ukrainian and Russian literature are
usually bent upon establishing such ties, and seek out common ideas, subjects and themes from various works that

---

[17]See, for example, I.K. Bilodid, *Rosiys'ka mova - mova mnohonatsio-
nal'noho spilkuvannia narodiv SRSR* (Kiev: "Radians'kyi pys'mennyk,"
1962), p. 11.

[18]Kolasky, *op. cit.*, p. 69.

[19]G. Lomidze, *Edinstvo i mnogoobrazovanie* (Moscow: "Sovietskii pisatel,"
1957). Although we have no verification of his ethnic background,
Lomidze's name indicates that he is probably Georgian.

support the theory of Russian primary influence.[20]

Similar demands reflecting the theme of cultural authenticity were expressed in all branches of the arts. We need
examine only one branch, cinema, to illustrate the patterns.

Early post-Stalin demands for authenticity in Ukrainian
cinema were made as a protest against numerous films in
which the leading motif was the "friendship" of the Ukrainian and Russian peoples. Exemplary of this genre was the
motion picture "Live, Ukraine!", a documentary produced by
the Kiev Studio of Motion Picture Chronicle in celebration
of the 40th anniversary of the establishment of Soviet rule
in the Ukraine. The camera pans repeatedly to the monument
of Bohdan Khmelnytsky in Kiev, then to his right hand
holding a mace pointed east to Russia, "from whence," the
narrator assures the audience, "help always came to our
people in difficult times."[21] The Biblical symbolism of
this scene - "I look to the hills, from whence cometh my
help" (Psalms 121:1) - cannot be overlooked.

Throughout the late 1950s and early 1960s, there were
calls for films dealing with Ukrainian historical themes,
particularly the Zaporozhian Cossacks, as well as movies
that would accurately reflect the vernacular.[22] One per-
sistent problem has been that native Ukrainian scenario
writers familiar with authentic Ukrainian culture have been
at a premium; most scenario writers have been either Russians, or Russified Ukrainians trained in Moscow.[23]

[20]*Literaturna hazeta*, November 22, 1957; *Vitchyzna*, No. 5(May, 1958),
pp. 206-10, and No. 5(May, 1959), pp. 163-78.

[21]From a description to the author of the film by a recent Ukrainian
emigre in Paris.

[22]See letters to the editor in *Radians'ka Ukraina*, October 17, 1956,
and *Radians'ka kultura*, No. 6(June, 1956); also see *Novyny kinoekranu*,
No. 6(June, 1956), p. 6.

[23]On these problems, see discussions in *Radians'ka kultura*, July 24,
1960; *Iskusstvo kino*, No. 12(1958), pp. 7-9; and *Literaturna hazeta*,
January 13, 1961.

The most outspoken demand for authenticity in cinema was
that of the Ukrainian film director Mykola Makarenko. Entitled "Looking at the Roots," his article covers all the
demands listed above as characteristic of the movement for
national authenticity, and in addition, accuses film
directors and scenario writers of being unaware of the
culture and daily life of the people they portray.[24]

Makarenko's article was debated and criticized in the
Presidium of the Association of Cinematographic Workers of
the Ukraine. Makarenko's critics, particularly Oleksandr
Levada, self-appointed ideological guardian of Ukrainian
cinema and then Deputy Chairman of the Association's
orgburo, urged that the blame be put where it belonged:
on the poor qualifications of directors, and excessive
emphasis on national peculiarities, and failure to be
guided by "the compass of Leninist nationalities policy."[25]
In another article, Levada criticized Makarenko's demands
for authenticity in terms of nationalities policy, arguing
in effect that the pursuit of authenticity as an end in
itself is not a legitimate concern of Soviet art. He then
denied that Ukrainian art and literature had been de-nation-
alized in any event:

> ...Makarenko stretches the idea that
> the native language is the most impor-
> tant element in the national form of art
> to the point of absurdity. As regards
> Ukrainian writers and artists, the whole
> world knows that it was during Soviet
> times that they were given the unlimited
> opportunity to create in their own lan-
> guage, develop the language, and generously
> draw on its wealth and treasure.[26]

[24]*Sovetskaia Ukraina*, No. 1(January, 1961), pp. 109-35.

[25]*Radians'ka kultura*, April 20, 1961, p. 2.

[26]*Komunist Ukrainy*, No. 6(June, 1961), pp. 61-67.

Levada has drawn here on one of the most potent themes of
of the myth of proletarian internationalism, namely that the
Soviet regime enabled minority cultures to develop their own
languages and cultures. This, too, corresponds to the
"flowering" thesis of the dialectic discussed in the previous chapter. This theme is potent because, first, of
course, there is a substantial element of truth to it, but
secondly, because the existence of the "flowering" thesis as
part and parcel of the proletarian internationalism myth
permits assimilationists to disarm their critics, as Levada
has done here, by refuting their arguments as groundless.
The fallacy is that while it is true that the Ukrainian
language is freer today than it was under the notorious
ukases of Valuev (1863) and Ems (1876), this hardly implies
that there is no Russification.

The issue of national authenticity in cinema remained a
controversial one, and periodically attracted the close attention of the Party.[27] Controversy in the field of drama
was similar,[28] as it was in music and the graphic arts,
although in these fields interest in folk themes and disputes over the extent of independent development of Ukrainian art as opposed to the influence of Russia were prominent.[29]

---

[27]See criticisms and counter-criticisms in *Mystetstvo*, No. 5(September,
1965), p. 3; *Radians'ka Ukraina*, May 17, 1968, p. 1; *Literaturna
Ukraina*, January 22, 1971, p. 2; August 15, 1972, p. 4; and September
29, 1972, p. 3.

[28]Calls were made, for example, for revisions in repertoire to include
Ukrainian classics rather than translations from Russian and foreign
plays. See *Literaturna hazeta*, October 20, 1959, p. 4; translation in
Digest of the Soviet Ukrainian Press, 3:12:22-23; *Literaturna hazeta*,
May 10, 1957, p. 2; *Radians'ka kultura*, October 31, 1963, p. 2.

[29]*Radians'ka kultura*, August 9, 1959, p. 4, and October 24, 1963, p. 3;
Molod Ukrainy, March 15, 1963, p. 3. The authors of such articles are
almost always ethnic Ukrainians, to make it appear that the move to
emulate Russia and hold the native culture in contempt is a Ukrainian
initiative, rather than a Russian-imposed imperative.

CULTURE AND HISTORIOGRAPHIC NATIONALISM

All myths are backward looking. The employment of folklore
motifs, the artistic representation of parochial national
"ways," the search for national "roots" in antiquity, and
the striving for cultural "authenticity," all represent
efforts to give expression to the myth of national moral
patrimony. It is, therefore, the interpretation of the
past that forms the crucial nexus between national cultural
expression and nationalities policy in the Soviet Union,
and this is probably true in general of "mobilization societies" which stake their legitimacy on a single, monolithic political myth.

Criticisms of the glorification of national peculiarities
are most often phrased in terms of "opposing one nationality to another," that is, not mere glorification of Soviet
Ukraine - this appears to be not only accepted but encouraged - but rather, drawing deliberate or implicit contrasts
between Ukrainians and other nationalities, particularly
Russians, or over-indulgence in the elements of Ukrainian
culture that set it apart from other cultures, are proscribed. This generally means folk and historical themes.[30]

The sins of ommission and commission that constitute
historiographic nationalism, whether in the actual writing
of history, or in *belles lettres* and other arts, have been
explicitly set forth. These, it will be seen, are in effect
proscriptions of revisions of the myth of proletarian internationalism, and more especially of the myth of Russian
primacy.

---

[30]The burden of this prohibition falls disproportionately on ethno-
graphers, whose subject matter forces them to deal with such themes.
Ukrainian *samvydav* sources report that the editors of *Narodna tvorchist'
ta etnohrafiia* are repeatedly censured because their journal "idealizes
the past," specifically through the publication of poetry, folk songs,
folk tales, proverbs and sayings. Academician P. Babyi is reported to
have criticized the journal simply because it publishes in Ukrainian.
See *Ukrains'kyi visnyk 7-8* (Smoloskyp, 1975), pp. 135ff.

Unacceptable historiographic nationalism consists of the
following:

1. Idealization of the patriarchal feudal past, and of the
past in general.

2. Underevaluation of the progressive significance of the
joining of various peoples to Russia.

3. Attempts to whitewash nationalist and separatist movements.

4. Underevaluation of the friendly assistance and progressive role of the Great Russian people and the Russian proletarian "vanguard."[31]

Historiography, then, is a field in which the Party per-
ceives that it has a great stake in defending the myths on
which its legitimacy rests. Historical journals and historical writings have not only the force of science behind
them, but, under censorship conditions as well, the implicit authority of the Party. Because of the trauma of
rewriting history in the artificial propagation of the
"friendship of peoples" myth, it can be assumed that writers
take their cues from historiographers when they wish to be
above reproach ideologically.

The politics of Ukrainian historiography has been treated
in depth elsewhere,[32] therefore we shall not analyze it in
detail, beyond noting the principal areas of contention.

Among the more contentious issues have been debates over
the origins of the East Slavs, and over the patrimony of
the city of Kiev. The Ukrainian historian Mykhaylo

---

[31]*Voprosy istorii*, No. 2(1961), pp. 223-24.

[32]See, for example, Stephan M. Horak, "Soviet Historiography and the New
Nationalities Policy: Belorussia and Ukraine," in Jane P. Shapiro and
Peter J. Potichnyj, eds., *Change and Adaptation in Soviet and East Eur-
opean Politics* (New York: Praeger, 1976); Stephan M. Horak, "Problems
of Periodization and Terminology in Ukrainian Historiography," *Nation-
alities Papers*, Vol. 3, No. 2, pp. 5-24; Lubomyr R. Wynar, "The Present
State of Ukrainian Historiography: A Brief Overview," *Nationalities
Papers*, Vol. 7, No. 1, pp. 1-23; Jaroslaw Pelenski, "Soviet Ukrainian
Historiography after World War II," *Jahrbücher für Geschichte Osteuropas*,
Vol. 12, No. 3, pp. 375-418.

Hrushevsky (1866-1934) - who, more than any other figure,
perhaps, can be regarded the father of Ukrainian nationalism - is associated with the theory that Kievan Rus' of the
9th to 13th centuries was a uniquely Ukrainian state, distinct from the later Russian state. This question is crucial to the myth of Russian primacy, because it is indis-
putable that Kievan Rus' antedated the Muscovite state, so
that the myth of Russian primacy demands that Kievan Rus'
and the East Slavs be regarded as having derived from a
proto-Russian people, rather than from independent origins.[33]
In recent years, the Soviet Ukrainian archaeologist Mykhailo
Braichevs'kyi (b. 1934) has produced monographs, some of
the officially published, which, while he dissociates himself from Hrushevsky, in fact support the thesis of the
Ukrainian patrimony of Kievan Rus'.[34]

Equally contentious, and of indubitable symbolic significance, has been the question of the Treaty of Pereiaslav
(1654), at which time, in the official Soviet version, the
Ukraine was reunified with Russia through an official treaty
between *Het'man* Bohdan Khmelnytsky and Tsar Aleksei
Mikhailovich. Contention over the Treaty involves the
question of whether it is to be interpreted as a temporary
military alliance against Poland, or as permanent accords
of incorporation.[35]

Regardless of the questions of *Realpolitik* that may have
been involved, and despite scholarly disputation both in
Soviet and Western academic circles, the official interpretation was enshrined in the Central Committee Theses

---

[33]See, for example, Kost' Huslystyi, "On Bourgeois Nationalist Distortions in the Study of the Ethnogeny of the Ukrainian People," in
Narodna tvorchist' ta etnohrafiia, No. 1(January-February, 1971), pp.
41-51; excerpts translated in *Digest of the Soviet Ukrainian Press*,
15:10:12-17.

[34]See his *Pokhodzhennia Rusi* (Kiev: "Radians'kyi Pys'mennyk," 1963).

[35]Various early Soviet treatments can be found in P.P. Gudzenko, ed.,
Vossoedinenie Ukrainy s Rossiei (Moscow, 1953).

advanced during the 1954 tercentenary celebration of the
Treaty, and provided guidelines for all subsequent interpretation of Ukrainian history.[36]

It was again Braichevs'kyi in the late 1960s who dis-
puted the official interpretation, in an article entitled
"Annexation or Reunion?" ("Pryiednannia chy vozziednannia?").
Braichevs'kyi examined a number of scholarly treatments of
the Treaty and, adding his own analysis, concluded that the
Treaty was regarded as merely a military union by the Cossack leadership at the time, but as an act of annexation by
the Tsarist leadership. Braichevs'kyi's article, written
in 1966, was refused publication, but received exceptionally
wide circulation in *samvydav*, where it came to the attention
of Ukrainian Party Central Committee ideological secretary
A.D. Skaba, who is reported to have personally rebuked
Braichevs'kyi.[37]

A third problem in Ukrainian historiography has been the
nature of the Zaporozhian Sich. The extreme sensitivity of
the Soviet regime to the Cossacks undoubtedly stems from the
latter's popular reputation for having been rebellious,
untamable, and probably unwilling subjects of the Tsar,
valuing above all else their independence. This popular
image conflicts with the myth that the Ukrainians were historically eager for "reunification" with Russia. The correct

---

[36]"Theses on the 300th Anniversary of the Reunification of Ukraine and
Russia (1654-1954), Approved by the Central Committee of the Communist
Party of the Soviet Union," *Pravda* and *Izvestiia*, January 12, 1954,
pp. 2-3; translation is in *Current Digest of the Soviet Press*, 5:51:3ff.

[37]See *Suchasnist'*, No. 7(1968), p. 123. Braichevs'kyi's article appears
in Roman Kupchinsky, ed., *Natsional'nyi vopros v SSSR: sbornik dokumentov* (Munich: Suchasnist', 1975), pp. 66-124. For a translation, see
Annexation or Russification: Critical Notes on One Conception, translated and edited by George P. Kulchycky (Munich: Ukrainisches Institut
für Bildungspolitik, 1974). A Ukrainian edition was published in
Toronto by "Novy dni" in 1972. According to *Khronika tekushchikh
sobytii*, Braichevs'kyi was dismissed in 1972 from the Institute of
Archaeology, Academy of Sciences of the Ukrainian SSR: No. 28 (New
York: Khronika Press, 1974), p. 20. Braichevs'kyi probably never regarded himself as a "dissident," and had written his scholarly article
with publication in mind.

ideological interpretation of the Zaporozhian Sich was set
forth in a book that appeared in Russian in 1957 by the
Ukrainian historian V.A. Holobuts'kyi. Although primarily
concerned with criticism of "bourgeois nationalist" interpretations of the Sich, the message is modern: the Cossacks
were not latter-day *samurai* nor fighters for independence,
but rather vigilant and stalwart fighters on behalf of the
Ukrainians for reunification with Russia.[38]

The final concern of Ukrainian historiography that is
relevant to the modern quest for authenticity in culture
is the revolution in the Ukraine, 1918-1922. The question
is important because of the symbolic significance of the
Ukraine's early "national communists": Mykola Khvylovyi,
S.V. Kosior, Vlas Chubar', Mykola Skrypnyk, and others.

The concept of national communism was a particularly
sensitive one for the Soviet regime in the aftermath of
Tito's defection in 1948, the 1956 Hungarian uprising, and
the defections of Albania and Rumania. That it remains a
sensitive question is evident from the 1968 Soviet invasion
of Czechoslovakia, and the Soviet reaction to the polycentrism espoused by European communist parties at the Berlin
conference of 1976. If, as has been suggested, the Union
Republics look jealously upon the sovereignty of East European socialist states,[39] the Soviet leadership cannot be
uncognizant of the danger of polycentrism arising within
the Soviet Union and the breakdown there as well of the
myth of Russian primacy. Great effort is therefore expended
to discredit the Ukrainian national communists.[40]

---

[38] V.A. Holubyts'kyi, *Zaporozhskoe kozachestvo* (Kiev, 1957), pp. 71-78.

[39] See Vernon V. Aspaturian, "Nationality Inputs in Soviet Foreign
Policy: The USSR as an Arrested Universal State," in Aspaturian, ed.,
Process and Power in Soviet Foreign Policy (Boston: Little, Brown and
Co., 1971), pp. 449-50.

[40] See H. Ovcharov, "On the Occasion of Light Shed on the Problem of
Borot'bism," *Komunist Ukrainy*, No. 2(1958), pp. 36-47; translation in
Digest of the Soviet Ukrainian Press, 1:7:1-5; *Radians'ka Ukraina,*

THE AMBIGUITY OF NATIONAL SYMBOLS: ESTABLISHMENT
INTELLECTUALS AND THE CRYSTALLIZATION
OF THE DISSIDENT MOVEMENT

It is the ambiguity of national symbols themselves and the
differential degree to which Ukrainian intellectuals publicly articulate their attachment to such symbols that makes
it impossible to draw an analytical distinction between an
"establishment" and an "opposition" in the Ukrainian context
before about 1965. Mass arrests began under the Brezhnev
regime, however, and it became important for Ukrainian intellectuals to take an unambivalent stand on one side or the
other. After 1965, we can speak of the "opposition" as
those individuals who either: a) were arrested, imprisoned,
or otherwise harassed by the state (this is a definition by
the regime of the individual as in opposition); or b)
circulated their writings in illegal channels of communication, or *samvydav* (thereby, the individual defines himself
as in opposition). These categories are not, of course,
mutually exclusive.

This artificial distinction, we must keep in mind, cam-
ouflages the extent of shared values and symbols between
opposition and establishment intellectuals, and *de facto*
community of interest between political elites interested
in decisional autonomy and cultural elites interested in
expanded cultural expression. It also glosses over the
developmental character of the crystallization of nationalist dissent. Virtually all of the individuals identi-
fiable as nationalist dissenters, non-conformist as they

April 17, 1958, pp. 3-4; *Komunist Ukrainy*, No. 7(July, 1968), pp. 26-38;
F. Iu. Sherstiuk, "Exposure and Rout of the Nationalist Deviation by
the CPU in 1926-1928," *Ukrains'kyi istorychnyi zhurnal*, No. 3(1958),
pp. 73-83; translation of excerpts in *Digest of the Soviet Ukrainian
Press*, 2:12:1-3; also see criticisms of Roman Andriiashyk's controversial novel of the KPZU, *Poltava* (published in *Prapor*, August-Septem-
ber, 1969), in *Radians'ka Ukraina*, December 8, 1970, p. 2, and
Literaturna Ukraina, January 26, 1971, p. 3. These are typical examples
of this genre of criticism; the list could, of course, be extended
indefinitely.

may have been, were certainly, in their own and in their
fellows' eyes, members of the cultural establishment up to
1965, and few failed to try to publicize their views through
legitimate channels before resorting to *samvydav*.

Although most establishment intellectuals seem to be
unambiguous in their outward hostility to ideas that hint
of ideological unorthodoxy, there have been a few whose
views have been liberal enough to place them on the border-
line. Foremost among these have been Maksym Ryls'kyi
(1895-1964), outspoken in his early defense of the "Young
Writers;"[41] Viktor Nekrasov (b. 1911), a Russian writer
native to Kiev and now living in Paris;[42] and Oles' Honchar
(b. 1918), whose novel *Sobor* we discuss below. Two writers,
Ivan Drach (b. 1936) and Mykola Kholodnyi (b. *ca.* 1936),
appear to have been on both sides, later recanting their
views.[43]

The so-called "Young Writers" divided the Ukrainian
Writers' Union, less by age than ideologically and
aesthetically. That older establishment writers such as
Ryls'kyi and Nekrasov frequently came to their defense is
evidence of at least some shared viewpoints, and many of
the values of the Young Writers, particularly as they per-
tained to the preservation of the Ukrainian language, were
reflected in oblique protests on the part of establishment
intellectuals at the end of the 1960s and early 1970s at

---

[41]*Literaturnaia gazeta*, August 23, 1962, p. 5; *Literaturna Ukraina*,
January 29, 1963, p. 1.

[42]See, for example, Nekrasov's appreciation of Mikhail Bulgakov's novel
of the revolution in the Ukraine, *The White Guard* (published in the
West by Fontana Modern Novels, 1971), in *Novyi mir*, No. 8(1967), pp.
132-42, and appended to the Fontana edition in translation.

[43]On Drach, see *Znannia ta pratsia*, No. 1(1965), p. 2; *Molod Ukrainy*,
December 29, 1965; and *Radians'ka Ukraina*, January 22, 1971. Kholodnyi's
recantation is in *Literaturna Ukraina*, July 7, 1972. For discussions
of Kholodnyi, see *Ukrains'kyi visnyk 3* (Smoloskyp, 1971), pp. 44-63,
and *Ukrains'kyi visnyk 6* (Smoloskyp, 1972), pp. 123-25.

Writers' Union congresses.[44]

The most important and controversial characteristic of the Young Writers at first was innovation. Their concerns were less with politics than with art, and less with nationalism than with universal human concerns, although national sentiment and a concern with authenticity in art and literature were evident in some early works. The style of the Young Writers reflected romanticism, idealism, candor, and self-conscious honesty. It was in the latter that the Young Writers at first had the blessing of the Party through de-Stalinization: many of the early works of the Young Writers were criticisms of the "cult of personality" and of the Stalinist bureaucracy, clearly influenced by young Russian writers of the "thaw," most especially Evtushenko.[45]

The most outstanding of the Young Writers were the poetess Lina Kostenko (b. 1930), the poet Mykola Vinhranovs'kyi (b. 1930), the physician-poet Vitalyi Korotych (b. 1936), Ievhen Hutsalo (b. 1937), the novelist Volodymyr Drozd (b. 1939), and the poet Ivan Drach (b. 1936).[46] Equally outstanding and somewhat more controversial were the literary critics Ivan Svitlychnyi (b. 1929), Ievhen Sverstiuk (b. 1928), and Ivan Dzyuba (b. 1931). Older

---

[44] On the Writers' Union as a forum of protest, see Ivan Koshelivets, "Khronika ukrainskogo soprotivleniia," *Kontinent*, No. 5(1975), pp. 173-99; Ivan Koshelivets, *Ukraina 1956-1968* (Paris: Instytut Literacki, 1969); "Ukrainian Writers Protest," Radio Free Europe Research Paper F-100, February 19, 1975; and "Writers' Congress in the Ukraine," Radio Free Europe Research Paper 1043, June 16, 1971.

[45] Examples are Ivan Drach's "Ode to an Honest Coward," *Prapor*, No. 1 (1963), and Andrii Malyshko's "Ballad of the Anonymous Informer," *Literaturna hazeta*, July 28, 1961. Drach was attacked for his poem: see *Literaturna Ukraina*, March 28, 1963, pp. 6-7. Also see Ivan Svitlychnyi's justification of the Young Writers in *Dnipro*, No. 4(1962), pp. 144-52.

[46] For surveys of the works of these and other Young Writers, see "The Birth of Ukrainian Opposition Prose," Radio Liberty Daily Information Bulletin, August 24, 1962, and Jaroslaw Pelenski, "Recent Ukrainian Writing," *Survey*, No. 59(April, 1966), pp. 102-112.

writers who in style, orientation and outspokenness were
close enough to the Young Writers to be considered a part of
them in spite of the generation difference included Borys
Antonenko-Davydovych (b. 1899), and Andrii Malyshko
(b. 1912).

The Party's response to the Young Writers was one of
guarded enthusiasm from the beginning. In 1962, the Ukrainian Writers' Union began to waive its membership requirements, and many of the Young Writers were also taken into
the Party, in the apparent hope of co-opting their energy
and innovativeness. An all-Union Congress of Young Writers
was held in Moscow in December, 1962, for the purpose of
feeling out the demands of the Young Writers, and posing
constructive dialogue with the literary establishment.[47]

Although severe and concerted criticism of the Young
Writers as a group did not begin until 1963, some criticism
began as early as 1960, and came not from ideological
organs, but from older establishment intellectuals who felt
threatened by the popularity of the Young Writers.[48] This
is especially apparent, for example, in criticisms by the
extreme pro-Russian establishment poet Pavlo Tychyna (1891-
1967), appointed in 1962 by the Writers' Union Presidium to
act as ideological watchdog over the Young Writers.[49]
Tychyna upbraided the Young Writers for their precocious
disrespect, likening them to "cubs," and to "birds just
learning to fly."[50] Early attacks on the Young Writers
were accompanied by attacks on the "liberal journals" that

[47]*Molod Ukrainy*, December 5, 1962, p. 2. For a criticism of the Ukrainian delegation to the conference, see *Komunist Ukrainy*, No. 12(1963),
pp. 42-49.

[48]Viktor Nekrasov, personal interview, Paris, June 27, 1976.

[49]Nekrasov interview. Nekrasov also alleges that Drach's "Ode to an
Honest Coward" was written about Tychyna.

[50]*Radians'ka Ukraina*, December 27, 1963, p. 3.

published their works - *Vitchyzna, Zhovten, Dnipro* and *Prapor*.[51]

The problem of the defiance of the Young Writers was deemed of sufficient importance to merit a CPUk Central Committee Plenum on August 9-11, 1962. Central Committee Secretary for Ideological Affairs A.D. Skaba launched a scathing criticism of the Ukrainian intelligentsia for their "tendencies to idealize the past" and for fostering hostility to Russians. He accused the Young Writers of openly flirting with Ukrainian "bourgeois nationalism," as well as with "decadent Western artistic notions," and reproached older writers for failing to counter sufficiently the rebelliousness of the young and, in some cases, for openly defending them.[52] The Plenum marked the end of the regime's patience with the Young Writers and the beginning of harsh criticism led by ideological officials.

*The "Shestydesiatnyki" and the Myth of
National Moral Patrimony*

Those representatives of the Young Writers who did not capitulate to the criticism of the Party in 1962-1963 came later to style themselves as the "*shestydesiatnyki*" (literally, the "people of the sixties"). The label is symbolic in itself, for in Soviet historiography, the radical intelligentsia of the 1860s - the intellectual precursors of the revolution - are so styled. The name, therefore, evokes the historical role of the intelligentsia as in active opposition to the government. In this case, the dissenters have co-opted a pregnant symbol from the regime.

---

[51] See, for example, *Komunist Ukrainy*, No. 12(1958), pp. 81-87; *Radians'ka Ukraina*, April 28, 1960, p. 1, and April 30, 1960, p. 1; *Literaturna hazeta*, June 23, 1961, p. 4; *Vitchyzna*, No. 9(1961), pp. 205-10; and *Literaturna Ukraina*, February 16, 1962, pp. 1-2.

[52] *Radians'ka Ukraina*, August 15, 1962, p. 2.

The importance of the *shestydesiatnyki* is that they represent the first kernel of a deliberate, committed, and self-identified nucleus of opposition among the mobilized and Soviet-educated generation. They form the core, and the origin, of the overt opposition that emerged when they were driven "underground" by the mass arrests under the Brezhnev regime; their orientations, values, and the symbols to which they were attached formed, therefore, the issues and orientations of the Ukrainian nationalist opposition later. If the intellectual bases of the Organization of Ukrainian Nationalists (OUN) during and after World War II were to be found in a version of "integral nationalism" acquired by diffusion from Central Europe in the interwar period, the ideology of modern Ukrainian nationalism is a "humanist," demotic nationalism, almost an idealized internationalism, that grew out of the intellectual concerns of the Young Writers and the *shestydesiatnyki*.

The most important of the *shestydesiatnyki* was the poet Vasyl Symonenko (1935-1963), for three reasons: a) he was the first to have specifically tied the humanistic and aesthetic concerns of the Young Writers to nationalist aspirations; b) the events following his death were the immediate catalyst of the 1965-1966 wave of arrests which force the *shestydesiatnyki* into opposition; and c) he became a symbolic rallying point to unite the opposition. Like Shevchenko, he became the focus of symbolic struggle by January, 1965 as the regime vainly attempted to foster an official Symonenko cult in order to co-opt his popularity and neutralize the nationalist content of the symbol. Because of Symonenko's importance as a symbol, we shall examine him and the events that followed his death in some detail.

Born to peasant parents in Poltava *oblast*, Symonenko worked after graduation from the Journalism Faculty of Kiev University as a newspaperman in Cherkasy, writing poetry in his spare time. Having published only one volume of poetry, *Tysha i Hrim* (Silence and Thunder) in 1962, he

died of cancer on December 13, 1963, at the age of 29.[53]
Symonenko's prohibited works, including poems and his *Diary*,
have been published *in toto* in *samvydav*. [54]

Symonenko's poetry is not Aesopic in its open nationalism:

> My nation exists, my nation will
> always exist!/No one will scratch
> out my nation!/All renegades and
> strays will disappear,/and so will
> the hordes of conquerer-invaders.../
> My nation exists! In its hot veins/
> Cossack blood pulses and hums.[55]

Subsequent eulogies by Sverstiuk and Svitlychnyi attest
to the degree that the Young Writers were impressed by
Symonenko's outspokenness, and both emphasized that he had
laid down an example of "moral courage," and that everyone
had an obligation to follow that example in the struggle
for national dignity.[56] The fact that Symonenko died of a
disease, not from persecution, and in fact had not been
persecuted at all, except by the censor, did not prevent
his followers from making him into the symbol of a martyr
to the cause of Ukrainian national liberation. Such a symbol appears in retrospect to have been necessary to lend
unity and coherence to what was in fact an *ad hoc* movement.
The *shestydesiatnyki* never identified with the OUN, attest-
ing to the regime's success in making that particular symbol

[53]His second collection, *Bereh chekan'* (The Shore of Expectations), was
published in the West by Suchasnist' (Munich, 1965), and again in 1966
by Prolog (New York). Another collection, *Zemne tiazhinnia* (The Grav-
itation of the Earth) was published post-humously in the Soviet Union
in 1964.

[54]See *Ukrains'kyi visnyk 4* (Smoloskyp, 1971), pp. 79-107. This issue
also includes tributes to Symonenko by Dzyuba (pp. 119-31), Sverstiuk
(pp. 113-19), and Svitlychnyi (pp. 108-121). It also includes an
anonymous biography of Symonenko (pp. 73-78).

[55]*Ibid.*, p. 128.

[56]*Ibid.*, pp. 108-119.

very unattractive, and they were too young as well to identify with the Ukrainian national communists of the pre-war
years. Symonenko's appeal as a rallying symbol faded with
time of course, and he was replaced in that role toward the
end of the decade by Moroz.

On January 16, 1965, Ivan Dzyuba delivered an oration at
a post-humous celebration of Symonenko's birthday in the
Republican Building of Literature in Kiev, which alerted
the literary and ideological establishment to the potency
of Symonenko as an anti-regime symbol:

> It is no secret that Vasyl Symonenko
> was first and foremost a poet of the
> national idea.... It is true that
> Leonid Mykolaevych Novychenko, who is
> sitting at this moment at the table,
> assures us that the concepts 'national
> idea,' 'national consciousness,' are
> now unlawful and illegal, antiquated,
> and anti-Marxist.... Of course the
> national idea exists and will exist.
> It is real for us today and it means
> a concept of a fully sovereign state
> and cultural existence for the Ukrainian
> socialist nation, of a fullness and
> sovereignty of her national contribution
> toward the cause of peace, democracy,
> and socialism.[57]

Dzyuba then went on to explain that there were periods in
history when poets and writers became stale because they
were forced by history to dwell on the national idea. The
present epoch, however, is one of the kind that "does not
squeeze out but *catalyzes* all other universal human ideas."[58]

Finally, in what, given the context, could only have been
interpreted as a call for resistance, Dzyuba summarized the
"moral lesson" of Symonenko:

---

[57]*Ibid.*, pp. 123-24.

[58]*Ibid.*, p. 124.

> People are not waiting for anything
> as much as they are waiting for the
> example of heroic public conduct.
> People need this example because
> they need the assurance that even
> today such heroic action is possible,
> and that today it is not fruitless...:.
> Therefore today, perhaps more than ever,
> it is possible and necessary to fight.[59]

Spirituality as the National Moral Patrimony

A fundamental assumption of the myth of national moral patrimony is that the nation is the ultimate repository and embodiment of all human spiritual values. Judging from *samvydav* writings and the consensus of our informants, the underlying thrust of the Ukrainian cultural revival is the feeling on the part of many intellectuals that de-national-ization deprives a people not only of cultural forms and language, but by doing so, and in the manner in which it is done, it deprives a people of the vehicle for the expression spirituality - of the medium through which ideas, traditions and interpretations which are valued over and above their everyday utility, give meaning to life, and provide comfor-table zones of stability, are preserved and transmitted. This medium for the expression of spirituality is the national culture.

Thus, in an eloquent description of the effects of what we have called the "maximization of redundancy," Valentyn Moroz maintains that "devaluation of the word" is the main moral problem left over from the Stalin era; stereotyped phraseology, epithets, superlatives and the like reached such a pitch that any criteria for judging reality or spiritual reality disappeared. No one, he writes, believed in any reality, and emotions disappeared, too; the only

[59] *Ibid.*, p. 126.

emotions expressed were those "tickled out" by official
propaganda. "Devaluation of the word," he continues, led
to the devaluation of all values; aim, ideal, heroism, etc.,
were replaced by nihilism. For the Ukraine, as well as for
the other nations of the Soviet Union, the concepts "nation,"
"patriotism," "native language," "motherland," and the like
were similarly devalued.[60]

It is a mistake to equate the myth of national moral
patrimony, as it has been articulated inside the Soviet
Ukraine, with the assumption peculiar to "integral nationalism" that a given nation, i.e., one's own, is superior to
all others, and is mystically destined to "fulfill history"
through the subjugation or destruction of "inferior" species
or peoples. Perhaps because the OUN and UPA are so closely
identified with this view - rightly or wrongly - it is sin-
gularly lacking in the ideology of modern Ukrainian nationalism. Because we are basing our conclusions solely on
written material - and material written by educated and
articulated people at that - we have no means of judging
what concept of the nation exists in the popular mind, and
we do not discount the possibility that, were Ukrainian
nationalism a popular ideology, the premise of the nation
as the repository of moral value might be translated into
the simpler ideology of the nation as the only value.

Modern Ukrainian nationalism as it has been articulated
is distinguished from wartime integral nationalism in the
following ways:
1. The absence of the glorification of youth, vitality,
violence, and armed struggle as the expression or culmi-
nation of national vigor. Civil disobedience, not terrorism
or militarism, is the form of action that is espoused.
2. The absence of any appeal to the irrational as a principle, which was a characteristic of integral nationalism.

---

[60]Valentyn Moroz, "Sredi snegov," (in Russian), AS 596, SDS Vol. VIII.
This and all subsequent references to *samvydav* documents follows Radio
Liberty's "Arkhiv Samizdata" and "Sobranie Dokumentov Samizdata"
classification system, now in wide use.

The intellectuals that comprise the Ukrainian nationalist dissent movement are certainly romantics, but nonetheless, intellectualism and rationalism remain prominent characteristics of their value system.

3. The absence of an exclusivist orientation to civil life. Although the approach to Ukrainian identity is an ethnic one, it is not a racialist one. It is in this sense that the nationalist dissidents, whether Marxist-Leninist as Dzyuba, or not, as Moroz, have been profoundly affected by their socialization under the Soviet regime; that the Soviet concept of citizenship is a demotic, rather than a "root" one, has influenced the Ukrainian dissenters' concept of ethnic identity.

Modern Ukrainian nationalism arose out of dissatisfaction on the part of cultural elites with official proletarian internationalism, and out of the perceived failure of the officially sponsored culture to satisfy felt cultural needs. It is less the affirmation of parochial ethnicity for its own sake, than rejection of the *official* rejection of ethnicity. More directly stated, it is the rejection of the Russification of culture under the guise of proletarian internationalism. To the degree that Russification has come increasingly to be interpreted as "oppression," modern Ukrainian national self-assertion has the same sources as nationalism in the Third World: the call for communal solidarity of a group with perceived immediate commonalities (language, culture, myth of common descent and fate) as against a group that is perceived as alien along the same dimensions, and can be construed to be an "exploiter." This "reactive" feature of Ukrainian nationalism is the linkage between the distinctive features of minority nationalism in the Soviet Union, and the more familiar nationalisms of other parts of the world.

The earliest statement in the post-Stalin period that the nation is the repository of spiritual values was the line in Sosiura's previously discussed poem, "Love Ukraine:"

> Your lover will not love you,
> If you do not love Ukraine!

Statements of this type, as we have discussed above,
were tolerated by the regime until the mid-1960s, so long
as they did not glorify the Ukraine more than the Soviet
Union itself, or set the Ukraine up as an object of adora-
tion against the Union itself or against other nations.
Many of Symonenko's poems - those which did not allude to
Russian "conquerer-invaders" - in spite of their Ukrainian
patriotism, were published after his death, with only the
most offensive lines expunged.

The premise also underlay the early calls for authenticity in Ukrainian culture, and became increasingly explicit as an element of symbols relating to authenticity.
The most sensational public exposition of the thesis, however, came in a novel written not by a dissident but by
Oles' Honchar, then and (after a short hiatus) now Chairman
of the Presidium of the Ukrainian Writers' Union.

All of our informants agree that Honchar's allegorical
1968 novel *Sobor* (The Cathedral)[61] was the most significant
event in the Ukraine in the post-Stalin period, because it
was written by an establishment intellectual and at first
accepted by the establishment, for its content and literary
quality, and for the reaction it produced.

The novel abandons all canons of socialist realism; it is
anti-modernization in tone, and unambiguously opposed to
Russification. It concerns a young Ukrainian, Ivan Bahlai,
who is killed in the struggle to save an ancient Cossack
cathedral, which is being torn down by the state, in the
fictional town of Zachiplianka on the Dnipro river. The
town is clearly modelled on Dnipropetrovs'k - one of the
most Russified cities in the Ukraine - and the cathedral is

---

[61]Oles' Honchar, *Sobor* (Kiev: "Radians'kyi pys'mennyk," 1968). The
novel was first published in *Vitchyzna*, No. 1(1968). An offset was
published in the United States by the Museum of the Ukrainian Orthodox
Church (New York and S. Bound Brook, N.J., 1968).

a symbol of Ukrainian culture being dismantled by the Russification policies of the Soviet regime.

Of exceptional literary quality, the novel was initially
highly praised, first in the Dnipropetrovs k papers *Zoria*
and *Prapor iunosti*,[62] and later by the establishment critic
Leonid Novychenko in the all-Union *Literaturnaia gazeta*.[63]
It also received a favorable review in Warsaw's Ukrainian
language newspaper *Nasha kultura*.[64]

Later, however, the novel came under severe attack as
ideologically faulty: it glorified the Cossack past, it
wrongly opposed workers to bureaucrats, it was not "Party-
minded" and, as evidence that the novel's symbolism had not
escaped the critics, it had a "very dubious subtext."[65]

The turnabout came as the result of a conference of secretaries of local Party organizations in Dnipropetrovs'k.
The Faculty of History and Philology at Dnipropetrovs'k
University - of which Honchar is a graduate - was forbidden
to celebrate Honchar's 50th birthday, and a public campaign
against the novel was begun with a series of letters,
allegedly from Dnipropetrovs'k workers, protesting Honchar's
"negative treatment" of the working class.[66] There are
reports that at least a dozen Dnipropetrovs'k journalists

[62]Reported in *Khronika tekushchikh sobytii*, 7:23-24 and 10:30,39.

[63]*Literaturnaia gazeta*, March 20, 1968, p. 2.

[64]*Nasha kultura* (Warsaw), No. 5(1968), p. 2.

[65]See criticism by M. Iurchuk and F. Lebedenko, *Radians'ka kultura*,
April 26, 1968, p. 2, and M. Shamota, *Radians'ka Ukraina*, May 16, 1968,
p. 3. The critics and journals which had earlier praised the novel
were also criticized.

[66]See *Robitnycha hazeta*, April 28, 1968. Also see *The Ukrainian Bulletin*, Vol. XXI, No. 13-6(1968), and Radio Free Europe Research Bul-
letins: "Ukrainian Novel Raises a Storm," July 1, 1968, and "Russification and Socialist Legality in the Dnepropetrovsk Area," March 10,
1969. The latter also appears in *The Ukrainian Review*, Vol. XVI,
No. 3(1969), pp. 46-52.

who came to the public defense of *Sobor* received sanctions
ranging from reprimand to dismissal from the Party.[67] It is
also reported that the campaign against the novel touched
of student riots in Dnipropetrovs'k and Kharkiv.[68]

The aftermath of the campaign produced a remarkable document in the summer of 1968. An anonymous letter, signed
only "The Creative Youth of Dnipropetrovs'k" was sent to
Shelest, Shcherbitsky, Ovcharenko and Writers' Union Secretary D. Pavlychko. The lengthy letter protested not only
the campaign against *Sobor* and its defenders, but also Russification of culture and education in Dnipropetrovs'k and
other large cities of the East Ukraine, and also detailed a
number of scandals and petty larcenies among members of the
Dnipropetrovs'k Party organization, suggesting that local
Party members must have at least talked to the writers of
the letter about these matters.[69]

In 1970, Ievhen Sverstiuk wrote and circulated in *samvydav* channels an essay, *Sobor u ryshtovanni* (The Cathedral
in Scaffolding), loosely centered around the symbolic theme
of Honchar's novel.[70] The essay is a defense of the view
that spiritual values must be centered in national culture.
The type of civic personality created by the conditions of
Stalinism, Sverstiuk writes, is an irresponsible and oppor-
tunistic one, and this has facilitated the erosion of the
nation as a repository of values. When neither the ideology
nor proletarian internationalism is capable of providing
enduring values, the only source of such values is the

---

[67]*Posev* (Frankfurt), No. 9(September, 1969), p. 10.

[68]"Russification and Socialist Legality..."

[69]*"List tvorchoi molodi Dnipropetrovs'koho,"* (1968), AS 974, SDS Vol.
XVIII. Also see *Ukrains'kyi visnyk 1* (Smoloskyp, 1970), pp. 26-27.
For a report on the trial of one of the signers and a lengthy commen-
tary on the case, see *Ukrains'kyi visnyk 2* (Smoloskyp, 1970), pp. 7-21.

[70]Ievhen Sverstiuk, *Sobor u ryshtovanni* (Baltimore: Smoloskyp, 1971).
For a translation, see Ievhen Sverstiuk, *Clandestine Essays* (Littleton,
Colo: Ukrainian Academic Press, Libraries Unlimited, 1976).

national tradition as it is embodied in the past.[71] Not
only the vehicle, but the content of human spirituality is
the national tradition. For Sverstiuk, the intent and the
effect of government sponsored denationalization is to
"root in dogma the provincial and imitative character of
Ukrainian culture,"[72] that is to say, to reinforce what we
have called the myth of Russian primacy.

Finally, as far as "idealization of the past" is concerned, Sverstiuk argues that it is the artificial "friendship of peoples" myth that in the strictest sense "idealizes"
the past. Addressing his words to the literary critic
Mazurkevych, who had criticized the intelligentsia for
idealization of the Cossack republic,[73] he writes that the
real question is not one of "idealization," but "was there
or was there not in fact a Christian Cossack republic?"

SYMBOLS OF THE NATIONAL PATRIMONY
IN POPULAR CULTURE

There are a number of elemental symbols of national identity, and generically many of these are common to ethnic
communities throughout the world: architectural forms, language, folk music, art, legendary men - to name only a few.
Such symbols serve to differentiate the group from others,
lend the group a sense of pride in its own genius and,
transmitted through primary socialization, to perpetuate
the national identity. In the Soviet Union, where such
symbols are entrenched in the national cultures, the regime
has not tried to obliterate them, but rather to co-opt them
and lend them a new, Soviet content. When this is success-

[71]*Ibid.*, p. 33.

[72]*Ibid.*, p. 41.

[73]*Radians'ka osvita*, May 18, 1968, p. 8.

[74]*Sobor u ryshtovanni*, p. 46.

ful, the reverence and emotion attached to the symbol will,
presumably, be transferred to the regime. We have no way
of judging the success of these efforts in the popular mind
so long as survey research on such questions is prohibited
in the Soviet Union. We can only examine the public dialogue that has taken place between spokesmen for the regime
and the nationalist intellectuals over the content of
national symbols.

We shall briefly examine the manipulation of three such
entrenched symbols: the legendary Ukrainian poet Taras
Shevchenko, the issue of the preservation of monuments of
antiquity, and Ukrainian folk choral societies.

Taras Shevchenko

Shevchenko (1814-1861) is without question the foremost
literary symbol of the pride and dignity of Ukrainians.
Only Ivan Franko (1856-1916), Lesia Ukrainka (Larysa Kosach-
Kvitka, 1871-1913), and the historian Hrushevsky even
approach his stature in this regard. Born a serf, Shevchenko's freedom was purchased in 1838, and he enrolled in
the St. Petersburg Academy of Fine Arts. He published his
first book of realist poetry, *Kobzar* (The Bard) in 1847,
and later, for his poetic protests against serfdom and
against Russification, was exiled to Siberia. Freed in
1858, he was prohibited to live in the Ukraine, and died in
St. Petersburg in March, 1861.

The Soviet regime has interpreted Shevchenko as a "revolutionary democrat," emphasizing that his protests against
Russification of the Ukraine were aimed at Tsarist policies,
not against the Russian people, for whom it is alleged he
had a great love. He is often said to have been influenced
by Russian revolutionary writers, and is said to have been
opposed to Ukrainian nationalism. This interpretation began in the late 1930s, at the same time that Russian history
was being re-evaluated in the light of Russian patriotism;

prior to that time, Shevchenko had been officially considered to be a "bourgeois democrat, and ideologist of the
petty bourgeois peasantry, with religious and nationalist
remnants."[75]

The latest round of controversy over the interpretation
of Shevchenko began in the preparations for the celebration
of the 150th anniversary of his birth in 1964. An incident
involving the creation of a stained-glass window for the
vestibule of the Shevchenko Kiev State University illustrates the subtlety of the Shevchenko symbol.

Four young artists, Liudmyla Semykina, Panas Zalyvakha,
Halyna Sevruk and Alla Hors'ka,[76] were commissioned to
create the window. When completed, it depicted not a
saccharine poet, but an angry, gaunt Shevchenko holding in
one arm a battered woman symbolizing the Ukraine, and in
the other hand a book, held high. The window bore the
following inscription:

I shall glorify these small dumb slaves,
I shall put the word on guard beside them.

(Vozvelychu malikh otykh rabiv nimykh,
Ia na storozhi kolo ikh postavliu slovo.)

[75]"Theses of the Division of Culture and Propaganda of the Central
Committee, Communist Party of Ukraine," quoted by Yaroslav Bilinsky,
The Second Soviet Republic, p. 191. Bilinsky discusses in detail the
controversy surrounding the interpretation of Shevchenko up to 1957,
which we are not summarizing here. For representative versions of the
modern version of Shevchenko as a revolutionary democrat, see *Komunist
Ukrainy*, No. 2(1961), pp. 51-56, and No. 5(1961), pp. 75-84. Also see
"Bard of Freedom and Brotherhood" (in English and Ukrainian for foreign
readers. Kiev: Ukraina Society, 1976).

[76]Alla Hors'ka and Panas Zalyvakha subsequently became involved in dissident activities. Zalyvakha was sentenced to a labor camp. Hors'ka
was brutally murdered (decapitated) under still mysterious circum-
stances on November 28, 1970; *samvydav* sources make a credible argument
that her death was the work of the KGB; see *Ukrains'kyi visnyk 4*
(Smoloskyp, 1971), pp. 14-20.

There were immediate objections to the window, and the
Decorative-Monumental Art Section of the Artists' Union met
in Kiev in April, 1964 to determine the disposition of the
project. A piecemeal transcript of the meeting was circulated in *samvydav*.[77] Criticism of the window proceeded
almost tentatively, various individuals criticizing it at
first on aesthetic grounds: too abstract, too harsh. The
most direct criticism, however, was that the window was
"ideologically harmful" because of the ambiguous symbolism.
The window was later destroyed at night, in what was officially described as an act of vandalism.[78] It is clear
that the depiction of Shevchenko as a defender of the
Ukrainians, implicitly against the Russians, was unacceptable.

As with everything written abroad about the Ukraine, the
Soviet regime is markedly sensitive to the overtly nationalistic interpretation placed on Shevchenko by Ukrainians
living in the West. The establishment of a monument to
Shevchenko in Washington, D.C. in 1964, for example,
prompted an angry letter to the emigration signed by 34
Soviet Ukrainian cultural figures protesting such "malicious
attempts to use the works of this poet against our country...."[79] These and other hostile reviews of the treatment of Shevchenko in the West are evidence that these
interpretations are available to Soviet readers, or that
the regime believes they may be. It is quite likely that
they are, the Soviet borders being, as we have noted, rather

[77]*Ukrains'kyi visnyk 4* (Smoloskyp, 1971), pp. 12-14.

[78]John Kolasky maintains that the window was smashed on the orders of
V.A. Boychenko, a secretary of the Kiev *obkom*, in order to prevent the
commission from examining it, and that this happened on March 9, before
the commission met. This is not consistent with the *samvydav* account,
which clearly implies that the commission examined the window in April.
See Kolasky, *Two Years in Soviet Ukraine*, p. 92.

[79]*Literaturna hazeta*, November 29, 1963.

permeable; this of course complicates the regime's efforts
to neutralize the nationalist content of the symbol.

Ukrainian *samvydav* sources allege that beginning in 1964
the regime began deliberately expunging symbols of Shevchenko from popular culture:

> A special directive has been issued
> calling for strict supervision of con-
> certs and other ceremonies honoring
> Shevchenko, in order to maintain them
> at a very basic level, lest...the sincere
> message of the Bard surface and awaken
> thoughts of the Ukraine, 'our own, but
> vassal land.' Many articles and poems
> about Shevchenko are being excised from
> newspapers and magazines because censors
> see in them implied criticism of the
> colonial status of the Ukraine.[80]

The Jubilee Celebration of Shevchenko's birthday in
March, 1964 was a festive but co-opted occasion, attended
by the entire Ukrainian Party Politburo and numerous eminent guests, including Khrushchev.[81] The celebration was
marked by the presence of large numbers of policemen in
anticipation of agitation by the *shestydesiatnyki*. This
turned out to be unnecessary, as the *shestydesiatnyki*
largely boycotted the event. They gathered instead at the
Shevchenko monument in Kiev two months later, on May 22,
to celebrate the anniversary of the return of Shevchenko's
body from St. Petersburg to the Ukraine. The import of
this act of defiance was that it was meant to symbolize the
demand for the "return" of Shevchenko's heritage as well as

---

[80]"Z pryvodu protsesu nad Pohruzhal's'kym," AS 911, SDS Vol. XVIII.
This document is primarily concerned with the May 24, 1964 fire in the
Ukrainian Library of the Academy of Sciences of the Ukrainian RSR, in
which 600,000 volumes of Ukrainian archival materials and books were
destroyed.

[81]*Radians'ka Ukraina*, March 10, 1964, pp. 1-4. An all-Union celebration
was also held in Moscow, and a statue of Shevchenko was erected in Moscow, across from the Ukraina Hotel. See *Radians'ka Ukraina*, March 10,
1964, pp. 1-2, and June 11, 1964, pp. 1-2.

his corpse. May 22 became an annual event, marked sometimes by the reading of Symonenko's poems and inflammatory speeches against Russification of Ukrainian culture and language. At first the regime attempted to co-opt the event, organizing official festivals marked by the presence of police, *komsomol* officials and *druzhynnyky*, but there was always an unofficial celebration afterwards, which usually led to arrests.[82] Employers were ordered not to permit their employees to leave the premises on May 22, and a number of individuals were dismissed after 1968 for disobeying this injunction.[83]

Shevchenko continues to be a potent symbol of the Ukrainian nation, and ironically the Party is partly responsible for this. In efforts to co-opt the symbol, they keep it potent. This potency, when exploited by the opposition, adds to the symbol's intrinsic appeal.

Monuments and Antiquity

Monuments are symbols of national authenticity insofar as they represent the continuity between a people's contemporary perception of itself and myths of past association and differentiation from other groups. To the extent that they symbolize the myth of common ethnic descent and shared historical experiences, they "authenticate" the national myth.

Beginning in the early 1960s, there was a revival of interest in antiquity in all the Slavic areas of the USSR.

[82]*Ukrains'kyi visnyk 2* (Smoloskyp, 1970), pp. 40-41.

[83]Nadezhda Svitlychna and R. Motruk, for example, were dismissed from their jobs; *Ukrains'kyi visnyk 1* (Smoloskyp, 1970), p. 77. Three employees of the Kiev Hydroelectric Station received prison terms for distributing leaflets asking citizens to ignore the proscription on observing May 22; *Ibid.*, pp. 14-17. For other accounts relating to the May 22 observances, see *Khronika tekushchikh sobytii*, 5:19, 6:5, 8:35, 27:17, and 28:21.

In the RSFSR, this took the form of voluntary societies for
the preservation and restoration of old cathedrals, churches
and monasteries which, owing to official hostility to religion, are at best in a state of neglect, and often vanda-
lized or else used, for example, as storage depots by state
enterprises.[84]

In the RSFSR, these voluntary groups were often closely
associated with groups that espoused neo-Slavophile or Russian nationalist ideologies.[85] In the Ukraine, there have
been calls for preservation of monuments and relics, but
there is no report of actual voluntary groupings on the
scale that Medvedev reports for Russia. We advance two explanations for this. First, Soviet officials have tolerated
Russian nationalist groups to a great extent, hoping that
they would neutralize more anti-regime movements, and because, despite the fact that Russian nationalism rests on
the same *type* of myth that Ukrainian nationalism does, the
former is more reinforcing of the proletarian internationalist myth of Russian patrimony of the Union.

A second and more immediate explanation is that the Party
acted more decisively in the Ukraine than in the RSFSR to
co-opt the interest in antiquity, precisely because of its
potentially nationalist overtones. The Voluntary Society
for the Preservation of Monuments of History and Culture of
the Ukrainian SSR, organized under the Ukrainian SSR Council
of Ministers, has 12,000 primary organizations in enterprises, collective farms and universities, and a Republic-
wide membership of over two million.[86] Ukrainian *samvydav*

[84]*Literaturna Ukraina*, April 23, 1968, p. 4; translation in *Digest of
the Soviet Ukrainian Press*, 11:6:17-19.

[85]On such groups, see Roy Medvedev, *Kniga o sotsialisticheskoi demokratii* (Amsterdam and Paris: Herzen Foundation and Editions Grasset et
Fasquelle, 1972), pp. 104-110 and *passim*.

[86]On the Society, see *Kultura i zhyttia*, August 22, 1965; *Literaturna
Ukraina*, June 17, 1966; and March 8, 1968; *Pamiatnyky kultury*, No. 1-2
(1969), pp. 13-14; and *Molod Ukrainy*, April 28, 1971, p. 2. The
Society also receives extensive publicity in Soviet publications intended for Ukrainian readers abroad.

116

sources report that the Society has been given directives
to concentrate on the preservation of "historical-revo-
lutionary" monuments, particularly those relating to Lenin,
rather than on churches and monasteries, and that in 1973,
100 monuments recommended by the Society for state protection, nearly all of them churches, were taken off the
list. Those that receive state protection, it is reported,
are not in fact restored, but merely have an explanatory
plaque attached to them. These sources also list recent
incidents of the removal of monuments dedicated to Shevchenko, Franko and even Khmelnytsky, and their replacement with memorials to revolutionary figures.[87]

The most notable *samvydav* document on the nexus between
antiquity and national identity is Valentyn Moroz's account
of the efforts of the Hutsuls, a small mountain people
living in the foothills of the Carpathians, to regain 99
relics borrowed in 1963 for use as props in the film
Shadows of Forgotten Ancestors, and never returned.[88]
Moroz's essay is significant less for the plight of the
Hutsuls *per se* than for the argument he makes for the
necessity of the preservation of traditional culture in a
period of modernization. For Moroz, modernity can only be
dealt with on the basis of the nation as the modernizing
agency, for in the nation alone reside the values that prevent modernization from leading to a spiritually empty
"mass culture."

Moroz argues that Soviet nationalities policy must fail,
because culture can only be built slowly and incrementally;
"it cannot be built on the five-year plan, like a canal."[89]
Secondly, for Moroz, there can be no such thing as a

[87]*Ukrains'kyi visnyk 7-8* (Smoloskyp, 1975), pp. 151-54.

[88]Valentyn Moroz, "Khronika soprotivleniia," (in Russian, 1970). AS
411, SDS, Vol. VI. This was one of three articles for which Moroz, now
in the U.S., was sentenced to a fourteen year term.

[89]*Ibid.*, p. 10.

"cultural revolution:" revolutions do not create traditions, but rather destroy them. Finally, any attempt to deprive a people - whatever the size of the entity - of their national identity through depriving them of their culture also deprives them of their only source of dignity and spirituality.[90] For Moroz, then, as for Sverstiuk and the other nationalist dissidents, the nation must be preserved, not for its own sake, but because it is the only moral patrimony, and the national culture is the only vehicle of the higher human values.

Choral Societies

Folk music, and folk culture in general, is also a symbol of national authenticity. It has been believed for over a century in Russia and other Slavic countries that the simple *narod* - the folk - particularly the peasantry, is the repository of eternal human values. The Ukrainian nation that is romanticized and revered by individuals interested in national authenticity as a value is the *rural* Ukraine.

Ukrainian folk culture, like the Russian, is rich in songs and dances. The revival of interest in antiquity mentioned above was accompanied by an increased urban interest in folk music.[91] The regime has acted to co-opt this as well, through the establishment of national choral societies associated with enterprises, factories and universities. These societies are funded by the Council of Ministers, and directed by reliable Party members; oversight is through the Ministry of Culture. The emphasis is on works by Soviet composers written in the lyrical folk

[90]*Ibid.*, pp. 14-15.

[91]See also John A. Armstrong's discussion of the utilization of choral societies and other cultural activities by nationalists in the occupied Ukraine; *Ukrainian Nationalism 1939-1945*, pp. 223-27.

style, but not upon traditional folk songs from the oral
tradition.[92]

The state has discouraged active ethnological research
in folk music, particularly when it has been undertaken
independently of Party auspices. The journalist Ivan
Prokopov, for example, in the period 1959 to 1966 collected
over 4,000 ballads and ditties sung by the Hutsuls, and
recorded a number of wedding ceremonies in villages in the
Carpathians, but was unable to publish them.[93] Similarly,
collections by Lesia Ukrainka, Mykhaylo Pavlyk and Marko
Vovchok have not been published. Moroz was harassed by
militia and KGB officials when trying to record Easter
songs in the Hutsul village of Kosmach in April, 1970.[94]

Periodically, establishment intellectuals have urged
greater state interest in authentic folk music. The official reason given for refusal to publish folk music and
sponsor research in the area is that it is too tiresome,
too esoteric for general interest, and economically un-
feasible.[95] The following case study of the *Homin* Ethnographic Choral Ensemble, however, strongly suggests that
authentic folk music is strongly evocative of the myth of
national moral patrimony, and, as an elemental symbol of
national identity, must be co-opted, neutralized, or suppressed.

The *Homin* ("sound of voices") group began in Kiev in
1968, an offshoot of the older *Zhaivoronok* ("Lark")
Itinerant Student Choir, directed by Valentyna Petrienko
(d. 1972) until finally denied premises for rehearsal by

[92]*Literaturna Ukraina*, September 29, 1972, pp. 3-4.

[93]*Literaturna Ukraina*, April 11, 1967, p. 2.

[94]"Zaiava hromadian s. Kosmach prokuroru Ivano-Frankiv'skoi oblasti pro vypadok na tserkovnyi terytorii," (1970), AS 990, SDS Vol XVIII, p. 3.

[95]*Literaturna Ukraina*, April 11, 1967, p. 3. Research or programs in folk arts and crafts are discouraged for similar ostensible reasons.

the state in 1965.[96] A number of separate groups of young
people, many of them former members of *Zhaivoronok*, had been
gathering in private homes to sing folk songs and to re-
hearse for Christmas carolling (*koliaduvannia*). These
groups consolidated under the directorship of the folk-
lorist Leopol'd Iashchenko, and began conducting outdoor
singouts; soon, they were invited to give performances in
various villages outside Kiev. Members of the group included students, factory workers, teachers and scientists.

At the beginning of 1970, the group was being regularly
harassed by the KGB, and accusations that it was a "nationalist" group began; the accusation was first publicly made
by a certain Ruban, *partorg* of the Kiev University Faculty
of Journalism. He characterized it as an "underground"
organization, and demanded the dismissal of Iashchenko
from the Composers' Union.

In September, 1971 *Homin* was officially prohibited from
holding rehearsals or concerts at their regular meeting
place, the *kharchovyk* culture palace, and the *kharchovyk's*
director, Kraseva, invited the group to join the culture
palace's own folk ensemble, where they "sing the songs of
Soviet composers." For failing to heed Kraseva's advice,
and because a member of the choir had read a poem by Symonenko at the Shevchenko monument on May 22, Iashchenko was
dismissed from the Composers' Union.

Ukrainian Minister of Foreign Affairs Shevel' is reported
to have urged at a meeting of the Agitprop Department that
Ukrainian bourgeois nationalism is the "number one ideological problem," and that *Homin* is an agent of it because
it "conducts propaganda among the youth by singing folk
songs." All of Iashchenko's compositions were removed from
radio broadcasts and record stores, and his arrangements of
Ukrainian folk songs were expunged from the 1972 edition
of *Spivaie narodny khor* (Kiev: "Muzychna Ukraina"). The
ambiguity of national symbols is ironically reflected,

[96]*Ukrains'kyi visnyk 6* (Smoloskyp, 1972), pp. 116-119.

120

however, in the fact, reported in *samvydav*, that Iashchenko submitted *Homin's* repertoire to a Republican competition on folk music compositions, not under his own name but under a number, as contest rules required, and was awarded four prizes in the first judging.

Pressure was put upon individual members to leave the choir under threat of sanctions ranging from ostracism to dismissal from employment. *Ukrains'kyi visnyk* reports that 38 individuals were so threatened, and five actually dismissed for participation in the choral group. The same source reports that a kindergarten teacher, Raisa Mordan', was fired for taking her pupils to a performance of the group in a park. "This is a nationalist chorus," she was told at the *partkom*, "it sings hostile songs; it is riddled with nationalists. And *you took children there!*"[97]

Reprisals are also taken against other groups that display a public interest in folk music outside the sponsorship of the Party. It is reported that an old traditional custom was revived in Kiev, for example, whereby groups of young people go from home to home on New Years singing traditional folk carols (*shchedrivky*). Twenty such groups were counted in Kiev in 1971, some of whom appeared in traditional dress, including the costume of the Cossack *mamai*. These groups are arrested on the street on charges of "hooliganism" and reprisals are taken against them at their jobs and schools. Similarly, a group of *bandura* players led by Vasyl Lytvyj was disbanded after an unofficial concert, and its members deprived of the right to reside in Kiev.[98]

[97]*Ukrains'kyi visnyk 6* (Smoloskyp, 1972), pp. 133-41.

[98]*Ukrains'kyi visnyk 4* (Smoloskyp, 1971), pp. 148-49.

CONCLUSIONS

We have attempted in this chapter to trace the evolution of
the Ukrainian cultural revival by examining its manifes-
tation in elemental symbols of distinct Ukrainian identity,
public debate over the significance of these symbols, the
manner in which they have been exploited by cultural pluralists and the nationalist opposition, and the efforts of
the Party to co-opt such symbols where possible in order to
neutralize them or transfer their entrenched emotional
connotations to the regime's internationalist myth. We
have also attempted to show the precise way in which symbols of national identity are related to the myth of national moral patrimony.

Historically, cultural revival has preceded or accompanied mass national movements. This does not imply, of
course, that there is a revolutionary situation in the
Ukraine today; in all likelihood, passionate attachment to
national symbols and the willingness to resist are limited
to a small proportion of the intelligentsia. Although we
have almost no information about the attitudes of the
unmobilized peasantry, it is true that in terms of social
and occupational mobility, the incentives are in the direction of further denationalization rather than the reverse.
An assessment of the degree of attachment of the Ukrainian
population as a whole to national symbols other than language would require the study of socialization in primary
groups - especially the family - and the use of survey
research techniques which are at present impossible in the
Soviet Union.

IV
SYMBOLISM AND STATUS:
THE UKRAINIAN LANGUAGE

Language is an important elemental symbol of national identity. In the Soviet Union, conflict over the symbol dis-
places conflict over the substance of nationality rights
and privileges, and much of this conflict occurs in the
area of "language planning."

Joshua Fishman has defined language planning as the "organized pursuit of solutions to language problems."[1] Jonathan Pool, in an article on the problems of language planning in Soviet Central Asia, sees language planning as consisting of two types: "language status planning," referring
to efforts to fix the status, role and functions of languages (and thus, he notes, the choices among languages
that users make); and "language corpus planning," involving
intervention in "the content and structure of languages
themselves: vocabularies, sound systems, word structures,
sentence structure, writing systems, and stylistic reper-
toires."[2]

Our concern in this chapter is with language planning
in the Soviet Ukraine, and with the perceptions that
Ukrainian intellectuals hold of the role of their language.
Ukrainian nationalist dissenters have articulated the belief
that the Ukrainian language is a crucial part of the Ukrainian national moral patrimony, and there is indirect evidence
that this belief is shared by many establishment figures.

---

[1]Joshua A. Fishman, *Language and Nationalism: Two Integrative Essays*
(Rowley, Mass: Newbury House Publishers, 1973), p. 55.

[2]Jonathan Pool, "Developing the Soviet Turkic Tongues: The Language of
the Politics of Language," *Slavic Review*, Vol. 35, No. 3(September,
1976), p. 406.

This concern with the Ukrainian language is connected with the belief that: a) the language is threatened in various ways with dilution or extinction, and b) it merits state-sponsored efforts to alleviate these threats, both for its own sake as a medium of communication, and as a symbol of Ukrainian identity and the bearer of Ukrainian culture.

As a symbol of ethnic identity, a national language fulfills three symbolic functions. First, it serves as a symbol of *authenticity*: like the cultural forms and expressions discussed in the previous chapter, it authenticates the myth of a historic communal bond. Aside from physical features when these are relevant, language is the most obvious and the most tenacious bond linking the members of a community to one another and - through literature, written records and the oral tradition - it authenticates the myth of a common past and a common fate.

Secondly, language serves as a symbol of *differentiation* of the ethnic community from other groups. The differentiation function of language becomes particularly relevant when, as in the case of the Ukrainians who are culturally and religiously relatively close to the Russians, there are few other unambiguous symbols of differentiation available.

The third symbolic function of language is in the distribution of *status*. Among large parts of the urban population of the Ukraine, the Russian language enjoys higher prestige than the Ukrainian, many Russians being openly contemptuous of Ukrainian as a "vulgar peasant dialect." The status-distribution function of language comes into play expressively and instrumentally, in that the use of Russian serves to lend prestige - or at least acceptance - to the speaker in highly Russianized areas of the Ukraine, and also seems to be a necessary condition of social mobility. A side of this question which merits further research is the differential prestige of the Russian and Ukrainian languages in less Russianized cities, and among non-Russian and non-Ukrainian national minorities in the Ukraine.

After briefly considering the language question in the

official ideology and some concrete aspects of the status
of the Ukrainian language, we shall examine controversy
generated by Soviet language planning efforts in two areas:
language and education, and language culture and purity.
The first is an aspect of "language status planning," the
second of "language corpus planning." Our focus in both
instances is upon conflict relating to the symbolic functions of language, as defined above.

THE LANGUAGE QUESTION IN OFFICIAL
NATIONALITIES POLICY

In the official ideology, one of the important concomitants
of the eventual merger (*sliianie*) of nations in the USSR is
to be the adoption of the Russian language as at least the
lingua franca throughout the Soviet Union, and at best, as
the "native language" of the minority nationalities. Mean-
while, officially articulated policy stipulates that
national languages are to be allowed to develop, and guar-
antees "full freedom for every citizen of the USSR to speak
and educate his children in any language, without permitting
any privileges, limitations or compulsions in the use of
one language or another."[3]

Throughout the interwar period, it had been believed
that the final "merger" of nations would be accompanied by
the "merger" of languages, with a *new* language emerging
after the victory of communism. This doctrine was associated with the theories of N. Ia. Marr (1864-1934), who
held that there were no language groups or families, only
class languages arising out of the economic bases of societies. The position of Russian as the "language of
international discourse" rests upon Stalin's rejection of

---

[3]"The Program of the Communist Party of the Soviet Union," *Pravda* and
Izvestiia, November 2, 1961, pp. 1-9; translation in Charlotte Saikowski
and Leo Gruliow, eds., *Current Soviet Policies IV* (New York and London:
Columbia University Press, 1962), p. 26.

Marr's theories. Stalin pronounced that language is not, as Marr had maintained, part of the "superstructure," but rather a classless attribute of nations and peoples which can be utilized by bourgeois and proletarian classes alike. The result of "merger," therefore, will not be a new, amalgamated language; rather, one will come out on top, its grammatical and lexical corpus intact. In the process, national languages will give way to "zonal languages," and these will eventually give way to a single, international language, although Stalin conceded that this process might take centuries.[4] The suggestion was very strong in Stalin's writing that Russian would be a zonal language in the Soviet Union and Eastern Europe.

Stalin's theses on linguistics were significant for the Ukrainians on practical grounds for two reasons. First and favorably, they recognized that national languages, intact and undiluted, were legitimate media of communications; this legitimized language planning efforts for the preservation and even enrichment of the Ukrainian language. Secondly and ominously, Stalin's pronouncements legitimized the exceptional claim of Russian to be the language of international discourse. The ambiguity inherent in Stalin's dialectic provided the leeway for conflict over language policy and appropriate language planning efforts.

Justifications for Russian as the *lingua franca*, rather than any other national language, are of three types: 1) It is spoken as a native language by a majority of the inhabitants of the Soviet Union - up to 60% - as well as by more people than any other language; 2) it is close to the other two Slavic languages, Belorussian and Ukrainian, and the East Slavs comprise up to 75% of the population of the USSR; and 3) "subjective factors." One author defines "subjective factors" as follows:

---

[4]J.V. Stalin, *Marxism and Linguistics* (New York: International Publishers, 1951), pp. 11ff.

> As far as subjective factors are con-
> cerned, they include the fact that the
> Russian socialist nation has achieved
> the heights of worldwide science and
> culture, that the Russian language has
> created a completely unique...repository
> of the achievements of civilization...
> that the Russian language is itself an
> unusually rich and beautiful language,
> and finally, that Russian was the language
> of Vladimir Illich Lenin.[5]

The Soviet regime at the current time strongly promotes
a policy of bilingualism, rather than one of complete linguistic assimilation. The emergence of diglossia patterns
has not threatened native languages in areas of the world
where speakers of small languages do not feel that their
language is threatened. Where the native language is insufficient (for social intercourse and/or mobility), but
people feel that the native language is threatened, however,
bilingualism emerges accompanied by linguistic nationalism.[6]
This has been the pattern in the Ukraine in the period
under study.

[5]V. Kuznetsov, "The Language of International Discourse," *Pravda Ukrainy*, September 12, 1972, p. 2; translation in *Digest of the Soviet Ukrainian Press*, Vol. 1972:11:21-23. Proclamations of the love of minority nationalities for the Russian language are commonplace in the republican and all-Union press. For other explicit discussions of Russian as the *lingua franca*, see *Current Soviet Policies IV*, p. 27, and Iu. Desheriev and M. Melikiian, "Development and Mutual Enrichment of the Languages of the Nations of the USSR," *Ukrains'ka mova i litera-tura v shkoli*, No. 12(December, 1965), pp. 3-13; translation in *Digest of the Soviet Ukrainian Press*, Vol. 1966:2:23-25.

[6]Joshua A. Fishman, "National Languages and Languages of Wider Communi-cation in the Developing Nations," *Anthropological Linguistics*, No. 11 (1969), pp. 111-135.

PRESENT STATUS OF THE UKRAINIAN LANGUAGE

The threat to the vitality of the Ukrainian language is
perhaps overestimated by Ukrainian dissidents. Ukrainian
was claimed as the native language by 91.4% of Ukrainians
in the 1970 census, down 2.1 percentage points from the
1959 census.[7] A slightly different picture emerges when
these data are grouped according to urban and rural residence of the respondents:

Table 4.1

*Percentage of Ukrainian Population of Ukrainian
SSR Reporting Ukrainian as Native Language*

	URBAN			RURAL	
1959	1970	% point change	1959	1970	% point change
84.7	82.8	-1.9	98.6	98.7	+0.1

Sources: Itogi vsesoiuznoi perepisi naseleniia 1959 g. Ukrainskaia SSR.
(Moscow: "Gosstatizdat," 1963), pp. 174-91; *Itogi vsesoiuznoi perepisi
naseleniia 1970 g.*, Vol. IV (Moscow: "Statistika," 1973), pp. 170-91.

Table 4.2

*Percentage of Ukrainian Population of Ukrainian
SSR Reporting Russian as Native Language*

	URBAN			RURAL	
1959	1970	% point change	1959	1970	% point change
15.3	17.1	+1.8	1.3	1.3	0.0

Sources: Same as for Table 4.1.

[7]*Itogi vsesoiuznoi perepisi naseleniia 1959 g., Ukrainskaia SSR* (Moscow:
"Gosstatizdat," 1963), pp. 174-191; *Itogi vsesoiuznoi perepisi naseleniia 1970 g.*, Vol. IV (Moscow: "Statistika," 1973), pp. 152-53.

Table 4.3

Percentage of Ukrainian Population of Ukrainian SSR
Giving Ukrainian as Native Language: by Oblast

OBLAST	URBAN			RURAL		
	1959	1970	% point change	1959	1970	% point change
Ternopil*	98.2	98.9	+0.7	99.9	99.7	-0.2
Ivano-Frankiv'sk*	97.9	98.3	+0.4	99.9	99.97	+0.07
Volyn*	97.7	98.2	+0.5	99.9	99.9	---
Rivne*	95.7	97.6	+1.9	99.8	99.9	+0.1
Kiev (oblast)	96.9	97.1	+0.2	99.6	99.9	+0.3
Cherkasy	95.5	96.9	+1.4	99.7	99.9	+0.2
Lviv*	94.7	96.5	+1.8	99.9	99.95	+0.05
Khmelnyts'kyi	95.4	96.4	+1.0	99.8	99.95	+0.15
Zakarpattia*	95.7	96.1	+0.4	99.5	99.6	+0.1
Poltava	95.9	95.9	---	99.6	99.9	+0.3
Kirovohrad	94.4	95.6	+1.2	99.4	99.8	+0.4
Vynnytsia	94.4	95.2	+0.8	99.7	99.9	+0.2
Chernivtsi*	92.6	94.2	+1.6	99.7	99.8	+0.1
Zhytomyr	93.9	94.0	+0.1	99.6	99.9	+0.3
Chernyhiv	85.8	91.3	+5.5	95.0	95.8	+0.8
Sumy	91.2	89.2	-2.0	94.2	94.1	-0.1
Dnipropetrovs'k	89.2	86.3	-2.9	99.2	99.5	+0.3
Kherson	64.1	83.4	+19.3	98.6	98.6	---
Zaporizhzhia	81.9	78.4	-3.5	97.2	97.5	+0.3
Kiev (city)	71.9	77.4	+5.5	NA	NA	NA
Kharkiv	60.8	75.7	+14.9	99.0	99.3	+0.3
Mykolaiiv	74.4	73.3	-1.1	98.4	98.3	-0.1
Voroshylovhrad	63.7	72.7	+9.0	97.7	96.7	-1.0
Odesa	69.4	67.9	-1.5	98.3	98.6	+0.3
Donets'k	74.9	65.4	-9.5	95.5	94.2	-1.3
Krym (Crimea)	42.7	44.9	+2.2	64.8	71.9	+7.1

*=West Ukraine

Sources: Itogi vsesoiuznoi perepisi naseleniia 1959 g., Ukrainskaia SSR
(Moscow: "Gosstatizdat," 1963), pp. 174-91; Itogi vsesoiuznoi perepisi
naseleniia 1970 g., Vol. IV (Moscow: "Statistika," 1973), pp. 170-91.

Tables 4.1 and 4.2 show that the Ukrainian language
gained slightly in the countryside, and its losses in the
cities, taking the Republic as a whole, were modest. Table
4.3 illustrates that the stability of the Ukrainian language is strongest in the oblasts of the West Ukraine.
Ukrainian also made dramatic gains in the urban areas of

Kherson, Kharkiv and Voroshylovhrad, and moderate gains in
Kiev city and Chernihiv *oblast*. The most important fact
illustrated in Table 4.3, however, is that the losses to
the Ukrainian language in cities - net Russification - have
occurred in only six out of the 25 *oblasts*: Sumy, Dnipropetrovs'k, Zaporizhzhia, Mykolaiiv, Odesa and Donets'k. All
other *oblasts* showed a net gain in adherence to the Ukrainian language.

Of the *oblasts* that exhibit net Russification in the
cities, only Dnipropetrovs'k has shown a significant de-
crease in the ratio of Ukrainians to Russians (net Russianization). In the other five, the ratio in the 1970 census
is comparable to that for 1959, as shown in Table 4.4.

Table 4.4
Ratio of Ukrainians to Russians by Oblast

OBLAST	RATIO 1959	RATIO 1970	% POINT CHANGE
Ternopil	7.25	10.5	+44.8
Volyn	6.0	7.5	+25.0
Ivano-Frankivs'k	6.4	7.5	+17.2
Chernyhiv	6.6	7.3	+10.6
Zakarpattia	6.4	6.8	+ 6.3
Cherkasy	5.8	6.4	+10.3
Rivne	3.85	6.1	+58.4
Khmelnyts'kyi	5.3	6.0	+13.2
Kiev *(oblast)*	6.1	6.0	- 1.6
Poltava	6.8	5.5	-19.1
Kirovohrad	5.0	5.5	+10.0
Vynnytsia	4.6	5.4	+17.4
Sumy	5.3	5.3	0.0
Zhytomyr	4.7	5.0	+ 6.4
Lviv	3.4	4.6	+35.3
Chernivtsi	2.6	3.8	+46.2
Mykolaiiv	2.9	2.9	0.0
Kherson	3.2	2.9	- 9.4
Kiev (city)	2.6	2.8	+ 7.7
Dnipropetrovs'k	3.3	2.7	-18.2
Kharkiv	1.9	1.8	- 5.3
Zaporizhzhia	1.9	1.7	-10.5
Odesa	1.2	1.3	+ 8.3
Donets'k	1.3	1.1	-15.4
Voroshylovhrad	1.2	0.1	-91.7
Krym	0.25	0.28	+12.0

Sources: Same as for Table 4.3.

Table 4.4 also reveals other anomalies in the relationship of Russification to Russianization. There was dramatic (twelvefold) Russianization of Voroshylovhrad *oblast* between the two censuses, accompanied, however, by a dramatic gain for the Ukrainian language. Equally significant gains in adherence to Ukrainian occurred in Kherson and Kharkiv, and to a lesser extent in Chernihiv and Kiev city, where there were no substantial changes in the ratio of Ukrainians to Russians. Similarly, a number of *oblasts* in which the ratio of Ukrainians to Russians has increased have shown no dramatic gains for adherence to Ukrainian.[8]

The policy of promoting bilingualism has been rather more successful. In 1970, 48.5% of the urban and 25.1% of the rural Ukrainian population of the Republic reported fluency in Russian as a second language, although we have no way of gauging the quality of this fluency. Ukrainian is also strong as a second language, however. Between 52.4% and 52.5% of those Ukrainians who declared Russian as their native language also declared Ukrainian as a second language.[9] To the extent that this group can be supposed to be equally fluent in Russian and Ukrainian, having declared Russian as native out of deference or social pressure, it reduces the extent of actual Russification; this, of course, can only be a supposition. Unambiguous linguistic assimilation can only be attributed with certainty to those Ukrainians who speak Russian but not Ukrainian; only 8.2% of the urban Ukrainian population falls into this more restricted category.[10]

---

[8]Statistical analysis yields no significant correlation of these variables.

[9]*Itogi vsesoiuznoi perepisi naseleniia 1970 g*, Vol. IV, pp. 158-59. Data on the declaration of a second language are not available for 1959.

[10]Calculated from data in *Itogi vsesoiuznoi perepisi naseleniia 1970 g.*, Vol. IV, pp. 158-59. 8.2% is that percentage of the urban population speaking a native language other than Ukrainian (for 99.8% of whom that language is Russian), who do not declare Ukrainian as a second language; i.e., they speak Russian, but not Ukrainian.

Minority nationalities in the Ukraine - other than Jews
and Russians - which come from other republics, tend to
adopt Russian rather than Ukrainian as a native or a second
language, when declaring a language other than their own:
this is probably explainable simply in terms of migration,
as they learned Russian before they migrated to the Ukraine.
Czechs and Poles, however, who have lived on Ukrainian territory for generations, tend to assimilate to Ukrainian
rather than to Russian.[11] Finally, 25.9% of Russians and
39% of Jews living in the Ukraine report Ukrainian as a
second language. The adoption of Ukrainian as a second
language by Russians living in urban areas (27%) is higher
than by those in rural areas (20%).[12] At first gloss, one
might expect the reverse, as Ukrainian is more necessary
for dwellers in rural areas; perhaps the explanation is
that Russians in the villages are frequently itinerant
officials, while those in the cities are relatively settled.

The data we have presented attest that rampant linguistic denationalization is not taking place in the Ukraine;
except for a few urban areas in the East Ukraine, the
Ukrainian language is in fact gaining. There was a net decline for the Ukraine as a whole, but a very modest one.

But the figures also show that Ukrainians are speaking
Russian as a second language. This aspect of Soviet
nationalities policy is showing success. Brian Silver has
argued that bilingualism may be viewed as "a stable form of
accommodation between ethnic groups," but for the long term,
he is not confident that bilingualism will not threaten the
maintenance of the native tongue for some Soviet nationalities, such as the Ukrainians, for whom factors that

[11]*Itogi vsesoiuznoi perepisi naseleniia 1970 g.*, Vo. IV, pp. 152-53.
For a more sophisticated statistical treatment, though Union-wide and
not by *oblast*, see Brian Silver, "Ethnic Identity Change among Soviet
Nationalities: A Statistical Analysis," PhD Thesis, Department of
Political Science, University of Wisconsin-Madison, 1972.

[12]*Radians'ka Ukraina*, April 25, 1971; also, *Itogi vsesoiuznoi perepisi
naseleniia 1970 g.*, Vol. IV, pp. 152-53, 158-59, 164-65.

reinforce the native language are weak.[13] But while
officially-sponsored or encouraged discrimination against
the Ukrainian language certainly exists, it is not reflected
in any significant decline in adherence to the language
overall.

Discrimination against the Ukrainian language is in part
the result of social processes, particularly in highly
Russianized areas, and in this case is to be attributed to
the differential prestige of the Russian and Ukrainian languages.[14] State policy can be said to discriminate against
the Ukrainian language when (to use Joseph Gusfield's concept) policies pursued by the state tend to favor one side
of a "status" issue.[15] Official Soviet policies in the
Ukraine have tended to reinforce the prestige of Russian
over Ukrainian, and to encourage the adoption of Russian by
Ukrainians seeking upward mobility. These policies have
generated significant controversy on the language question.
The entire period, for example, has been marked by demands
for greater use of Ukrainian in the mass media and the arts,
and there is considerable documentation - both Soviet and
Western - of the fact that publishing and broadcasting in
Ukrainian is not proportional to the percentage of Ukrainian speakers in the Republic.

Both establishment intellectuals and dissidents have
taken part in the controversy over language. Commitment to
the preservation of the Ukrainian language is the clearest

[13]Brian Silver, "Bilingualism and the Maintenance of the Mother Tongue
in Soviet Central Asia," *Slavic Review*, Vo. 35, No. 3(September, 1976),
p. 424.

[14]Russian contempt for the Ukrainian language has been well-documented.
See, for example, John Kolasky, *Two Years in Soviet Ukraine, passim;*
Yaroslav Bilinsky, *The Second Soviet Republic,* pp. 156ff; and dissident
writings, especially Ivan Dzyuba, *Internationalism or Russification?*
(New York: Monad Press, Inc., 1974), pp. 149ff.

[15]Joseph R. Gusfield, *Symbolic Crusade* (Urbana: University of Illinois
Press, 1963), p. 11.

substantive link between establishment intellectuals, dissidents, and even some Ukrainian Party officials. We turn
our attention to an examination of controversy over state
policies affecting language as they relate to two issues:
language and education, and language culture. As they concern the symbolic role of language in the maintenance of
ethnic identity, the former is particularly a question of
differentiation and status, the latter primarily of authenticity.

CONTROVERSY OVER LANGUAGE
IN THE SOVIET UKRAINE

Language and Education

In the field of education, state policy effectively dis-
criminates against the Ukrainian language. It does so
directly, by requiring the study of Russian in primary
schools (since 1972, also in kindergartens) and by conducting instruction in Russian, and indirectly through the
structure of incentives: because the better institutes of
higher education conduct much, if not most, of their instruction in Russian, parents wishing to provide their
children with the best opportunities for upward mobility do
well to send their children to Russian schools.[16] The
education system thus produces bilingualism, which is an
articulated goal of state policy, but it is inescapable
that early socialization on this pattern will lower still
further the prestige of the Ukrainian language; education
is a prime medium for the transmission of symbols, and symbols are the vehicles of values.

The education system works against the Ukrainian language as a symbol of differentiation and status in three

---

[16]The 1977 Constitution (Article 45) limits the guarantee of native
language instruction to schools, excluding any right to its use in
higher education (except, of course, for native Russian speakers).

134

ways: 1) by retarding the pupils' facility with the language; 2) by communicating, largely through example and
nuance, negative symbolic associations with Ukrainian and
positive ones with Russian; and 3) by making an irresistible
appeal to the students' self-interest, as they learn that
there is a premium attached to the mastery of Russian, and
a social stigma attached to speaking Ukrainian in some con-
texts.

Khrushchev's 1958-59 school reforms abolished the com-
pulsory instruction of children in both the republican language and in Russian, leaving the choice of sending their
children to national or to Russian schools to the parents.[17]
Seemingly innocuous, the decree in fact meant that most
parents would opt for Russian schools, mainly to enhance
their children's prospects, but also perhaps because of
social pressure, and because Russian schools have better
facilities. Opposition to the change was great. The Kiev
Writers' Union passed a resolution against implementation
of the reform,[18] and a number of Ukrainian Party officials
are said to have pleaded that the reform not be instituted.[19]
Sviatoslav Karavans'kyi wrote and circulated an article
somewhat later, describing the decree as "fundamentally
discriminating" in its intent and effects, and demanding

[17]See Section 9 of the "Decree on strengthening ties between school and
life, and continued development of public education in the Ukrainian
SSR," *Radians'ka Ukraina*, April 19, 1959, pp. 2-3; translation of excerpts in *Digest of the Soviet Ukrainian Press*,3:6:1. For a discussion
of the reforms, see Yaroslav Bilinsky, "The Soviet Education Laws of
1958-59 and Soviet Nationality Policy," *Soviet Studies*, Vol XIV,
(October, 1962), pp. 138-57; and "Education of the non-Russian Peoples
of the USSR," *Slavic Review*, Vol. 27(September, 1968), pp. 411-37; also
see Harry Lipset, "The Status of National Minority Languages in Soviet
Education," *Soviet Studies*, Vol. XIX (October, 1967), pp. 181-89.

[18]*Literaturna hazeta*, December 19, 1958.

[19]V. Borysenko, "Ukrainian Opposition to the Soviet Regime," *Problems
of the Peoples of the USSR*, No. 6(1960), p. 40. The reform *dropped* the
requirement of education in the national language, and was therefore
probably not perceived as coercive in the minds of most parents.

it be rescinded.[20]

Many of the feared effects of the reform were in evidence before it was instituted, however. Considerable concern had been publicly expressed in the period 1957-1959 over the quality of mastery of Ukrainian language and literature on the part of applicants to universities. Summarizing the results of admissions examinations to Shevchenko Kiev State University, one educator concluded that the lowest levels of mastery of Ukrainian were shown by those who finished city schools with Russian as the language of instruction, and in particular, schools for working youth. These applicants tended to think in Russian and then translate their sentences into Ukrainian, making frequent syntactic errors and employing a large number of Russicisms.[21] Similar generalizations were made about applicants to the University of Chernivtsi in 1960.[22]

It is therefore difficult to gauge the extent to which the reforms were actually responsible for the effects feared for them. There was, however, an increase in the number of Russian schools in the Ukraine, and articles began appearing urging parents to send their children to Russian schools. Travellers and emigres report that considerable social pressure is brought upon parents not to send their children to Ukrainian schools.

Statistics on the number of Ukrainian schools and Russian schools are frequently published, along with the percentage

[20]Sviatoslav Karavans'kyi, "Po odnu politychnu pomylku," (September, 1965), AS 916, SDS Vol. XVIII.

[21]A.M., "About Admissions Examinations in Ukrainian Language and Literature at the T.H. Shevchenko Kiev State University," *Ukrains'ka mova v shkoli*, No. 6(1958), pp. 91-93; translation in *Digest of the Soviet Ukrainian Press*, 3:4:19.

[22]I.I. Slynko, "Results of Entrance Examinations in the Ukrainian Language to the University of Chernivtsi," *Ukrains'ka mova v shkoli*, No. 5(1960), pp. 90-93; translation in *Digest of the Soviet Ukrainian Press*, 4:12:23. Numerous articles of this type appeared during this time period.

of schools in the Ukraine these represent. It was reported
in 1958, for example, that there were 25,000 Ukrainian
schools in the Republic,[23] constituting 83% of the Ukraine's
30,236 schools of general education, with a total enrollment
in all schools of 5,468,000 pupils.[24] Rarely published,
however, are figures for the percentage of pupils attending
Ukrainian schools.[25] Although the majority of schools are
Ukrainian schools, many of these are located in rural areas
and small towns, and are smaller than average. The last
time, to our knowledge, that such figures on enrollments
were published with official approval for the entire
Republic was for the 1955-56 school year:

Table 4.5

Language of Instruction, 1955-1956
Ukrainian SSR

LANGUAGE OF INSTRUCTION	No. OF SCHOOLS	%	No. OF PUPILS	%
Ukrainian	25,034	85.32	3,845,754	72.79
Russian	4,051	13.81	1,392,270	26.35
Moldavian	159	.54	27,102	.51
Hungarian	93	.32	16,622	.31
Polish	4	.01	1,875	.04

Source: L.V. Cherkashyn, *Zahal'ne navchannia v Ukrains'kii RSR v*
1917-1957 (Kiev, 1958), p. 61. Cited by John Kolasky, *Education in*
Soviet Ukraine: A Study in Discrimination and Russification (Toronto:
Peter Martin Associates, Ltd., 1968), p. 51.

It is clear from these figures that Russian schools,
with an average of 344 pupils per school, are larger than

[23] *Radians'ka osvita*, No. 18(May 4, 1957).

[24] *Radians'ka osvita*, No. 22(June 1, 1957). The figures do not include
372,600 youths in 3,915 schools for working and farming youth.

[25] Dissidents, too, have complained about the scarcity of data on this
subject; see *Ukrains'kyi visnyk 6* (Smoloskyp, 1972), p. 63. The pre-
sumption is that the regime considers the information sensitive.

Ukrainian schools, with an average of 154 pupils per school. Later figures are fragmentary, but the number of Russian schools had increased by 1964-65 to over 4500, or over 15% of the total,[26] while, by 1967, the percentage of Ukrainian schools had declined to 81.1%.[27]

In an unusual exception to the rule, figures were published in 1970 for enrollment in Ukrainian schools in Zakarpattia. The following figures are for general schools in the *oblast*:

Table 4.6

*Language of Instruction
in Zakarpattia, 1970*

LANGUAGE OF INSTRUCTION	No. OF SCHOOLS	%	No. OF PUPILS	%
Ukrainian	614	82.6	163,000	81.4
Russian	15	2.1	11,000	5.7
Hungarian	70	9.4	21,500	10.7
Rumanian	12	1.6	4,300	2.1
Mixed	32	4.3	200	0.1

Source: A.M. Ignat, "Zdiisnennia lenins'koi polityki v shkolakh Zakarpattiia," *Radians'ka shkola*, No. 6(1970), pp. 43ff. The figures do not include 482 middle and eight-year schools with unknown attendance

The exceptional publication of these statistics may well have been designed to counter charges of the Russification of education, as the figures show an unusually low percentage of enrollment in Russian schools. Zakarpattia is, however, a largely rural *oblast* with a low Russian presence and a large Hungarian and Rumanian presence. Nationality controversy in the city of Uzhhorod is less concerned with Ukrainian-Russian relations than with relations with the East European nationalities, and the control of contacts of

[26]*Radians'ka Ukraina*, December 5, 1964.

[27]P.P. Udovychenko, "Rastsvet narodnogo obrazovaniia, nauki, i kul'tury," *Sovetskaia pedagogika*, No. 10(1967), pp. 38-48.

138

the latter with the neighboring home states.[28]

In 1969, there appeared a *samvydav* document with interesting statistics on relative Ukrainian and Russian school attendance in the centrally-located *Lenins'kyi* district of the city of Kiev:

Table 4.7

General Education Schools in Lenins'kyi
Raion - Kiev, circa 1969

UKRAINIAN SCHOOLS		
SCHOOL NUMBER	TYPE	NUMBER OF STUDENTS
117	English-Ukrainian	350
92	middle	350
87	middle	330
132	middle	130
58	middle	200
	TOTAL:	1360

RUSSIAN SCHOOLS		
SCHOOL NUMBER	TYPE	NUMBER OF STUDENTS
57	English-Russian	1600
86	middle	1000
58	middle	900
48	middle	1000
79	middle	1000
33	middle	1000
78	middle	1200
147	middle	1000
?	middle	300
?	middle	800
?	middle	800
	TOTAL:	10,600

Source: H.H., "Pid shovinistychnym presom," *Ukrains'kyi visnyk 6* (Smoloskyp, 1972), pp. 66-67.

[28]Confidential interview.

It can be seen from Table 4.7 that, while 31.3% of the schools in the *raion* are Ukrainian schools, they are attended by only 11.4% of the students in the district. We do not have information on the ratio of Ukrainians to Russians in the *raion*, but we have the *samvydav* author's assurance that the percentage of students in Russian schools is considerably higher than the percentage of Russians in the *raion*. This source also notes that School No. 57 is a "Central Committee" school, attended by the children of Shelest, Shcherbitsky, Drozdenko, Paton and other elites. The children and grandchildren of Podgorny and other elites attend School No. 78.[29]

Data in the same document for Kurenivka *raion* in Kiev show five Russian schools attended by 5,000 students, and five Ukrainian schools attended by 4,945 students in 1969.[30] These data are even more revealing, because the population of Kurenivka, a working class district, was almost 100% Ukrainian in 1969. Thus, approximately 50% of the Ukrainian pupils in this *raion* attend Russian schools. The same source reports that facilities in the Ukrainian schools are poor compared to those in Russian schools, and that there are few Ukrainian kindergartens.[31]

The quality of instruction in the Ukrainian language in both Ukrainian and Russian schools is also an issue that has drawn criticism. School textbooks in the Ukrainian language have been found to contain Russified spellings and grammatical forms, which persist edition after edition. Similarly, the culture of the teachers' language comes under frequent attack; the most frequently cited shortcoming is

[29]H.H., "Pid shovinistychnym presom," *Ukrains'kyi visnyk 6* (Smoloskyp, 1972), pp. 66-67.

[30]*Ibid.*, p. 70.

[31]*Ibid.* Also see the *samvydav* document "Tovaryshi bat'ky shkoliarev," (1964), AS 909, SDS Vol. XVIII, a complaint signed by 17 mothers of kindergartners to the Ukrainian SSR Minister of Health, protesting the use of Russian in the kindergartens.

the so-called *surzhyk* (hodgepodge) - the mixture of Russian and Ukrainian words. This problem is greater in the East Ukraine than in the West Ukraine; there have been some complaints, in fact, about the quality of teaching *Russian* in the West Ukrainian schools.[32]

Part of the general difficulty has been poor training of teachers. The peculiarities of teaching Ukrainian, it is complained, are not properly taught in pedagogical institutes. A *samvydav* document, written in Russian but with numerous misspellings and grammatical errors, by the Chairman of the State Examining Committee of the Crimean Pedinstitute, complains that courses in the Ukrainian language at the Institute are taught in Russian, often by teachers who do not know Ukrainian themselves.[33]

Higher education in the Ukraine is conducted for the most part in Russian. Iuryi Nikolaevych Dadenkov, Ukrainian Minister of Higher and Secondary Education (February, 1960-November, 1973), proposed far-reaching Ukrainization of higher education in a speech before the rectors of a number of institutions in August, 1965; he subsequently submitted his proposals to the CPSU Central Committee. Dadenkov's proposals, illuminating for what they reveal about the state of higher education in the Ukraine, were described by Viacheslav Chornovil in a *samvydav* document which reached the West in late 1972.[34]

Dadenkov informed the conference of rectors that 317,529 students were enrolled in the 50 institutions of higher

[32]V. Raukov, "Sreda zaela," *Uchitel'skaia gazeta*, December 24, 1966, p. 2; B. Khandros, "Chtoby sreda ne zaela," *Uchitel'skaia gazeta*, February 21, 1967, p. 2; "Luchshe uchit' russkomu iazyku vo vsekh shkolakh strany," (editorial), *Narodnoe obrazovanie*, No. 7(1970), pp. 125-27.

[33]V.N. Skrypka, "Pro stanovyshche ukrains'koi movy v Kryms'komu Ped-institutu," *Ukrains'kyi visnyk 6* (Smoloskyp, 1972), pp. 73-78. Although the title is in Ukrainian, the article is in Russian.

[34]Viacheslav Chornovil, "Iak i shcho obstoiue Bohdan Stenchuk?" *Ukrains'kyi visnyk 6* (Smoloskyp, 1972), pp. 12-56.

education under the Ukrainian Ministry for Higher and Secondary Technical Education, of whom 177,050, or 55%, were
Ukrainians. Since, in 1965, 1.3 million students were
enrolled in higher and secondary schools in the Ukraine,[35]
approximately 982,471, or 75.6%, of the students in the
Ukraine were enrolled in institutes under the authority,
not of the Ukrainian government, but of various USSR min-
istries. Dadenkov's figures thus apply to only 24.4% of
students in institutes in the Ukraine.

In the 50 institutes, Dadenkov reported that 8,832, or
48.7%, out of the total teaching staff of 18,132 were
Ukrainians. At the eight universities in the Republic,
45,954 (61%) of the 75,207 enrolled students were Ukrainians; of the teaching staff of 4,400, 2,475 (56%) were
Ukrainians. However, only 34% of the teaching staff delivered their lectures in Ukrainian; at Odesa, 10% did; and at
Uzhhorod University, where 71% of the student body was
Ukrainian, 43% delivered lectures in Ukrainian.[36]

Further, according to Dadenkov, the language of instruction is Russian at the Kiev Institute for National Economy
and the Kharkiv Legal Institute, the only schools in the
Ukraine educating personnel in these fields for the Republic. Finally, of 36 specialized technical schools under
Dadenkov's authority, the language of instruction was
Russian in 30, and both Russian and Ukrainian in the remaining six.[37]

Dadenkov then made ten proposals, the effect of which
would have been to shift the language of instruction to
Ukrainian in stages, to require all professors to learn
Ukrainian, to require the publishing houses of Kiev,
Kharkiv and L'viv Universities and *"Radians'ka shkola"* to

[35]*Radians'ka Ukraina*, February 5, 1966, p. 4.

[36]Chornovil, *op. cit.*, pp. 25-27.

[37]*Ibid.*, p. 26.

142

publish texts primarily in Ukrainian, and that all administrative business in universities and institutes be shifted
from Russian to Ukrainian.[38]

Chornovil reports that the CPSU Central Committee was
inundated with protest letters from Russians and Russified
Ukrainians in Kiev, and that Moscow was displease with the
proposals in any event; under pressure from Moscow, they
were filed away and forgotten.

As Chornovil argues, it is unlikely that Dadenkov would
have made the proposals without Shelest's knowledge and
support.[39] Shelest's interest is quite credible; it was at
this time that his contacts with nationalist-oriented intellectuals were becoming noticeable, and in subsequent
years he called for publication of college textbooks in
Ukrainian, and openly defended the Ukrainian language at
the 5th Congress of the Ukrainian Writers' Union in 1966.[40]

A few months prior to Dadenkov's speech before the rectors, Sviatoslav Karavans'kyi filed a lengthy complaint with
the State Prosecutor of the Ukrainian SSR, demanding that
Dadenkov, as Minister of Higher Education, be brought to
trial for violation of the law, for having permitted the
Russification of higher education. Karavans'kyi based his
complaint on Article 66 of the Criminal Code of the Ukrainian SSR ("Violation of National and Racial Equality") and
Article 167 (relating to violation of Leninist norms in the
organization of higher education).[41] The complaint did not,
of course, produce an indictment, and it was intended graphically to bring the problem to public attention in legalis-
tic form. A copy of the complaint did, however, reach

[38]*Ibid.*, pp. 28-29.

[39]*Ibid.*, p. 30.

[40]*Literaturna Ukraina*, September 6, 1968, and November 17, 1966.

[41]Sviatoslav Karavans'kyi, "Klopotannia prokurorovi URSR pro seriozni
pomilky i progoloshennia rusyfikatsii ministrom vyshchoi ta sred'noi
osviti URSR Iu. M. Dadenkova," (February 24, 1964), AS 915, SDS Vol.
XVIII.

Dadenkov and Shelest, and they are reported to have been immensely disturbed by it.[42] If this is true, it is significant evidence of effective interest articulation outside normal channels.

Language Culture and Purity

Language planning, as Joshua Fishman has emphasized, is not inherently a nationalist activity; in pre-nationalist times, both opponents and proponents of language planning, in Fishman's words, "reveal a typical lack of central concern for the ethnic, the authentic, the indigenously unique spirit and form."[43] Instead, the concern was primarily with "dimensions such as beauty, parsimony, efficiency, feasibility...."[44] Nationalist language planning, however, is concerned with the pursuit of ethnic authenticity and differentiation through the effort to exclude external linguistic influences: the pursuit of linguistic purity. But while nationalist-oriented language planners, in the effort to reconcile modernization and authenticity, are usually reluctant to admit foreign words into the language (attitudes toward calques vary), they are not averse to borrowing modern - and often foreign - concepts and ideas. What they seek to protect, therefore, is the *vehicle* in which such concepts are couched, precisely for its value as a symbol of authenticity, unity and differentiation.

In the Ukraine, the external influence against which Ukrainians wish to protect the language is, of course, Russian. Because the two languages are etymologically

[42]Viktor Nekrasov, personal interview, Paris, June 27, 1976; corroborated by Leonid Plyushch, personal interview, Paris, July 6, 1976.

[43]Joshua A. Fishman, *Language and Nationalism: Two Integrative Essays* (Rowley, Mass: Newbury House Publishers, 1973), p. 72.

[44]*Ibid.*, p. 73.

closely related, and because Ukrainian enjoys a lower status
than does Russian, the Ukrainian vernacular is often characterized by lexigraphical and grammatical Russicisms, and
in science and technology the tendency is simply to borrow
Russian terms for new concepts rather than to base new
words on Ukrainian roots. The extensive introduction of
Russicisms into the Ukrainian language (and, indeed, into
all Soviet languages) is in fact a part of official policy.
At an All-Union Conference on Problems of Terminology in
Moscow in 1959, it was emphasized that supplementation of
lexicons of national languages is to be guided by the principle of "minimal differences" - that new words for new
scientific and technological concepts in national languages
should be based on the same roots (either Russian, or the
foreign word borrowed by Russian) - to facilitate inter-
republican scholastic communications.[45]

Following the 20th Party Congress, Ukrainian intellectuals sought to revive interest in and respect for the
Ukrainian language among the urban population. Among the
intellectuals who were concerned with popular language culture and outspoken in their defense of the language were
Mykyta Shumylo, Maksym Ryls'kyi, Ivan Dzyuba, Valentyn
Moroz and Sviatoslav Karavans'kyi. Among the most outspoken and prolific of the defenders of the language, however, has been the linguist Borys Antonenko-Davydovych.[46]
He has sometimes been explicit, and astute, in his analysis
of the psychological basis of reactive linguistic nationalism. He writes of his high school days:

[45]*Literaturna hazeta*, May 21, 1959. Also see Vitalii Rusanivs'kyi,
"New Prospects for the Development of National Languages," *Literaturna
hazeta*, July 28, 1959, pp. 1-2; translation in *Digest of the Soviet
Ukrainian Press*, 3:9:20; and I.K. Bilodid, in *Radians'ka Ukraina*,
August 31, 1963, p. 3

[46]See his *Iak my hovorymo* (Kiev: "Radians'kyi pysmennyk," 1970). Also
see articles in *Zmina*, March, 1964; *Dnipro*, No. 9(1960), pp. 142-52;
Literaturna Ukraina, January 19, 1965, and March 5, 1965. For criticisms of Antonenko-Davydovych, see *Literaturna Ukraina*, March 30, 1965.

> There was something odd: the more the
> authorities of the high school relegated
> the Ukrainian language from use, the
> deeper it penetrated not only into our
> usage, but into our hearts as well.
> Moreover, when we were in the higher
> grades and became acquainted with the
> foremost Russian literature...using the
> Ukrainian language among ourselves became
> a badge of our nationality, democracy,
> almost a revolution.[47]

Perhaps because of his age, his concerns, and his
position in the establishment, Antonenko-Davydovych is ven-
erated by nationalist dissidents. He published, for
example, an article in 1968 in which he advised putting
back into the alphabet the letter "ґ," which had been
dropped in the standardization of Soviet Ukrainian orthography in the early 1930s.[48] The old letter "ґ" was a
voiced, plosive back-palatal consonant, equivalent to the
Russian "г" (both transliterated "g"), and used in relatively few words. The Ukrainian "г," however, is a voice-
less, fricative back-palatal consonant (transliterated "h").
Antonenko-Davydovych's argument was that Russians and even
many Ukrainians pronounce the Ukrainian "г" like the Russian "г," mistaking the identical orthography for identical
pronunciation and saying, for example, "Grushevs'kyi,"
rather than the correct "Hrushevs'kyi." Restoration of the
"ґ" might help eliminate the confusion, he believed. Also,
we may note, the distinctive Ukrainian pronunciation of
"г" is an element of differentiation, and its preservation
a matter of authenticity.

Antonenko-Davydovych's article produced only mild re-
buffs and good-natured ridicule from establishment critics

[47]*Dnipro*, No. 11(1961), pp. 135-45.

[48]"Litera, za tokoiu tuzhat'," *Literaturna Ukraina*, November 4, 1969.
The use of the letter "ґ" was continued in the Polish Ukraine until
its annexation by the USSR.

such as V. Rusanivs'kyi.[49] The suggestion was not criticized on ideological grounds. It is reported, however, that
the proposal prompted a lively debate in *samvydav* channels
over the intra-linguistic effects of Russification, and a
number of petitions asking that Antonenko-Davydovych's suggestion be put into effect.[50]

As against intellectuals who have defended the Ukrainian
language, I.K. Bilodid deserves brief mention as the Ukrainian champion *par excellence* of Russification. Bilodid was
the Ukrainian Minister of Education who presided over the
implementation in the Ukraine of Khrushchev's 1958-59
education reforms and, in his capacity as a philologist and
head of the Ukrainian Academy of Sciences' *Instytut movo-
znavstva* (Institute of Linguistics), he has championed the
Russian language and opposed language planners' efforts to
preserve the language.[51]

Protest against Russification has from time to time been
registered a various official forums. A Republican Conference on the Problems of the Culture of the Ukrainian
Language, held in Kiev February 11-15, 1963, for example,
produced numerous unscheduled speakers protesting, to great
applause, the Russification of education, public business
and government transactions, scholarly works, and the arts.
Apparently, the participants sent a list of their demands
to the Central Committee.[52] Similarly, Koshelivets reports
outspoken protest at a Republican Conference of Teachers in

[49]V. Rusanivs'kyi, "Za chym tuzhyty?" *Literaturna Ukraina*, November 28,
1969, p. 2.

[50]For a survey of the *samvydav* discussion, see *Ukrains'kyi visnyk 3*
(Smoloskyp, 1971), pp. 92-95.

[51]See Kolasky's graphic description of Bilodid in *Two Years in Soviet
Ukraine*, pp. 66-71.

[52]See S. Dobhal, "A Fight for the Language," *Problems of the Peoples of
the USSR*, No. 18(June, 1963), p. 47. Also see Kolasky, *Education in
Soviet Ukraine*, pp. 193-94. The events at the Conference were not
reported in the Soviet press, but a participants report was published

Kiev in 1963.[53]

Kolasky reports having witnessed an argument at a meeting
of the Presidium of the Ukrainian Writers' Union in 1964,
between V. Rechmedin and Andrii Malyshko on the one hand,
and A.D. Skaba, CPUk CC Secretary for Ideological Affairs,
on the other. He reports that Skaba directed them to write
up their complaints and submit them to the Central Committee.[54] This is significant; Skaba is widely reputed to
have directed Dzyuba, too, to write out his complaints and
submit them.[55] It suggests that during his tenure, Skaba
was either screening intellectual protest from Shelest, or
deliberately evading a confrontation in which he, Skaba,
did not feel intellectually competent. The former interpretation is reinforced by Shelest's appointment of F.D.
Ovcharenko to replace Skaba as ideological secretary in
March, 1968. The outstanding qualification of Ovcharenko,
a chemist by profession, was his extensive close personal
friendships with Kiev intellectuals.[56]

Other aspects of the "intra-linguistic" effects of Russification have also been of concern. Intellectuals have
complained, for example, about distortions in Ukrainian
onomastics. As the study of the origins of proper names,
onomastics preserves in the popular memory names, usages,
and dialects, and the emotional connotations that go with
them, which are historically rooted and therefore crucial
to the national myth. Under the Soviet regime, Russified

in *Nasha kultura* (Warsaw), March, 1963, pp. 5-6.

[53]Ivan Koshelivets, "Khronika ukrainskogo soprotivleniia," *Kontinent*,
No. 5(1975), p. 188.

[54]Kolasky, *Education in Soviet Ukraine*, p. 194.

[55]Although Nekrasov and Plyushch, both of whom knew Dzyuba well, told
us that this piece of conventional wisdom is false: that Dzyuba wrote
and submitted his manuscript without directive or invitation.

[56]Ivan Koshelivets, personal interview, Munich, June 11, 1976. The information was corroborated by Nekrasov, Paris, June 27, 1976.

and Sovietized versions of Ukrainian place names have come
into common usage: *Rovno* instead of *Rivne*, *Severodonets'k*
rather than *Pivnichnodonets'k*. In some cases of Sovietization, the result is incongruous. *Krasnyi* in Russian means
"red" and is strongly suggestive of bolshevism; in Ukrainian (as in Old Russian), *kras'nyi* still means "beautiful;"
the appropriate translation of "red," as in "Red Army,"
"Red Guards," etc., would be *chervonyi*. Yet the Ukraine is
studded with place-names like *Krasnyi Lyman*, *Krasnoloka*,
Krasnoarmiyske, and the like.[57]

The underdeveloped nature of Ukrainian linguistics and
the role of Ukrainian linguistics and slavistics have been
another area of concern. Demands for a special Ukrainian
linguistics journal were voiced at a conference on linguistics in Kiev, May 27-31, 1958.[58] This demand was not
satisfied until the creation in January, 1967 of the journal
Movoznavstvo (Linguistics), devoted to such problems as the
connection between thought and language, contacts among
languages, and the structural peculiarities of language.
The creation of the journal was not accompanied, as had
been demanded, by the establishment of a special department
of language culture in the Institute of Linguistics of the
Ukrainian SSR Academy of Sciences.[59]

Considerable controversy over the publication of Ukrainian dictionaries marked the entire period. Publication of
a six-volume Ukrainian-Russian dictionary, several technical and scholastic Ukrainian-Russian dictionaries, and a
ten-volume "explanatory" dictionary of the Ukrainian language were held up for many years, drawing numerous protests

[57]*Literaturna Ukraina*, October 1, 1963. In Kiev, however, the thorough-
fare is popularly called *Chervonoarmiis'ka*.

[58]*Ukrains'ka mova v shkoli*, No. 5(1958), pp. 90-94.

[59]*Literaturna Ukraina*, September 27, 1966. The subject was officially
considered too narrow to justify a special department.

from intellectuals.[60]

Delays in the preparation of dictionaries are the result
of controversy over the question of "minimal differences"
versus authenticity, and over which literary works are
appropriate as standards of usage; there has been controversy as well over the extent of inclusion of passive vocab-
ulary: obsolete words, archaisms, rarely used words, and
colloquialisms. The viewpoint of spokesmen for proletarian
internationalism is that such emphasis on authenticity and
differentiation artificially impedes internationalization
and "drawing together" (*sblizhenie*), and is thus ideologically faulty.[61]

Finally, there has been considerable controversy in
recent years over language culture in science. This is an
important aspect of language as a vehicle and as a symbol
of national distinctiveness. Intellectual, and particularly
scientific, excellence on the part of representatives of a
nationality can serve as a displacement symbol for more
explicit symbols of national greatness.[62] The same, we may
note parenthetically, is true of sports. It is especially
disconcerting to persons conscious of their Ukrainian
nationality that Ukrainian achievements in science and
technology are classified with and subordinated to *Soviet*

[60]*Literaturna hazeta*, August 15, 1961; *Literaturna Ukraina*, October 5,
1962; September 17, 1963; and February 2, 1968.

[61]I.K. Bilodid, "The Role of Native Language in the Development of
Education and Culture of a People," *Ukrains'ka mova i literatura v
shkoli*, No. 6(1967), pp. 1-8; translation in *Digest of the Soviet
Ukrainian Press*, Vol. 1967, 9:18-20; I.K. Bilodid, "Flowering of Lan-
guage in the Ukrainian Soviet Nation," *Ukrains'ka mova i literatura v
shkoli*, No. 12(1967), pp. 5-11; translation in *Digest of the Soviet
Ukrainian Press*, Vol. 1968, 4:20-21; L.L. Humets'ka, "Fifty Years of
Linguistics in the Ukraine," *Ukrains'ka mova i literatura v shkoli*,
No. 5(1968), pp. 85-87; translation in *Digest of the Soviet Ukrainian
Press*, Vol. 1968, 7:23-24; and Andrii Buriachok, "Concerning the
Selection and Treatment of Words in the Explanatory Dictionary of the
Ukrainian Language," *Literaturna Ukraina*, May 30, 1972, p. 4; trans-
lation in *Digest of the Soviet Ukrainian Press*, Vol. 1972, 7:15-16.

[62]This is particularly true of Ukrainian nationalistically-oriented

achievements. Such Ukrainians perceive this Russian co-
optation of Ukrainian achievements to be particularly strong
in international scientific interaction.[63]

Most Ukrainian scientists speak and write in Russian.[64]
Higher education is conducted in Russian, and many scientists are trained in the RSFSR. The necessity for communication with colleagues, not only Union-wide but in the
Ukraine, and the desire to gain Union-wide recognition,
make fluency in Russian essential for Ukrainian scientists,
and for scholars in general.

Ukrainian scientists are particularly concerned over the
tendency to adopt Russian or other foreign words for technical concepts, rather than Ukrainian or "Ukrainian-
sounding" terms. The field of cybernetics, which is highly
developed in the Ukraine, has shown, they argue, that the
Ukrainian language is quite adequate for conveying complex
technical ideas.[65]

A *samvydav* article written in 1969 argues that Ukrainian
science is undergoing a "crisis" in regard to scientific

intellectuals. We propose (but do not attempt to demonstrate) as a
general hypothesis that any activity which carries status will be employed as a displacement symbol of national greatness when direct symbols of national distinctiveness are oppressed.

[63]See, for example, the extensive debate sparked by the criticisms of
Ukrainian and Soviet science made by Vitalii P. Shelest, an atomic
physicist and the son of Petr Shelest, in an article entitled "Arkh-
imedy prosiatsia za party," *Literaturna Ukraina*, May 5, 1970, p. 1.
For a summary of the debate, see "The State of Soviet Basic Sciences:
An Unusual Criticism by Ukrainian Academicians," Radio Liberty Research
Paper CRD 335/70, September 16, 1970. Petr Shelest is thought to have
been influenced by his son, who was a link between the former First
Secretary and the Kiev intellectuals: John Basarab, personal interview,
Munich, June 7, 1976.

[64]John A. Armstrong notes that everywhere he travelled in the Ukraine
and Belorussia, scholars conversed among themselves in Russian rather
than in their native language; "The Soviet Intellectuals: Observations
from Two Journeys," *Studies on the Soviet Union*, Vol 1(1961), pp. 30-33.

[65]Serhii Plachenda, "A Genre Awaiting its Flowering," *Literaturna
Ukraina*, April 5, 1968; translation in *Digest...*, Vol. 1968, 5:16-18.

use of the Ukrainian language. The author alleges that the
Ukrainian Academy of Sciences is acting in an "unpartylike"
manner in permitting the Russification of the language
through science, insofar as it is the Party's policy to
promote the "flowering" of national cultures. He also
directs his complaints to the *"Naukova dumka"* publishing
house, 212 of whose 375 books (57%) published in 1969 were
in Russian.[66] The document is a letter - written, ironically, in Russian - addressed to the CPUk Central Committee,
the Presidium of the Supreme Soviet, the *partkom* of the
Ukrainian SSR Academy of Sciences, and to a number of newspapers.

CONCLUSIONS

Attachment to ethnic identity undoubtedly can and will persist even after a group has been linguistically assimilated,
as the ethnic experience in America has demonstrated. But
the native language, while it persists, is the most prominent badge of nationality. Soviet Ukrainian intellectuals
conscious of and placing importance on their distinct
Ukrainian identity have encouraged language planning efforts
that will enhance the Ukrainian language as a symbol of
ethnic authenticity and differentiation, and are concerned
about the status of the language. Many consider the prestige, the purity, and even the existence of the Ukrainian
language to be imperiled by official policies and attitudes,
of which Russification is the effect, whether intended or
unintended.

Regime policies, despite the officially articulated
policy of promoting national languages, have fostered the
erosion of the Ukrainian language, in large part through

[66]V.I. Kumpanenko, "Pis'mo s razmyshleniiami po voprosu o glubokom
krizise v primenenii Ukrainskogo iazyka v publikatsii nauchnykh
issledovanii i nauchnykh rabot AN USSR v 1969 g.," *Ukrains'kyi visnyk 3*
(Smoloskyp, 1972), pp. 94-109.

152

influencing the distribution of prestige attached to the use of Russian, as opposed to Ukrainian. These policies and their effects, however, along with increasing bilingualism, have not significantly affected the vitality of the Ukrainian language inside the Republic. Except in a very few highly Russianized and urbanized areas of the East Ukraine, adherence to the language between 1959 and 1970 increased, and the losses in the aforementioned Russianized areas were modest. In addition, increased Russianization of Ukrainian *oblasts* in the intercensus period appears to have had no effect on the rate of Russification.

Modernization and mobilization in the Ukraine have no doubt created great pressure for Russification, insofar as the path of upward mobility depends on mastery of Russian. Modernization and its effects are probably irreversible; the social processes generated by modernization will continue to exert pressure for the erosion of the Ukrainian language. In spite of this, however, the language has shown an encouraging vitality, and an articulate segment of the Ukrainian intelligentsia has been vocal in its defense.

V
SYMBOLIC ACTION:
NATIONALIST OPPOSITION AND REGIME RESPONSE

Symbolic action is action the effect of which is other than
the manifest, instrumental goal of such action. An elec-
tion, when there is only one candidate, is an example;
another is the conduct of a trial the purpose of which is
not to determine the guilt or innocence of the accused, but
to set an example or publicly to discredit the defendant
and others like him. Similarly, an appeal or a petition by
a dissident to an official instance when there is no hope
of redress is an action intended not to obtain remedy, but
graphically to confront officials with the contradiction between articulated and actual policy.

The dialogue between Ukrainian nationalist dissenters
and the regime has been largely in terms of actions which
are to varying degrees symbolic in this sense. This is the
result of severely restricted communications, highly controlled channels of interest articulation, and the sanctions
applied to the expression of demands the content of which
are uncongenial to the state. An increase in such symbolic
actions signifies a move away from the "subject-partici-
pant" political culture that has characterized Soviet
society. To the degree to which such actions break the
pattern of acquiescence and external consensus, they present
a challenge to the regime. The existence of dissent itself
is embarrassing to a state which bases its legitimacy on a
claim to unanimity of societal goals. The desire to suppress dissent without unduly publicizing its existence
forces the state to resort to forms of action which can also
be classified as symbolic within our meaning.

In this chapter, we shall examine the phenomenon of
Ukrainian nationalist dissent with regard to the structure

154

of the movement, its demographic bases, its systems of communications, and the strategies and tactics it has employed
in its search for effective means of interest articulation.
Likewise, we shall examine the response of the regime,
paying attention to the use of the judicial and penal systems, and to symbolic means by which the regime attempts to
discredit the dissenters publicly and detract from the
legitimacy of their demands for greater Ukrainian cultural
and political autonomy.

STRUCTURAL AND PROGRAMMATIC CHARACTERISTICS OF UKRAINIAN NATIONAL DISSIDENCE

Structurally, the dissent movement in the Ukraine in the
post-Stalin period has been inchoate, not coordinated as a
whole. The most notable instances of opposition have been
the acts of individual intellectuals, acting with the moral
support of other dissidents, but rarely as an organized
group.

Organized Clandestine Groups

Organized clandestine groups, when they have existed, have
been small, and apparently easily subdued by the state.
Not all of the organized groups have been outright secessionist organizations prepared for armed struggle; those
that have, however, have appeared exclusively in the West
Ukraine. The organization of groups outside the sponsorship of the Party (even apart from their programmatic
goals) is discouraged, so it is not surprising that clandestine groups are more extreme in their aims than the
ad hoc cultural opposition. *Samvydav* sources provide information on ten such organized groups with nationalist programs in the Ukraine in the period under study; we shall
briefly discuss each one.

1. *United Party for the Liberation of the Ukraine.*

This was a group of workers who formed an organization in Ivano-Frankivs'k in the late 1950s, devoted to the liberation of the Ukraine and the creation of an independent state. It is not known whether the group advocated violent means to this end. The members of the group were arrested in December, 1958 and sentenced in March, 1959.[1]

2. *The Ukrainian Workers' and Peasants' Union.*

This was a group of intellectuals and workers in L'viv, arrested at the end of 1960 and tried in May, 1961 for attempting to form a party along Marxist-Leninist lines and advocating the legal and non-violent secession of the Ukraine from the Soviet Union - a right specified in Article 17 of the 1936 USSR Constitution and Article 14 of the Constitution of the Ukrainian SSR - subject only to a popular referendum.[2] In addition to the advocacy of secession, Ivan Kandyba, a defendant in the case, listed the grievances of the Ukrainians on the nationality issue; these included the bans on Ukrainian cultural figures, the restriction of Ukrainian political and economic rights, the denial of the Ukraine's right to relations with other countries, discrimination against the Ukrainian language, and the "removal of 2/3 of her wealth" from the Ukraine.[3] Kandyba states that there were numerous such organized groups in the West Ukraine in the 1950s, but there is no information on them.[4]

[1]Ivan Kandyba, "List Pershomu Sekretarevi TsK KPU Shelestovi P. Iu: Za pravdu i spravedlisvist'," AS 904, SDS Vol. XVIII.

[2]For a discussion of the programmatic aims of the group, see AS 904 and AS 906. On Lukianenko, see "Anonimnoe soobshchenie "Lukianenko Lev Grigorevich," AS 2301. For a general discussion of the "Lawyers' Case," see *Ukrains'ki iurysti pid sudom KGB* (Munich: Suchasnist', 1968). Many of the documents relating to the case are translated in Michael Browne, ed., *Ferment in the Ukraine* (London: MacMillan, 1971), pp. 31-93.

[3]AS 904, SDS Vol. XVIII.

[4]*Ibid.*

Many of the members of the Ukrainian Workers' and Peasants' Union were Party members and held responsible positions in Party and government in L'viv, and they were relatively open in their activities. For this reason, their arrests and trials were significant as an object lesson for the nationalist movement: they demonstrated the futility of resort to constitutionally protected measures in pursuit of constitutionally guaranteed rights.[5]

3. *Ukrainian National Committee*

This was a group of twenty young workers in factories and state farms in L'viv *oblast*, who formed an organization the aim of which was to demand realization of the legal right of the Ukraine to secede from the Union. They were tried and sentenced in December, 1961. Two of the participants, Ivan Koval and Bohdan Hrytsyna, were shot.[6]

4. *OUN Cells*

While the Organization of Ukrainian Nationalists (OUN) was almost completely routed within five years after World War II, some isolated cells apparently escaped attention. Among the last of these was a complete cell discovered in a bunker in Ternopil' *oblast* in 1961. Although the *samvydav* account implies that the group had lived in the bunker continuously, it seems unlikely that they could have escaped attention in such a hideout for twelve years. In all likelihood, the bunker was used only occasionally. The participants forcibly resisted arrest, and shot themselves before surrendering. The self-inflicted wound of one of the participants, Mariia Pal'chak, was not fatal, and she was tried and condemned to death after complex surgery; on

[5]Levko Lukianenko also refers to several organized groups, including a group of six from Khodoriv *raion* in L'viv *oblast*, the Mykola Apostol group of five sentenced in Ternopil' in 1961, and the Bohdan Hohus group of five sentenced in Ternopil' in 1962. See AS 906, SDS XVIII.

[6]AS 904, SDS Vol. XVIII.

appeal, the death sentence was commuted to fifteen years in prison camps.[7] Her brother, Stepan Pal'chak, although not a participant, was sentenced to ten years for failing to report the cell to the authorities.[8]

Another cell, calling itself OUN-North (*OUN-Pivnych*), was organized among former prisoners of the Vorkuta prison camp still living in the town of Vorkuta (north of the Arctic Circle in Komi ASSR).[9] The group, including Bohdan Khrystynych, Volodymyr Leoniuk and Iaroslav Hasiuk, adopted the OUN philosophy, and engaged in propagandistic work, particularly the distribution of OUN literature via couriers in the Ukraine. All members were sentenced to fifteen year terms.[10]

5. *Serbenchuk Group*

Little is known of this group; *samvydav* sources report only that Rostislav Serbenchuk was released in March, 1972, after having served 8 years 5 months for attempting to create an anti-Soviet organization in Odesa.[11]

6. *Democratic Union of Socialists*

This was a small Marxist group formed by Mykola Drahosh (b. 1932), a mathematics teacher and headmaster of a working

[7] *Ukrains'kyi visnyk 3* (Smoloskyp, 1971), p. 88.

[8] *Ukrains'kyi visnyk 4* (Smoloskyp, 1971), p. 175.

[9] Many former OUN and UPA participants were interned at Vorkuta. In May, 1954, the Vorkuta labor camp was the scene of a mass uprising of Ukrainian and other prisoners, numbering seven thousand, led in part by former OUN member Mykhailo Soroka. The entire camp administration was driven from the camp and held at bay until the uprising was quelled by the army on June 26. The Ukrainians, believing that war with the United States was imminent, were certain that they would be slaughtered rather than permitted to remain on territory occupied by the enemy. See *Ukrains'kyi visnyk 6* (Smoloskyp, 1972), pp. 168-77.

[10] *Ukrains'kyi visnyk 3* (Smoloskyp, 1971), p. 87.

[11] *Khronika tekushchikh sobytii*, 25:36.

youths' school in Odesa. Two other teachers at the school, one a Russian, and three Moldavian students in Kishinev, were also members of the group. All were tried and sentenced in Kishinev in September, 1964.[12]

7. *Ukrainian National Front*

This group was active in Ivano-Frankivs'k *oblast* from 1964 to 1967. According to the *samvydav* account, events surrounding the arrest were sensational. There are indications that the group regarded itself as a successor to early post-war OUN groups. The group circulated OUN pamphlets dated 1947-49; one of the members of the group had found 7,000 of these pamphlets in three crates in the Carpathians. The group also produced its own *samvydav* journal, *Volia i bat'kyvshchyna* (Liberty and the Fatherland), about fifteen issues of which are reported to have appeared. The journal emphasized propaganda, not terror or forcible seizure of power, as a tactic. The journal also included an open letter to the 23rd Party Congress - reportedly actually sent to Party leaders and the press - and a statement regarding the case of a former OUN member, Dzhuhalo, who had allegedly been parachuted into the Ukraine in the 1950s. The members of the group were sentenced in November, 1967 to five and six year prison terms, followed by exile.[13]

8. *The Creative Youth of Dnipropetrovs'k*

Three prominent members of this group, whose only organized action was to sign a letter protesting Russification and the capaign against Oles' Honchar's novel *Sobor* in 1968 (see Chapter 3), were arrested and tried in 1969 and 1970; these were Ivan Sokul's'kyi, the drafter of the letter, N.G. Kul'chyn's'kyi, and V.V. Savchenko. They were

[12]*Khronika tekushchikh sobytii*, 15:32, 18:8, 20:26-27, and 23:16.

[13]*Khronika tekushchikh sobytii*, 17:26-28; also see *The Ukrainian Review*, Vol. XVI, No. 2(1969), pp. 9-12, for reports on this group. The trial received wide publicity in the USSR.

sentenced to terms ranging up to seven years plus exile.

Very little is known of the group outside of the letter,
and it is likely that the group's sole *raison d'etre* was
the drafting of the letter. Information in the letter concerning activities in the Dnipropetrovs'k *obkom*, however,
suggests that members of the group had connections with
elite circles.[14] The type of nationalism exhibited by
this group is autonomist, not secessionist: a defensive,
protective activism aimed against excesses of Russian
chauvinism and violation of civil rights, rather than
ethnic nationalism. Consequently, the Creative Youth of
Dnipropetrovs'k, as well as the Democratic Union of
Socialists, have more in common programmatically with the
larger all-Union civil rights movement than with secessionist groups, although their small size made them as vulnerable as the latter.

9. *Initiative Committee of Ukrainian Communists*

Very little is known of this group as an organized
entity outside of the contents of a letter sent to foreign
communist parties in its name in December, 1964, protesting
the violation of "Leninist norms in nationality policy"
through Russification of Ukrainian science, culture and
politics, and the revival of Stalinism.[15] The letter is
written from a Marxist standpoint, and cannot be classified

[14]See "List tvorchoi molodi Dnipropetrovs'koho," AS 974, SDS Vol.
XVIII; an English translation appears in *The Ukrainian Review*, XVI,
No. 3(1969), pp. 46-52. For a discussion of the events surrounding the
letter, see "Russification and Socialist Legality in the Dnepropetrovsk
Area," Radio Free Europe Research Paper USSR/39, March 10, 1969; an
informative comment on the case by a dissident is Mykola Plakhotniuk,
"Za nami - pravda," *Ukrains'kyi visnyk 2* (Smoloskyp, 1970), pp. 7-21;
also see *Ukrains'kyi visnyk* Nos. 2 (Smoloskyp, 1970), pp. 22-29, 31-32,
29-31, and 6 (Smoloskyp, 1972), pp. 117-118. Information on the fates
of those involved is in *Ukrains'kyi visnyk 1* (Smoloskyp, 1970), pp.
26-39, and *Khronika tekushchikh sobytii*, 7:25, 8:41, 10:39, 11:51-57,
12:13-14, 17:62 and 27:26.

[15]"Zvernennia do vsikh komunistiv narodno-demokratychnykh i kapitalistychnykh krain, do kerivnykh organiv komunistychnykh i robitnychykh
partii svitu" (1964), AS 912, SDS Vol. XVIII.

as separatist, but rather as autonomist. It is exceptional
if indeed, as it claims, it represents the viewpoint of a
large number of Ukrainian Communist Party members, but this
cannot be verified as no names are included, and none of
our informants were able to shed light on the composition
of the group, although they were familiar with the existence
of the letter.[16] While the group may, therefore, be little
more than a lofty signature to a document representing only
a few opinions, the possibility that the views reflected in
it may represent the feelings of portions of the elite
lends it some significance, particularly in light of such
statements as "...we painfully believe that, sooner or
later, blood will flow as a result of the egoistic, chauvinistic policy of the CPSU."[17]

10. *Union of Ukrainian Youth of Galicia*

This group, on whose activities we have no information,
was tried in the late 1960s in Ivano-Frankivs'k. Its members
included Dmytryi Hryn'kov (b. 1948), N.N. Motriuk, Ia. V.
Shovkovoi, D. Ia. Demidov, and R.V. Chuprei.[18]

Organized clandestine groups such as those discussed
are important primarily for their mere existence in a society which severely sanctions formal associations outside
the aegis of the Party. They attest to the existence of
perspectives and demands radically at odds with regime
goals, and the willingness to run risks to achieve them.
Groups such as these, however, have tended to be small,
isolated, and to hold forth little hope for effective
opposition.

---

[16]This includes Plyushch, Nekrasov, Koshelivets and others.

[17]AS 912, SDS Vol. XVIII. A Russian translation appears in *Natsional'-
nyi vopros v SSSR: sbornik dokumentov* (Munich: Suchasnist', 1975).

[18]*Khronika tekushchikh sobytii*, 33:49, 65-66.

Intellectual-Cultural Dissent

Considerably more important than clandestine groups, both
in terms of numbers and the attention they have received,
has been the inchoate, unorganized intellectual-cultural
dissent movement. We have discussed in Chapter 3 the
ambiguous dividing line between establishment intellectuals
who occasionally voice disapproval of regime policies, and
the dissidents. We are concerned here with dissidents, who
have been or who expect to be *persecuted* for their outspoken views.

It is fruitless to attempt to make a rigorous distinction between civil rights activists and nationalist
dissenters in the Ukraine, as the overlap between the groups
is very extensive. The Ukrainian dissidents, even when
initially or primarily concerned with civil rights, have a
concern for the national question that is missing - or at
least is not very prominent - among the concerns of civil
rights activists in the RSFSR, and this concern colors all
dissent to a greater or lesser degree. The failure of
Ukrainian nationalist dissenters to form an effective
common front with the civil rights movement in the RSFSR
and with the Union-wide movement for Jewish emigration is
undoubtedly partly due to fear that their national concerns
will be buried under civil rights concerns.

Other factors as well, however, have prevented such
united action: a generalized distrust of Russians on the
part of many Ukrainians; the fact that dissent at the
periphery, away from foreign correspondents and under a
more vigorous KGB, is more dangerous and difficult; and a
conscious regime policy to prevent a coalescence of the
Moscow groups with republican nationalist groups.

Ivan Koshelivets attributes the distance and lack of
coordination between the Ukrainian and the Russian opposition to the Russians, not to the Ukrainians.[19] Koshelivets

[19]Ivan Koshelivets, "Khronika ukrainskogo soprotivleniia," *Kontinent*,
No. 5(1975), p. 192.

undoubtedly has in mind the same criticism of the Russian
movement that the Ukrainians themselves have made, namely,
that Russian dissidents are insufficiently sensitive to
the nationality problem. It cannot be said, however, that
Russian dissidents have ignored the Ukrainians. The
Chronicle of Current Events (Khronika tekushchikh sobytii)
has reported consistently on both civil rights and nationalist dissent in the Ukraine, and frequently publishes
reviews of Ukrainian *samvydav*. In 1970, almost petulantly,
Ukrains'kyi visnyk carried a sharp rebuttal to the authors
of the "Program of the Democratic Movement of the USSR" -
a document that was signed anonymously by "The Democrats
of Russia, the Ukraine, and Baltic States" - denying that
this organization had the right to speak on behalf of the
Ukrainians, and asserting "with confidence" that no Ukrainian dissident had taken part in the formulation of the
Program.[20] Representatives of the Democratic Movement
responded in the underground journal *Demokrat*, pointing out
that when the Program was written, *Ukrains'kyi visnyk* did
not exist, and that the section of the Program on national
problems had in fact been written exclusively by Ukrainians
and Balts.[21] *Ukrains'kyi visnyk* similarly criticized a
letter of the RSFSR Initiative Group for the Defense of
Human Rights to the UN Commission on Human Rights,[22] for
its concentration of attention on oppressions in Russia;
the same article criticized several Russian dissidents,
including Sakharov, for "lack of clarity on the nationality
problem and its solution."[23] The *Chronicle* reprinted in

[20]*Ukrains'kyi visnyk 3* (Smoloskyp, 1971), p. 76. The "Program" is
AS 340, SDS Vol. V. Also see *Khronika tekushchikh sobytii,* 10:34.

[21]*Demokrat*, No. 5(1971); reported in *Khronika tekushchikh sobytii,*
25:40-41, and 14:37-38.

[22]AS 126, SDS Vol. II; reported in *Khronika tekushchikh sobytii,* 8:24.

[23]*Ukrains'kyi visnyk 1* (Smoloskyp, 1970), pp. 12-13.

1971 an editorial from *Ukrains'kyi visnyk 5* (No. 5 has not reached the West), criticizing the Moscow-based Committee for Human Rights for ignoring the national question.[24] The lengthy editorial also raised the interesting problem of internal passports, criticizing the Committee's demand for the abolition of the nationality entry; the authors wished to see the entry retained as an institutionalized protection of national identity.[25]

Not all Russian dissident groups, however, have been sympathetic to the Ukrainian nationalist dissenters. The *Political Diary (Politicheskii dnevnik)*, à remarkable Russian *samizdat* document thought to have circulated among Party officials, expressed alarm in 1965 at the increasing nationalist tendencies in the Ukraine, particularly among Party officials and the intelligentsia, although the *Diary* blamed these tendencies on the "chauvinistic policies of Khrushchev and Stalin."[26]

In addition to its failure to unite effectively with the all-Union civil rights movements, the Ukrainian nationalist dissent movement also failed to make common cause with Jews in the Ukraine agitating for the right to emigrate to Israel. While it is tempting to attribute this to the traditional hostility of Ukrainians to Jews, there is no evidence that modern Ukrainian nationalist dissidents are anti-Semitic. Two more immediate reasons probably account for this failure to unite. The first is, as with the civil rights movement, the fear of submergence of national concerns under Jewish concerns. Secondly, Soviet Jews in the Ukraine tend to be Russified, and they have a deeply ambiguous relationship to symbols of authentic Ukrainian

[24] *Khronika tekushchikh sobytii*, 22:33:35.

[25] *Ibid.* Also see a letter from a group of Ukrainian citizens to the Committee, describing arrests in the Ukraine: *Khronika tekushchikh sobytii*, 25:10-11.

[26] "Usilenie natsionalisticheskikh techenii i tendentsii na Ukraine," *Politicheskii dnevnik*, No. 9(June, 1965), AS 1002, SDS Vol. XX.

identity such as Khmelnytsky, who is widely reputed to have instigated anti-Jewish pogroms.[27] Modern Jews probably have not forgotten the fascist connections of the OUN, nor the anti-Jewish rhetoric and violence of some of the early Ukrainian nationalists.[28] In spite of this, an anomalous development of the last decade has been the appearance in the emigration of strong Ukrainian nationalists of Jewish origin. These Ukrainian Jews identify with the nationalist movement, however, not as a search for ethnic authenticity, but as a movement for the national rights of the Ukrainians that have been violated by the Soviet regime; that is to say, they see the national movement as a human rights problem.[29]

On the other side of the coin, the Jewish movement for emigration has been more successful than has the nationalist movement in achieving its aims, and it is not in the Jews' interest to compromise their own movement by association with the nationalists, or to associate with themselves the much more hostile symbols that the regime is able to bring to bear to discredit the nationalist dissidents.

In spite of thier failure to pursue effective common action with the Russians and the Jews, the Ukrainian

[27]This is another example of mythmaking through anachronism. It is inaccurate to ascribe to Khmelnytsky responsibility for pogroms of the type of the early 20th century (the monarchist Black Hundreds, for example). The 17th century was a violent period to begin with (witness the Thirty Years War), and religious violence was widespread; Catholics slaughtered Protestants and vice-versa, and Jews, too, were slaughtered by Russian Orthodox Christians. The Jews in Eastern Poland (now Western Ukraine), as agents and tax collectors for the Polish landlords, were particularly vulnerable to violence at the hands of Ukrainian peasants, from among whom the Cossacks were recruited. None of this, however, justifies regarding Khmelnytsky as the *instigator* of the violence.

[28]On Ukrainian-Jewish relations under Communism, see Stefan T. Possony, "The Ukrainian-Jewish Problem: A Historical Retrospect," *The Ukrainian Quarterly*, XXXI, No. 2(Summer, 1975), pp. 139-51; and Zvi Gitelman, "The Social and Political Role of the Jews in Ukraine," in Peter J. Potichnyj, ed., *Ukraine in the Seventies* (Oakville, Ontario: Mosaic Press, 1975), pp. 167-86.

[29]Personal conversations with John Basarab, Mykola Hoffman and Israel Kleyner, Munich, June-July, 1976.

nationalist dissidents frequently iterate that they bear
other nationalities no malice, and that Russian "colonial"
policies are as harmful to the Russians themselves as to
the Ukrainians.[30] An article entitled "Our Relationship
to the Russian People," written in 1949 by Osyp Diakov
(pseudonym O. Hornovoi, d. 1950), a member of the OUN, has
recently circulated in *samvydav*. Diakov, too, distinguished
between Russians as people and Russians as oppressors:

> In principle, our attitude to the Russian
> people in no way differs from our attitude
> to all other peoples. It stems from our
> basic ideological and political principles -
> peace to peoples; peace to men. All notions
> of chauvinism, still more of imperialism,
> are alien and hateful to the Ukrainian
> national revolutionary movement, which has
> arisen out of the soil of the national and
> colonial oppression of the Ukrainian people,
> and which expressed the people's desire for
> national liberation.[31]

Concerning the relationship of the nationalist dissident
movement with the Jews and other national minorities within
the Ukraine, Ivan Dzyuba, in a speech on September 29, 1966
at Babyn Yar (in which he explicitly identified Soviet with
Nazi totalinarianism), called for cooperation among all
oppressed peoples, but particularly Ukrainians and Jews.[32]

In 1976, the Ukraine did see the emergence of a human
rights organization with significant links to the all-Union
dissent movement. This was the Ukrainian Public Group to
Promote the Implementation of the Helsinki Accords, one of

[30]See, e.g., AS 198, SDS Vol. III, and *Ukrains'kyi visnyk 7-8* (Smoloskyp, 1975), p. 86.

[31]"Nashe otnoshenie k russkomu narodu," *Natsional'nyi vopros v SSSR:
sbornik dokumentov*, p. 11.

[32]"Vystup u Babynomu Iaru," AS 946, SDS Vol. XVIII. Dzyuba points out
that the great Ukrainian writers - Shevchenko, Franko, Lesia Ukrainka,
Hrinchenko, Vasylchenko and others opposed anti-Semitism, and that
prominent Ukrainian Jews defended Ukrainian national aspirations.

of five Soviet Helsinki Monitoring Groups - the other four
are located in Moscow, Georgia, Armenia and Lithuania. As
of this writing, the Kiev group has issued 18 Memoranda
documenting violations of the CSCE Final Act, relating to
human rights.[33] In 1977-78, the Soviet regime prosecuted
the leading members of the Helsinki Monitoring Groups,
handing out especially severe sentences - up to fifteen
years - to the Ukrainian participants.

At the height of the dissident movement in the 1960s and
early 1970s, the closest linkages of the Ukrainian nationalist dissidents with the all-Union civil rights movement
were through Viacheslav Chornovil, Leonid Plyushch, and
Sviatoslav Karavans'kyi.

Chornovil (b. 1938 in Kiev *oblast*), a journalist and a
former *komsomol* official, entered the civil rights movement
after having witnessed the 1965-66 trials of Ukrainian
intellectuals. He compiled a collection of materials on
violations of legality in these trials, along with the
biographies of twenty of the individuals involved, and sent
them as a petition of protest to government and Party
authorities.[34] Chornovil was arrested in November, 1967 and
served half his term before being released on general amnesty, but was re-arrested in January, 1972 under suspicion
of having been the editor of *Ukrains'kyi visnyk*. Chornovil
pleaded "not guilty" to all charges, including that of
editing the *Visnyk*.[35]

[33]The founding members of the Ukrainian Helsinki Monitoring Group were
Mykola Rudenko, Oles' Berdnyk, Petro Hryhorenko (General Petr Grigo-
renko), Ivan Kandyba, Levko Lukianenko, Oksana Meshko, Mykola Matu-
sevych, Myroslav Marynovych, Nina Strokata and Oleksiy Tykhyi. See the
Group's *Declaration and Memorandum No. 1*, published in English and
Ukrainian for the Ukrainian National Association by Svoboda Press,
1977; the document is available in Russian as AS 2839 (November, 1976).

[34]These items, AS 927 and AS 941, have been published in English as
The Chornovil Papers (New York: McGraw-Hill, 1968).

[35]See his statements in "My Trial," *Index on Censorship*, V, No. 1
(Spring, 1976), pp. 57-69.

Like most Ukrainian civil rights activists, Chornovil could not remain separate from the nationalist dissent movement. A friend of Dzyuba, he wrote and circulated in *samvydav* a lengthy point by point refutation of "Bohdan Stenchuk's"[36] polemical argument against Dzyuba's *Internationalism or Russification?*[37] Chornovil's refutation is a meticulously documented and tightly argued attack on "Stenchuk's" manipulation of the statistics on Russification and his tendentious interpretation of history.

Plyushch, well-known for his imprisonment in the Dnipropetrovs'k Psychiatric Hospital and final release and emigration in January, 1976 as a result of foreign, mainly French, pressure, was a member of the Moscow-based Initiative Group for the Defense of Human Rights. Plyushch, as his first act of defiance, wrote a letter in 1968 to *Komsomol'skaia pravda* challenging the veracity of its report of the Ginzburg-Galanskov trial, comparing it to similar violations of legality he had observed in Kiev in 1966. He became a member of the Initiative Group in 1969, signing its letter to the United Nations. His only polemical article to escape confiscation by the KGB was "Ethical Orientations," in which he compared the simultaneous victory and defeat of communism to the victory and defeat of Christ, and lamented the "drowning of the revolution in the blood of all its best representatives in internecine factional struggle."[38]

---

[36]"Bohdan Stenchuk" is thought to be a pseudonym for a collective of wrtiers. The booklet, *Shcho i iak obstoiue I. Dzyuba?*, was issued in July-August, 1969 by the Association for Cultural Relations with Ukrainians Abroad, and was not intended for Soviet readers.

[37]"Iak is shcho obstoiue Bohdan Stenchuk?" *Ukrains'kyi visnyk 6* (Smoloskyp, 1972), pp. 12-56.

[38]See an English translation of this article in George Saunders, ed., *Samizdat: Voices of the Soviet Opposition* (New York: Monad Press, 1974), pp. 268-72. On his early activities, see Plyushch's autobiography, *History's Carnival: A Dissident's Autobiography*. Edited, translated and with an introduction by Marco Carynnyk (New York: Harcourt, Brace Jovanovich, 1979).

Plyushch, born in 1939, graduated from the University of
Kiev in Mathematics in 1962, and worked in the Cybernetics
Institute of the Academy of Sciences of the Ukrainian SSR
until his involvement in civil rights activities in 1966.
Even after his emigration, Plyushch counts himself a
Marxist and a communist.[39] Asked by the author if he
considered himself a Ukrainian "nationalist," Plyushch
responded that he prefers the term "patriot," as "nationalism" connotes an exclusivist orientation to the rights of
other nations, and that it is unfair and inaccurate to
impute such orientations to the Ukrainian dissidents of the
1960s and 1970s.[40]

Plyushch relates that before 1966, he himself was a
"Russian chauvinist," (although he is Ukrainian), in that
he considered Russification a desirable phenomenon, as he
had been taught. A thorough and conscientious intellectual,
his experiences in 1966-68 caused him to re-examine his
views. He was apparently also influenced by non-Soviet
thinkers: among the items taken from his apartment during
a search, for example, was a copy of Rabindranat Tagor's
Nationalism.[41] Plyushch's Jewish wife, Tatiana Zhytnykova,
affirmed her husband's remarks, but added that in the
Western use of the term, "nationalism" is appropriate
because, to her mind, a nationalist is a person who loves
his nation and is above all concerned with the fate of its
people. To Mme. Plyushch, this does not imply that the
nationalist does not respect the rights of other nations,
despite the latter pejorative use of the term in the Soviet
Union. Mme. Plyushch commented that, if nationalists are
people who disrespect the rights of other nations, then the
real bourgeois nationalists are not the Ukrainians, but

[39]*Le Monde*, April 16, 1976, p. 2.

[40]Personal interview with Leonid Plyushch and Tatiana Zhytnykova,
Paris, July 6, 1976.

[41]*Ukrains'kyi visnyk 2* (Smoloskyp, 1970), p. 67.

rather the Russians in the Ukraine who display contempt for the language, culture and civil rights of Ukrainians.[42]

Among the most noted and prolific of the Ukrainian civil rights and nationalist dissidents has been Sviatoslav Karavans'kyi, born in Odesa in 1920. Karavans'kyi joined the OUN in the summer of 1941 while his native city was occupied by Rumanian troops. He was sentenced to a 25 year term in February, 1945, and served 16 years until his release on amnesty in December, 1960. Returning to Odesa, he worked as a calculator repairman, writing in his spare time for the magazine *Ukraina* and doing free-lance translations; he ultimately completed translations of *Jane Eyre*, Byron, Shakespeare, Kipling and Shelley into Ukrainian, and compiled a 1,000 page *Dictionary of Rhymes in the Ukrainian Language*. In 1961, he married Nina Strokata, a microbiologist, and enrolled in the correspondence department of the Faculty of Philology at Odesa University.

Karavans'kyi began writing petitions, complaints and publicistic works in 1965. We have already mentioned two of his protests against Russification in Chapter 4. He also wrote a number of petitions to Shelest, and one to Gomulka of Poland.[43] Rather than putting him on trial again, the Soviet General Prosecutor, Rudenko - presumably on the advice of the KGB - revoked Karavan'kyi's pardon and sent him back to prison camp to serve the remaining eight years and seven months of his original 25 year sentence. The legality of this was arguable, as Khrushchev had reduced the maximum allowable sentence to fifteen years.[44]

The tempo of Karavan'kyi's work, if anything, increased

---

[42]Plyushch interview.

[43]AS 900, AS 915, AS 916, AS 919, AS 942, AS 954 in SDS Vol. XVIII, and AS 198, SDS Vol. III, and others.

[44]*Khronika tekushchikh sobytii*, 7:6-7. Karavans'kyi protested the illegality of his sentence, to no avail, and in the same document protested the illegal treatment of a number of other prisoners. See AS 942, SDS Vol XVIII.

in prison. He has addressed over 20 petitions to various
official instances, not only protesting his own treatment,
but speaking out in defense of other prisoners, and of
minority nationalities such as the Jews, Chechens, Ingush,
Kalmyks, Karachays and others. A scholarly study while in
prison of the 1941 mass execution of Polish officers by
Soviet security police at Katyn Forest earned him an
additional five years in confinement. Karavans'kyi's wife,
Nina Strokata, refused to denounce him and, engaged in
samvydav and civil rights activities herself, was sentenced
in 1972 to four years in prison camps.

Perhaps the two most important figures in Ukrainian
nationalist intellectual dissent have been Ivan Dzyuba
(b. 1931) and Valentyn Moroz (b. 1936). Both have made
major contributions to the program and ideology of modern
Ukrainian nationalism. Dzyuba, a literary critic and a
historian, was the author of the celebrated *Internationalism
or Russification?*, a thoroughly researched and meticulously
documented indictment from a Marxist-Leninist standpoint of
Soviet violations of "Leninist nationality policy" through
Russification of Ukrainian social, cultural and political
life. Dzyuba's nationalist ideology can be described as
representing a "Mykola Skrypnyk" position, i.e., calling
for the full-fledged development of the Ukraine within the
Soviet federation. Dzyuba's specific grievances and his
program can be summarized as follows;

Grievances

1. The gradual but progressive loss of territorial sov-
    ereignty through "mass resettlement...of the Ukrainian
    population to Siberia, to the North, and other regions,
    where it numbers millions, but is quickly de-national-
    ized."

2. The loss of a common historical fate, "as the Ukrainian
    nation is being progressively dispersed over the Soviet
    Union, and as the sense of historic national tradition
    and knowledge of the historical past are gradually
    being lost due to a total lack of national education in
    schools and in society in general."

3. The maintenance of Ukrainian national culture in a "rather provincial position," its treatment as "second-rate," and the situation whereby "the Ukrainian language has been pushed into the background and is not really used in the cities of the Ukraine."

4. The circumstance that "during the last decades the Ukrainian nation has virtually been deprived of the natural increase in population which characterizes all present-day nations." [45]

Specific Program

1. The correction of the actual inequality or lagging behind of the smaller nations in various spheres of material and spiritual life.

2. Concessions from the larger nations of the USSR to the smaller ones.

3. The inadmissability of any one nation, language or culture being more highly privileged than others within the USSR.

4. Observance of the sovereignty of the republics and their protection from encroachments of centralizers on no matter what grounds.

5. The maximum national-cultural development of all republics on the basis of national languages, cultures and traditions.

6. A resolute struggle against Russian chauvinism as the main threat to communism and internationalism.

7. The development of communist self-awareness in all nations.

8. Internationalist education in the spirit of brotherhood and mutual assistance. [46]

Dzyuba, harassed and ill, partially recanted in 1969, after having been expelled from the Kiev Writers' Union. His recantation permitted him to remain a member of the Ukrainian Writers' Union. Because of his outspoken defense

---

[45] Ivan Dzyuba, *Internationalism or Russification?* 3rd Edition. (New York: Monad Press, 1974), p. 14.

[46] *Ibid.*, pp. 212-13.

of intellectuals arrested in 1972, however, Dzyuba was expelled from the Union in March, 1972, and arrested a month
later. He was sentenced to five years but, suffering from
incurable tuberculosis and agreeing to a total repudiation
of his book, he was released in late 1973.

Moroz, while not a member of the Party and not explicitly
Marxist-Leninist in his outlook, is not hostile to socialism
per se. He maintains, however, in common with Marxist-
Leninist dissidents, that Russian chauvinism and violation
of civil rights retards the development of true socialism.
During his first imprisonment in 1965-69, Moroz wrote and
circulated in *samvydav* an analysis of the situation of
Soviet society under the unbridled rule of the security
organs, describing in unflattering terms the mentality of
rulers and ruled alike in modern Soviet society.[47]

Following his release in 1969, Moroz wrote and circulated another article, one of three for which he was sentenced to another prison term,[48] in which he articulated
and defended the necessity for martyrdom and personal
scarifice on the part of the nationalist dissidents.[49] The
stimulus for writing the article was Dzyuba's December,
1969 recantation. Ironically quoting Dzyuba's own words at
a 1965 literary "evening" devoted to Symonenko, Moroz
insisted that what is necessary to restore value to the
"devalued word" is indeed "a living example of heroic civic
conduct." It is not enough, he argued, to make statements;

---

[47] "Reportazh iz zapovidnyka imeni Berii," AS 957, SDS Vol. XVIII.

[48] Moroz was sentenced in Ivano-Frankivs'k in November, 1970, to a total
of fourteen years deprivation of freedom, under Article 62 of the
Ukrainian Criminal Code ("Anti-Soviet Agitation and Propaganda"). For
petitions by Moroz and others on his behalf, see *Ukrains'kyi visnyk*,
Nos. 3(1970), pp. 1-28; 4(1971), pp. 31-61; and 6(1972), pp. 84-109.
Moroz was released in a prisoner exchange with the U.S. on April 27,
1979, and now resides in the United States.

[49] "Sredi snegov," (Russian translation of the Ukrainian original),
AS 596, SDS Vol. VIII.

it is also necessary to live by them and be ready to perish
for them. A total emotional commitment is required for
this:

> The essence of the matter is the degree
> of emotionality with which a person looks
> at this or that truth. One man simply
> knows it. Another lives by it...a verity
> warmed in one's soul to a certain temp-
> erature becomes a true value....Lesia
> Ukrainka termed this psychological state
> "obsession." (*oderzhimost*).[50]

It serves the regime best, Moroz urges, to have recantations from dissidents, so as to neutralize the legends
that grow up about them. For Moroz - and this is the
essence of his martyrdom creed - in the gray and contrived
world of a totalitarian society, values are determined and
cemented *symbolically*, and in the absence of the conditions
for a mass armed insurrection, the only weapon the dissidents have against the regime is the symbolic one.
Therefore, the "obsessed" must never recant: they must
never grant the regime that symbolic concession, for any
reason. It is not only immoral to do so, it is immoral to
enter the arena of dissent in the first place if one is not
prepared to sacrifice all other values - including family,
friends, and one's own life - to defending the cause of
which one has become a symbol, *because the symbolic gain to
the regime from a recantation is far greater than any harm
done the cause by passiveness.*
It is this that Moroz holds against Dzyuba. The latter
entered the fray, and became one of the foremost Ukrainian
nationalist spokesmen with his book - to the point, Moroz
points out, that for many people, to study Ukrainian
nationalism was to study Dzyuba. Having done so, Dzyuba
took upon himself an obligation, not necessarily to continue the struggle, but not to permit all his efforts to

[50] *Ibid.*

174

redound to the advantage of the regime through his own repudiation of it. Moroz is contemptuous of the defenders of
Dzyuba's statement who make the argument that by recanting
he was able to remain in the Writers' Union and exert further influence. This kind of "realism," for Moroz, merely
perpetuates the *status quo*; accused of "Don Quixotism,"
Moroz points to the "Don Quixotes" of the past who have
changed history.[51]

The influence of Lenin's early belief that the Russian
Revolution would catalyze the latent revolutionary potential
of the European workers is clearly reflected in Moroz's
creed of martyrdom. This call for total commitment and
self-sacrifice, if necessary, to galvanize the popular
consciousness, has its roots in Sergei Nechaev's austere
"Revolutionary Catechism," and in the culture of the Russian
revolutionary tradition, it has a component of virtue which
lends it a certain symbolic potency. We will discuss below
the symbolic counter-measures to which the regime must
resort to counter the potency of the dissidents' aura of
martyrdom. The strategy and the counter-measures both,
however, are predicated on the assumption that large numbers
of people share the national myth of the dissenters, but are
afraid to articulate it for fear of reprisals, or that they
are ambivalent about it but are subject to arousal.

In the previous chapter, we briefly discussed how Moroz
contributed to the myth of national moral patrimony. As
Moroz is perhaps the foremost ideologist of modern Ukrainian
nationalism, we shall flesh out here his concept of the
nation.

In an article criticizing the Belorussian poetess Evdokia
Los for her praise of Russia, Moroz maintains that only
with a "deep consciousness of nationality" can universal
human values be built. His conception of the value of

[51]For other explicit statements of Moroz's martyrdom creed (he does not
so label it), see "Otryvki iz pis'ma sem'e," AS 2083, and "Zamist'
ostann'oho slova," *Ukrains'kyi visnyk 6* (Smoloskyp, 1972), pp. 93-97,
in which he warns that persecution of him will "boomerang."

national particularity is strongly reminiscent of that of
Herder, with its emphasis on the value of diversity for its
own sake:

> Nationality is a truth as concrete as
> goodness, truthfulness and beauty. It
> is universal, but with a million facets,
> and every facet is assigned to a specific
> nation. The mission of a nation is to
> find that one side which no other nation
> can find, and to enrich mankind with it.[52]

There is a strong romantic element in Moroz: for full
spiritual development, the nation should be treasured above
all else. While individuals should know, intellectually,
that all people are equal, Moroz believes that emotional
values are higher, and in that realm of evaluation, he is
convinced that people must believe that "their nation has
been chosen by God and their people are the highest product
of history." And again:

> Where sacred things are concerned, logic
> has no meaning....The nation is something
> most holy. The nation is the synthesis of
> everything spiritual in man's realm. The
> Christian Shevchenko placed the nation
> above God (the formal, dogmatic God; the
> real, living God is the nation).[53]

Moroz can also love Russia, he says, because he doesn't
feel inferior to Russians. Moroz ridicules the Russifying
theory of the "inevitability of the fusion of nations," on
the grounds that a doctrine of inevitability ignores man's
autonomy and freedom of will. In connection with this, he
goes on to argue that since history cannot be programmed,

[52]"Moisei i Datan," AS 980, SDS Vol. XVIII. For years, only this anonymous summary of the article was available; the full article, however,
was published in late 1978 by Smoloskyp.

[53]*Ibid.* These, of course, are extreme views even for a nationalist.
They reflect, however, Moroz's extreme emotional aversion to the
de-nationalization of Ukrainian culture, and not chauvinism.

176

there is no guaranteed progress:

> There is no progress that automatically
> a nation the right to existence. A nation
> lives only when there are people ready
> to die for it.[54]

Thus, the ideology of Ukrainian nationalism articulated
by Moroz is ethnic nationalism, with a romantic conception
of the nation, and emphasis on the roles of religion,
ritual and tradition. It is tempered by acceptance of the
Enlightenment value of respect for diversity, and the de-
cidedly non-Marxist thesis of the unprogrammability of
history. There is, however, in Moroz's writings an optimism
that national liberation for the Ukraine *is* in fact inevitable, but whether this will take a benign form or will
involve stuggle and bloodshed will depend, in his view, on
the willingness of the authorities to accept change.[55]

DEMOGRAPHIC BREAKDOWN OF DISSIDENCE

The traditional home of virulent, separatist national sentiment has been the West Ukraine; over the last twenty years,
arrests in the West Ukraine for activities associated with
nationalism have outnumbered those in the East Ukraine by
about two to one. If we break down the geographical distribution of arrests, however, to those before and after the
emergence of the *shestydesiatnyki* as a major force in
opposition to the regime, some interesting variations became
apparent. Table 5.1 presents the geographical distribution
of arrests in the Ukraine for nationalist activity during
the Khrushchev period.

[54]*Ibid.*

[55]"Zamist ostann'oho slova," *Ukrains'kyi visnyk 6* (Smoloskyp, 1972),
pp. 93-97.

Table 5.1

Place of Arrest or Scene of Activity
of Political Crimes, 1956-1964

OBLAST	NUMBER OF ARRESTS[a]	PERCENT
L'viv	27	32.9
Ivano-Frankivs'k	8	9.8
Rovno	4	4.9
Volyn	4	4.9
Ternopil'	10	12.2
Chernivtsi	2	2.4
TOTAL, WEST UKRAINE	55	67.1
Kiev	9	11.0
Donets'k	6	7.3
Dnipropetrovs'k	3	3.7
Luhans'k	1	1.2
Sumy	1	1.2
Chernihiv	1	1.2
Zaporizhzhia	6	7.3
TOTAL, EAST UKRAINE	27	32.9
TOTAL	82	100.0

Sources: Ukrains'ke slovo, April 14-21, 1968, pp. 6,8; *Reestr osuzhdennykh ili zaderzhannykh v bor'be za prava cheloveka v SSSR* (Radio
Liberty Research Handbook No. 78, February, 1971).

[a]Some may have been religious arrests.

The table shows that during the Khrushchev period, most
of the arrests were in the West Ukraine, and of the total,
the largest number were in L'viv *oblast*. Of the arrests
during this period, 80% occurred in the period 1960-1962,
that is, during the reversal of Khrushchev's earlier liberal
nationalities policy.

With the exception of the Democratic Union of Socialists
and the Creative Youth of Dnipropetrovs'k, which were civil
rights rather than nationalist-oriented groups, all the
organized groups espousing separatist ideologies discussed
above were located in the West Ukraine. We have no

information concerning any group or individual originating
in the East Ukraine that has espoused a separatist ideology.
Subsequent tables, therefore, are concerned with the cul-
tural-intellectual opposition, representing the bulk of the
unorganized, *ad hoc* dissident movement in the Ukraine in
the 1960s and 1970s.

Table 5.2 presents comparative data on the place of
arrest or scene of major activity of the individuals arrested in the major waves of 1965-66 and 1969-72. These
data indicate that while in 1965-66, two-thirds of the
nationalist dissident activity took place in the West
Ukraine, there was a shift of activity by 1969-72, with
more than half the activity in this period in the East
Ukraine. Most marked was the shift from concentrated

Table 5.2

Place of Arrest or Scene of Activity of Political
Crimes, 1965-1966 and 1969-1972

OBLAST	1965-1966		1969-1972	
	ARRESTS	%	ARRESTS	%
L'viv	13	46.4	18	25.0
Ivano-Frankivs'k	4	14.3	7	9.7
Ternopil'	2	7.1	5	6.9
Volyn	1	3.6	-	-
Rovno	-	-	2	2.8
TOTAL, WEST UKRAINE	20	71.4	32	44.4
Kiev	6	21.4	30	41.7
Kharkiv	-	-	4	5.6
Odesa	1	3.6	2	2.8
Zhytomyr	1	3.6	-	-
Dnipropetrovs'k	-	-	3	4.2
Donets'k	-	-	1	1.4
TOTAL, EAST UKRAINE	8	28.6	40	55.5
TOTAL	29	100.0	72	99.9

Sources: The Chornovil Papers, pp. 81-226; *Ukrains'kyi visnyk* Nos. 1:14,
18, 23-27, 63, 80; 2:1-5, 66-75, 110-117; 3:2, 29-32, 64-90; 6:7-11,
122-129; *Khronika tekushchikh sobytii* 17:57-69; 27:2-12.

activity in L'viv to Kiev.   The data also show a greater
geographic spread of dissident activities in the late
1960s and early 1970s.   Combined with the data in Table
5.3, these data support the inference that West Ukrainians,
always the majority, have merely shifted their activity to
the East Ukraine.   The large "unknown" category, however,
makes it risky to draw definite conclusions.

Table 5.3
*Place of Birth of Individuals Arrested for Nationalist
Activities, 1965-1966 and 1969-1972*

OBLAST	1965-1966		% of those for whom data are available	1969-1972		% of those for whom data are available
	NO.	%		NO.	%	
L'viv	8	28.6	40.0	7	9.7	23.3
Ternopil'	4	14.3	20.0	-	-	--
Ivano-Frankivs'k	-	-	-	7	9.7	23.3
Volyn	1	3.6	5.0	2	2.8	6.7
TOTAL, WEST UKRAINE	13	46.4	65.0	16	22.2	53.3
Kiev	-	5.0	5.0	7	9.7	23.3
Donets'k	1	3.6	-	2	2.8	6.7
Chernihiv	-	-	10.0	1	1.4	3.3
Sumy	2	7.0	-	1	1.4	3.3
Luhans'k	-	-	-	1	1.4	3.3
Odesa	1	3.6	5.0	1	1.4	3.3
Zhytomyr	1	3.6	5.0	-	-	-
Kherson	1	3.6	5.0	-	-	-
Kharkiv	1	3.6	5.0	1	1.4	3.3
TOTAL, EAST UKRAINE	7	35.0	35.0	14	19.4	46.7
UNKNOWN	8	28.6	-	42	58.3	-
TOTAL[a]	28	100.1	100.0	72	100.0	99.8

Sources: Same as for Table 5.2.

[a]Percentages do not total 100 because of rounding off.

We have information on the family class background only
for the individuals arrested in 1965-1966, information provided by Chornovil. These data show that the largest
element of participants in these activities has consisted
of the sons of peasants, born (and probably educated) in
the West Ukraine.

Table 5.4

Family Background of Individuals Arrested on Charges
Related to Nationalist Activities, 1965-1966

FAMILY BACKGROUND	NO.	%	% of those for whom data are available
Peasant	11	39.0	64.7
Worker	3	10.0	17.6
Priest	1	4.0	5.9
Engineer	1	4.0	5.9
Teacher	1	4.0	5.9
UNKNOWN	11	39.0	-
TOTAL	28	100.0	100.0

Source: The Chornovil Papers, pp. 81-226.

The age of dissidents (see Table 5.5) at the time of
arrest has been quite stable between the 1965-66 and 1969-72
waves of arrests. The breakdown of the same sample in terms
of occupation is shown in Table 5.6. There appears to be no
differentiation in occupation between nationalist dissenters
and individuals who have engaged solely in civil rights
activities, as is evident from comparing Table 5.6 with
Table 5.7, a breakdown by occupational group of the signers
of a letter protesting the illegality of trials in the
Ukraine in 1968. The explanation for this lies no doubt
in the great overlap between these two groups.

We find, then, that the average nationalist dissident in
the 1960s and early 1970s was in his early 30s, the son of
a peasant or a worker in the West Ukraine, was at least a
secondary school graduate, and most likely a university

Table 5.5

Date of Birth and Age of Dissidents at Time
of Arrest, 1965-1966 and 1969-1972

YEAR OF BIRTH	AGE IN 1965	1965-1966			1969-1972			AGE IN 1970
		NO.	%	% of those for whom data are available	NO.	%	% of those for whom data are available	
1911-1915	50-54	1	3.6	5.0	1	1.4	2.2	55-59
1916-1920	45-49	2	7.1	10.0	1	1.4	2.2	50-54
1921-1925	40-44	2	7.1	10.0	4	5.6	8.9	45-49
1926-1930	35-39	4	14.3	20.0	3	4.2	6.7	40-44
1931-1935	30-34	1	3.6	5.0	6	8.3	13.3	35-39
1936-1940	25-29	10	35.7	50.0	19	26.4	42.2	30-34
1941-1945	20-24	-	-	-	3	4.2	6.7	25-29
1946-1950	15-19	-	-	-	5	6.9	11.1	20-24
1951-1955	10-15	-	-	-	3	4.2	6.7	15-19
UNKNOWN		8	28.6	-	27	37.5	-	
TOTAL		28	100.0	100.0	72	100.0	100.0	

1965[a]

Mean Age: 34
Median Age: 32
Modal Age: 27

1970[a]

Mean Age: 34
Median Age: 32
Modal Age: 32

Sources: Same as for Table 5.2

[a]Based on number known in respective years.

Table 5.6

Occupation of Individuals Arrested for Nationalist
Activities, 1965-1966 and 1969-1972

OCCUPATION	1965-1966			1969-1972		
	NO.	%	% of Known	NO.	%	% of Known
Manual Workers	1	3.6	4.0	5	6.9	8.3
White Collar	2	7.1	8.0	3	4.2	5.0
University Graduates:						
Teachers	3	10.7	12.0	5	6.9	8.3
Students	-	-	-	10	13.9	16.7
Journalists	-	-	-	1	1.4	1.7
University Graduates, Advanced Degree:						
History, Literature, Philology	10	35.7	40.0	17	23.6	28.3
Scientists and Engineers	6	21.4	24.0	3	4.2	5.0
Physicians	-	-	-	3	4.2	5.0
Artists and Musicians	3	10.7	12.0	1	1.4	1.7
Economists	-	-	-	1	1.4	1.7
Priests	-	-	-	1	1.4	1.7
Philosophers	-	-	-	3	4.2	5.0
Mathematicians	-	-	-	2	2.8	3.3
Professors, Unspecified	-	-	-	5	6.9	8.3
UNKNOWN	3	10.7	-	12	16.7	-
TOTAL	28	100.0		72	100.0	

Sources: Same as for Table 5.2.

Table 5.7

Occupational Backgrounds of the
139 Petitioners: April, 1968

OCCUPATIONAL BACKGROUND	NO.	%
Arts and Humanities:		
Cinematographers, Artists, Sculptors, Historians, Composers, Singers, Philologists, Writers	51	36.7
Scientists:		
Mathematicians, Physicists, Chemists, Biologists, Geologists	34	24.5
Engineers	11	7.9
Physicians	3	2.2
Lawyers	1	0.7
Teachers	3	2.2
Students	6	4.3
Manual Workers	26	18.7
Others	4	2.8
TOTAL	139	100.0

Source: "Appeal of the 139," Ukrains'kyi visnyk 1 (Smoloskyp, 1970), pp. 72-76.

student or university graduate in the field of history, literature or philology.[56] The *caveat* bears repeating, however, that the large "unknown" categories in many of these tables makes generalization hazardous.

The intensely romantic nationalist orientation of people in the liberal arts and the humanities in the USSR in the late 1960s is at least in part the result of Party-tolerated (and in the early part of the period under study, Party-encouraged) appeals for individuals trained in the arts: cinema, fiction-writing, graphic arts, and the calls discussed earlier for authenticity in the writing of history,

[56]Chornovil arrived at a similar profile of the typical person arrested in 1965-66 for "Anti-Soviet Agitation and Propaganda." See The Chornovil Papers, pp. 80-81.

the presentation of authentic national forms in art, literature, and so forth. These individuals received an intensely idealistic Soviet education, and they internalized the
internationalist myth. Thus, their "nationalism" reflects
much less the exclusivist orientations of "integral nationalism" than the internationalism that is, at least ideally,
espoused in Soviet nationalities policy. For this reason,
they have reacted bitterly upon recognizing the reality.
The reality is that mobilized Ukrainians, measuring success
in terms of movement to the cities and social and career
mobility there, have encountered Russians occupying the
positions and enjoying the status to which they aspired,
and fiercely protective of their privilege. Thus, the
dilemma of Soviet nationalities policy is that the very
mobilization polcies of the Soviet government, designed to
foster a new consciousness of membership in the larger
Soviet community, have instead given rise to increased
communal consciousness and ethnic hostility.

STRATEGIES AND TACTICS OF THE DISSIDENTS

The articulation of interests in the Soviet Union is circum-
scribed not only with respect to the channels of articulation, but with respect to the content of demands as well.
Whereas in Western democratic societies, while the state
may not meet the demands expressed, the articulation of
demands uncongenial to the state is not punished, in the
USSR the mere statement of certain demands is treated as
itself a crime; this is particularly true of demands of a
nationalist nature. Soviet nationalist dissidents, therefore, have been forced to make use of channels and methods
of interest articulation that are of marginal utility (such
as watered-down, Aesopic demands, as discussed in the previous two chapters, and efforts to exploit personal rela-
tionships with individuals close to the elite), and to seek
entirely different principles of interest articulation, in

order to overcome the impotence that the structure of the system imposes on them.

The principal strategy of the intellectual-cultural opposition has been symbolic behavior: the adoption of public behavior at variance with regime expectations or even in defiance of explicit rules. The goals of symbolic behavior are:

1. To point up to others, including, presumably, elites themselves, the possibility of alternatives to acquiescence; to make breaches in the popular regime-supportive consensus; and to galvanize popular support for the dissenters' demands.

2. Graphically to point up the discrepancies between officially articulated nationalities policy and the reality, and to point up the discrepancies between legally guaranteed rights and the actual behavior of the authorities.

In a word, the apparent purpose behind the kind of resistance the Ukrainian nationalist dissidents have engaged in is to test the legitimacy of actual regime nationalities policies by evoking an official response to behavior which is technically legal, but which is tacitly known to be punishable; differently stated, its purpose is to make the contradiction between myth and reality public and undeniable.

These strategies have included the following:

1. The opening of alternative channels of communication.

Samvydav (in Russian, *samizdat*), meaning "self-publishing," consists of typewritten, and sometimes unofficially reproduced, manuscripts of writings that would not pass the censor, passed clandestinely from hand to hand. In this manner, dissidents to a degree able to circumvent the officially imposed "maximization of redundancy" in political communications. By providing alternative sources of factual information, alternative interpretations, and alternative modes of symbol manipulation, *samvydav* literature serves to re-socialize part of the population, to lend coherence and

and a sense of purpose to the opposition, to rally support,
and to provide a means of mere expression. The mere fact
of its existence is bound to reinforce awareness of dissent. *Samvydav* literature also serves to inform the West of
events in the Soviet Union which official news agencies
do not report and, when rebroadcast back into the Soviet
Union by international radio stations, to further the ends
listed above.

The most important element of Ukrainian *samvydav* for
several years was the *Ukrains'kyi visnyk (The Ukrainian
Herald)*, which first appeared in January, 1970, and of
which eight issues have appeared. Modelled on the Moscow-
based *Khronika tekushchikh sobytii (Chronicle of Current
Events)*, the *Visnyk* has been a relatively dispassionate
chronicle of arrests, extra-judicial persecutions, and
other manifestations of the repression of nationalist-
oriented demands in the Ukraine. It is believed that
Viacheslav Chornovil was the editor of the first six issues
of the *Visnyk*, although he denies this.[57]

Combined issues 7-8 of the *Ukrains'kyi visnyk* took an
entirely different direction in terms of style and content
from those issues which appeared prior to CHornovil's arrest. Gone was the non-editorial reporting of events, and
in their place there appeared a virulent separatism, and
articles written more in the style of emigre Ukrainian
nationalists than in the style of Soviet Ukrainians.[58]

---

[57]Viacheslav Chornovil, "My Trial," *Index on Censorship*, V, No. 1
(Spring, 1976), pp. 57-69.

[58]Unlike all previous issues of the *Visnyk*, issue 7-8 employs language
that is reminiscent of that of Ukrainians in the West: *sovetskii*
rather than *radians'kyi*; *KGB* rather than *KDB*; *v Ukraini* rather than
na Ukraini, etc. (although it is true that in some parts of the West
Ukraine, speakers do say *v Ukraini*). The tone of the issue, and the
foreign policy issues raised, are also more characteristic of emigre
Ukrainians than of Soviet dissidents. None of this, of course, constitutes proof that the issue originated in the emigration; in view of
the additional fact, however, that the Moscow-based *Khronika tekushchikh
sobytii* has noted the existence and reviewed all issues of the *Visnyk*

2. The conscientious exhaustion of all legal approaches and remedies is a second strategy.

This strategy includes the lobbying of authorities at the local level; the wife of Ivan Rusyn, for example, obtained an interview with Shelest in November, 1965 in connection with her husband's trial.[59] At least one of the organized secessionist groups mentioned above, the Ukrainian National Front, drew attention to itself by sending a signed memorandum to the 22nd CPSU Congress.[60]

A very large proportion of *samvydav* documents consists of signed petitions and protests that have been sent to various official instances in connection with the arrests and trials of dissidents.[61] Similarly, petitions and appeals are made to international tribunals – particularly the United Nations – with reference to international law and conventions signed by the Soviet Union; frequently, too, such appeals are sent to Communist Parties in Eastern and Western Europe.[62]

3. Finally, there have been some instances of individual direct action.

There have been at least two cases of self-immolation in the Ukraine for nationalist causes. On December 5, 1968, Vasylii E. Makukha, a 50 year old teacher, burned himself to death in downtown Kiev, shouting as he did so "Long live free Ukraine!" On February 10, 1969, another teacher,

except this one, we feel that the authenticity of *Ukrains'kyi visnyk* 7-8 is at least open to reasonable doubt.

---

[59] *The Chornovil Papers*, p. 72.

[60] *The Ukrainian Review*, XVI, No. 2(1969), p. 11.

[61] In addition to those petitions included in the first six issues of *Ukrains'kyi visnyk* and in SDS Vol. XVIII, these include: AS 1990, AS 1948, AS 1949, AS 1989, AS 2006, AS 2082, and AS 2226.

[62] AS 261, SDS Vol. IV; AS 904, SDS Vol. XVIII; AS 919, SDS Vol. XVIII; AS 979, SDS Vol. XVIII; AS 989, SDS Vol. XVIII; and AS 1724, AS 1818, AS 1948, AS 2092, AS 2266, AS 2284, AS 2302, AS 2308, AS 2316, AS 2367.

Mykola Breslavs'kyi, set fire to himself on the grounds of Kiev University in protest against Russification, but his life was saved and he was arrested.[63] Finally, some instances of spontaneous mass demonstrations over Russification have been recorded.[64]

REGIME RESPONSE TO NATIONALIST DISSIDENCE

Judicial Mechanisms

The regime, by including all manifestations of Ukrainian aspiration for greater authenticity in culture and language, greater political autonomy, and opposition to Russification under the single rubric of "Ukrainian bourgeois nationalism," imposes a false unity of ends, rather than means, on the dissident movement, i.e., ultimate separatism, and has reacted to this largely chimerical end with judicial measures, rather than by attempting to respond to substantive demands. As a result, the regime has perhaps enjoyed short term success in quieting the most vociferous dissent, but no dialogue has been established, and the regime therefore has not responded in a constructive way to the challenge of nationalism. It has neither met the demands of the nationalists, nor taken steps to alleviate the conditions that give rise to nationalist discontent.

There is evidence that there were several years of hesitation and indecision at the highest levels over the appropriate means of dealing with growing Ukrainian dissent, in

---

[63]*Khronika tekushchikh sobytii*, Nos. 6:14, 8:15-16, 10:39; *Ukrains'kyi visnyk 1* (Smoloskyp, 1970), p. 3.

[64]Reports of spontaneous mass arousal are tantalizingly scanty. See, however, AS 1437 on riots in Dniprodzerzhins'k; *Khronika tekushchikh sobytii* 8:40 on a workers' demonstration in Kiev; *Khronika tekushchikh sobytii* 18:28 on the distribution of leaflets in Uzhhorod asking voters not to vote for the official candidate for Supreme Soviet deputy, but for a local writer; *Ukrains'kyi visnyk 2* (Smoloskyp, 1970), p. 84, on the distribution of leaflets at Kiev Polytechnic Institute, protesting the persecution of Dzyuba. There surely have been others.

the period following the 1965-66 wave of arrests in the
Ukraine.[65] Western sources have mentioned a secret Central
Committee resolution of December 30, 1971, to silence dis-
sent and quash the growing *samizdat* movement.[66]

The removal of Vitalyi F. Nikitchenko from the post of
KGB chief in the Ukraine in July, 1970, and his replacement
by V.V. Fedorchuk, coincided with the initiation of the
1971-72 offensive against the Ukrainian nationalist intelligentsia. Nikitchenko had been a personal friend of
Shelest, and quite possibly had been responsible for re-
straining the KGB from moving decisively against the dissidents in the period 1966-71. The replacement of Nikitchenko was apparently over Shelest's head,[67] and of course
preceded the purge of Shelest by only a short period.

Unionwide, the KGB had increased in power under the
Brezhnev regime. The KGB in the Ukraine appears to be
somewhat more autonomous in its operations, either because
it is given fuller rein by the center, or possibly because
there are simply fewer checks on police power in the periphery than in Moscow, under the eyes of foreign correspondents. Whatever the reason, Ukrainians - less than one
fifth of the total USSR population - account by most reports
for as many as half the political prisoners in the camps.[68]

[65]Christian Duevel, "Brezhnev at Odds with Podgorny: Development of
Socialist Democracy vs. Secret Police Oppression," Radio Liberty Research Paper CRD 231/70, June 22, 1970.

[66]*The Economist*, February 26, 1972, p. 149.

[67]"Ukrainian KGB Boss in Politburo?" Radio Free Europe Research Paper
No. 1900, October 8, 1973.

[68]Accounts vary. Andrei Amalrik reported to Anatole Shub in 1969 that
more than half the prisoners in the camps are of "minority nationalities," *International Herald-Tribune* (Paris), March 31, 1969, p. 3.
Mykhaylo Masiutko alleges that 60-70% of the prisoners in the Mordovian
camps are Ukrainians; see AS 950, SDS Vol. XVIII. Other estimates are
comparable; see A. Marchenko, "Moi pokazaniia," AS 106, SDS Vol. I, and
Ukrains'ka inteligentsiia pid sudom KGB (Munich: Suchasnist', 1970),
p. 170. The total number of political prisoners is equally uncertain,
but must number several thousands; see the open letter of A. Kosterin,

The Soviet authorities do not recognize the category of
"political prisoner," and prisoners who petition for the
right to be treated as political prisoners are usually punished for this.[69] Instead, dissidents are tried and sentenced as criminals. Almost all nationalist dissidents are
tried under either Article 62 of the Ukrainian Criminal
Code ("Anti-Soviet Agitation and Propaganda"), or Article
187-1 ("Dissemination of deliberately false fabrications
which discredit the Soviet state and social system").[70]

While the machinery of justice perhaps serves a didactic
and socializing function in all societies, the use of the
legal system to counter dissidence in the Soviet Union appears to have almost entirely an educational function. It
qualifies as symbolic behavior by our definition, insofar
as the manifest purpose of trials - to decide on the guilt
or innocence of the accused - is superfluous. The evidence
is overwhelming that the guilt of dissenters brought to
trial is decided politically, beforehand. The trials receive wide publicity, but unlike genuine criminal trials,
they are usually not open to the public; they are frequently closed even to relatives and close friends of the
defendants.

Besides the facade of legality which we may presume the
authorities wish to cloak their repression of dissent, legal
trappings reinforce the image of the dissidents as criminals
pitted against society, rather than as speaking for the

L. Bogoraz, P. Litvinov and others to world communist leaders of February 24, 1968, in *Problems of Communism*, XVII, No. 4(July-August,
1968), p. 69. Borys Lewytzkyj reports 670 persons arrested on political
grounds in 1960-1971: *Opposition in der Sowjetunion* (Munich, 1972),
p. 39; this number would have to be increased by at least 100 more
arrested in 1972 in the Ukraine: *Khronika tekushchikh sobytii*, 25:10
Radio Liberty reports 3,000 political arrests from the death of Stalin
to February, 1971: *Reestr osuzhdennykh ili zaderzhannykh v bor'be za
prava cheloveka v SSSR*, Radio Liberty Research Handbook No. 78, February, 1971, p. 1.

[69]See, e.g., AS 2087 and AS 2089.

[70]*Ugolovnyi kodeks Ukrains'koi SSR: nauchno-prakticheskii kommentarii*

society against the state. The image of the dissidents
that the state seeks to foster through juridical persecution is of criminals, craven traitors, and moral degen-
erates in the pay of imperialists. This version of the
dissidents as representing a form of deviance from which
the state is protecting the society is also served by the
practice of interning many political prisoners in psychiatric hospitals.[71] There is an overwhelming human
tendency to equate authority with rectitude; people whom
the state has jailed are assumed to be criminals, and
people who are committed to asylums are assumed to be
insane.

*Symbols Employed by the Regime to Discredit
the Nationalist Movement*

1. *Xenophobia: the Hostile West.*

The image of a hostile and implacable bourgeois West,
intent on subverting the Soviet regime, is perhaps the most
widely used symbol in official Soviet channels. This theme,
a descendant of Stalin's encirclement theory, is so common
in Soviet polemics that one need only pick up a newspaper,
almost at random, to find several instances of it.
Xenophobia - the fear and distrust of foreigners - is a
major facet of Soviet political culture, and it extends in
Russian culture far back into Tsarist times. The Soviet

(Kiev: Izdatel'stvo "Politicheskoi literatury," 1969), pp. 165-67, 403.

[71]On the psychiatric internment of dissenters, see AS 1265, AS 1266, AS
1267, AS 1268; V. Bukovsky and S. Gluzman, "A Manual on Psychiatry for
Dissidents," *Survey*, XXI, No. 1,2(Winter-Spring, 1974-75), pp. 180-99;
Georg Mann, "Abuses of Soviet Psychiatry," *Dissent*, Winter, 1975, pp.
90-92, 102; J.K. Wing, "Psychiatry in the Soviet Union," *British
Medical Journal*, I, No. 5905(Saturday, March 9, 1974), pp. 433-36;
Tatiana Khodorovich, *Istoriia bolezni Leonida Pliushcha* (Amsterdam:
Alexander Herzen Foundation, 1975); Roy and Zhores Medvedev, *A Question
of Madness* (New York and London: W.W. Norton, 1979); Leonid Plyushch,
History's Carnival, op. cit; Robert Bloch and Peter Reddaway, *Psychiat-
ric Terror* (New York: Basic Books, 1977).

regime makes extraordinary efforts to link ideologically
unorthodox positions with Western imperialism, either by
making the frequent argument that ideological wavering
plays into the hands of the West or, as we discuss below,
that dissidents are outright paid agents of Western imperialism.

The regime pays inordinate attention to everything that
is written in the West about the Ukraine, giving the strong
impression that these works must be read, not only by the
scholars who criticize them, but by elements of the public
as well. Were it not so, it seems that such a large-scale
public campaign to discredit them would be superfluous.

Periodically, polemics are carried on in public and in
scholarly channels with Western specialists on the Ukraine,
but the most vindictive rhetoric is directed against emigre
Ukrainians in the West engaged in literary activity of any
sort. Emigre Ukrainians are invariably characterized as
Ukrainian bourgeois nationalists in the pay of West German
or American fascists and imperialists. This device is reinforced in the popular mind by an extreme aversion in
Slavic culture to the concept of emigration, although this
aversion is less strong in the West Ukraine. Few Russians
or Ukrainians leave their homeland with alacrity, even when
aware of differential opportunities and many, when they do
leave, frequently express a longing for the homeland (not,
however, for the regime).

American activities also lend some credence to the myth
of a hostile West; the sometimes inflamed rhetoric of the
Cold War received good coverage in the Soviet press, as do
the activities of Radio Free Europe/Radio Liberty in
Munich, which broadcasts directly into the Soviet Union,
and reportedly has a wide audience not only among the
masses, but among higher Party officials, too. The fact
that the broadcasters are themselves emigres undoubtedly
reinforces the public perception - which the Soviet press
constantly reiterates - that they are turncoats in the pay
of imperialists.

The device of deliberate evocation of xenophobia as a
means of countering the appeal of Ukrainian nationalist
dissidents can be illustrated through the examination of
three key applications of the device: the Symonenko *Diary*
affair, the case of Dzyuba's *Internationalism or Russification?*, and the remarkable "Dobosh affair." Each of these
cases exemplifies one aspect of the manipulation of the
symbol of the hostile West.

The Symonenko *Diary* affair was the first overt use of
the evocation of xenophobia against Ukrainian dissidents.
It preceded in time the 1966 Siniavsky and Daniel trial in
the RSFSR, although whether it was part of the preparation
for that trial, or was inspired by the investigation of
Siniavsky and Daniel, or for that matter was unrelated to
it, remains unknown. The affair can nonetheless be said to
have established a Union-wide precedent of accusing dissidents of witting or unwitting collaboration with the West.

Ivan Svitlychnyi and Ivan Dzyuba were arrested in September, 1965 - although this was not reported in the Soviet
press for some time - and charged with having "smuggled"
the *Diary* of Vasyl Symonenko to the West. Symonenko, it
will be recalled, was the young Ukrainian poet who died of
cancer in 1963, and was subsequently lionized by the
shestydesiatnyki.

The *Diary* was published by Suchasnist' in Munich in
January, 1965, and the text was rebroadcast into the Soviet
Union by Radio Liberty. Svitlychnyi and Dzyuba were held
for several months, and subsequently released The background of the affair, as reconstructed in *samvydav* sources,
is that in April, 1965, *Radians'ka Ukraina* published a
letter from Hanna Shcherban, Symonenko's mother, a peasant
woman living on a collective farm in Cherkasy *oblast*, com-
plaining that Svitlychnyi and the young literary critic
Anatolii Perepadia had appropriated her son's *Diary* and
some of his poems, rather than permitting them to be turned
over to the Writers' Union as Symonenko allegedly had
directed in his will. Hanna Shcherban, it is reported, is

illiterate, and could not have written the letter. *Samvydav* sources allege that it was in fact written by Mykola Nehoda, a writer who had been incensed to learn that Symonenko had insulted him in the *Diary*. Nehoda wrote an open letter to *Literaturna Ukraina*, expressing his indignation. A Central Committee Department head in Kiev, a certain Kondufor, forebade publication of the letter, but it found its way into *samvydav* and received wide circulation anyway.[72]

It is not known for certain whether or not Svitlychnyi and Dzyuba actually assisted in the transmission of the *Diary* abroad, but it seems unlikely in view of Svitlychnyi's later comments on the case.[73] Nonetheless, a CPUk Central Committee letter was prepared and read at the Writers' and Artists' organizations, justifying Svitlychnyi's release without trial on the basis of his confession and extreme contrition.[74] The Western press also reported that he had confessed.[75]

The case of the Symonenko *Diary* is instructive in being among the first applications of the time-honored theme of the "hostile West" against the nationalist dissidents, but it leaves open the question of why Svitlychnyi and Dzyuba were released. It has not been the pattern for the KGB to release individuals detained for political crimes unless their recantation can be made to serve a political purpose. Svitlychnyi did not recant publicly, and Dzyuba - in this case - did not recant at all, so far as is known. Two not altogether mutually exclusive explanations appear plausible.

The first is that Dzyuba was released - and therefore

[72]*Ukrains'kyi visnyk 4* (Smoloskyp, 1971), pp. 131-35.

[73]AS 905, SDS Vol. XVIII.

[74]See *The Chornovil Papers*, p. 74.

[75]*New York Times*, International Edition (Paris), June 2, 1966, p. 2; *Neue Zuricher Zeitung*, June 3, 1966, p. 3; *Le Monde*, May 29-30, 1966, p. 3.

also Svitlychnyi — because of the former's close association with intellectuals who were protected by Shelest, through the intercession of Shelest's friend, the Ukrainian KGB head Nikitchenko.

A second explanation is that the regime itself was undecided on how to deal with the Symonenko cult. A concerted campaign had been underway to co-opt the popularity of Symonenko, and it is not logically consistent that at that time the regime should persecute Dzyuba and Svitlychnyi for sending abroad a work that was loudly proclaimed *not* to be anti-Soviet, and that the regime in fact praised. It will be recalled that the incident took place in the shadow of the trial of Siniavsky and Daniel, who were being prosecuted for publishing *anti-Soviet* works abroad.[76] This interpretation is reinforced by the appearance in *Visti z Ukrainy* (a journal published in the Soviet Union exclusively for Ukrainians in the West) of a review by Svitlychnyi, praising Symonenko's *Bereh chekan*, and emphasizing that the work was in no way anti-Soviet.[77]

Public Party reaction to Dzyuba's *Internationalism or Russification?* was so long delayed that it lends credence to hypotheses concerning Shelest's protection of Dzyuba, and high-level sympathy with at least some of the concerns that Dzyuba raised in the book. Public controversy over the book began not with its submission to the CPUk Central Committee in 1964, but with its publication in the West four years later.[78]

---

[76] It was only later, with the controversy over Solzhenitsyn's *Cancer Ward*, that publishing abroad came to be considered a crime without regard to content.

[77] *Visti z Ukrainy*, No. 26 (June, 1966), and No. 35 (August, 1966). It can be presumed that no Soviet writer may publish in this newspaper without special clearance.

[78] The first publication in the West was by Weidenfeld and Nicolson, London, 1968. It was published in Russian in 1968 by Suchasnist' (Munich), and in Ukrainian by the same publisher in 1973. The American (third) edition is published by Monad Press (New York, 1974).

Direct attacks on the book followed a year of indirect criticism of Dzyuba in the press.[79] Ukrainian *samvydav* alleges that Dzyuba was at first called before the KGB and asked to write a rebuttal to "bourgeois propaganda," but that Dzyuba refused, saying that the book in the first instance was Marxist, that he had had no part in its publication in the West, and that in any event the idea of writing a rebuttal based on KGB interpretations was not congenial to him.[80]

By 1969, the book was being openly attacked in the press.[81] At this time, "Bohdan Stenchuk's" booklet also appeared, followed closely in *samvydav* by Chornovil's rebuttal of "Stenchuk."

In the fall of 1969, the campaign against Dzyuba was carried to the Writers' Union. A call for his expulsion from that organization was published in *Molod Ukrainy* on September 10. On December 26, 1969, a vote was taken to expel him from the Kiev section of the Writers' Union, with the resolution that "a writer cannot be indifferent to whom he serves with his words, and why." Several members of the Writers' Union, including A. Holovko, B. Panch (who had previously criticized him), Iu. Smolych and I. Tsiupa, defended Dzyuba at the meeting, Tsiupa arguing that the whole affair be forgotten on the basis that "it is essential to pay attention to the international ramifications of an expulsion, so that Dzyuba not extend the problem, and the problem not be allowed to extend Dzyuba."[82]   On December 26,

[79]See, e.g., Vasyl Osadchy, "O mistere Stets'ko i velikomuchenits'ke liagushonke," *Perets*, No. 17(1966). See AS 905, SDS Vol. XVIII, for a letter to the editor of *Perets* from Chornovil and others protesting the inflamed rhetoric of the article.

[80]*Ukrains'kyi visnyk 1* (Smoloskyp, 1970), p. 6.

[81]See Liubomyr Dmyterko, "Mistse v boiu: pro literatora, iakyi opynyvsia po toi bik barakady," *Literaturna Ukraina*, August 5, 1969. For a protest by Stus, see *Ukrains'kyi visnyk 6* (Smoloskyp, 1972), pp. 7-8.

[82]Reported in *Ukrains'kyi visnyk 1* (Smoloskyp, 1970), p. 11.

Literaturna Ukraina carried some remarks Dzyuba had made in
his own defense before the Presidium (disclaiming connections with Ukrainian nationalists abroad), and termed them
a partial recantation, urging that Dzyuba could be readmit-
ted to the Writers' Union if he recanted completely.

This shadowy evidence hints at disagreement between the
Writers' Union and others (probably including Shelest) who
wanted to tone down the cultural battle in the Ukraine, and
those who wished to move decisively against the dissenters.
This interpretation is reinforced by the fact that, after
the fall of Shelest and the purge of his proteges, the
Party and the KGB did move decisively against the cultural
establishment and against the dissident movement, nearly
silencing it.

There is significant evidence that the "Dobosh affair"
was a provocation wholly concocted by the KGB in order to
substantiate charges that the Ukrainian dissident intellectuals were acting in alliance with emigre nationalist
groups abroad and their imperialist "bosses." By 1971, the
KGB had intensified its efforts to intimidate, infiltrate,
and isolate dissident circles in the Ukraine, particularly
to seize control of their channels of communication with
the West.[83]

Yaroslav Dobosh was a Belgian subject of Ukrainian an-
cestry (born in West Germany), and when he came to Kiev to
study, was a third year sociology student at Catholic University in Louvain. Dobosh was arrested by the KGB at Chop
on the Czechoslovakian border in early February, 1972, and

---

[83]Secondary and news sources reported, for example, that at least two
Soviet "nationality specialists" alleged to have KGB connections were
dispatched abroad in 1971 to study emigre nationalist groups, in an
effort to determine their connections with Soviet citizens, and to
assess their influence with Western policy-makers. Ukrainian students
from the West suspected of meeting with dissidents in the Soviet Union
were interrogated and expelled, and at least one Ukrainian dissident
in the Ukraine who had contacts with foreigners turned *agent provoca-
teur*. See, e.g., *Ukrains'ke slovo*, March 25, 1973; *Literaturna Ukraina*,
July 7, 1972, and *Rabitnycha hazeta*, July 8, 1972.

198

charged with being an agent of the OUN in the West.[84]

Dobosh at once implicated five intellectuals, who were
arrested and subsequently imprisoned: Ivan Svitlychnyi,
Leonid Seleznenko, Anna Kotsurova (a Czech student believed
to have been a KGB plant; she was not arrested, but deported to Czechoslovakia, where she was not molested),[85]
Stefaniia Hulyk, and Zinoviia Franko, the granddaughter of
the revered Ukrainian writer Ivan Franko (1856-1915).
Franko was subsequently released upon public confession and
a statement of self-criticism. Franko's public recantation
was followed by that of Seleznenko; both recantations further implicated the other defendants, and named other participants in illegal activities: Vasylyi Stus, Danylo
Shumuk, Ievhen Sverstiuk, and Z. Antoniuk, all of whom
received prison terms.[86]

On June 2, 1972, Dobosh held a televised press conference
in Kiev,[87] at which he confessed to being a paid agent of
ZCh-OUN (Foreign Units of the OUN), sent to the Soviet
Union by the organization to contact the individuals listed
above, and pay them for information to be used against the
Soviet Union in the West. Upon his return to Belgium,
Dobosh held a press conference on June 12, at which he
denied everything he had said at the Kiev press conference.

In 1975, Stus, one of the dissidents implicated in the
affair, wrote an article in prison arguing that the entire

[84]*Vechernyi Kiev,* February 11, 1972; reported in *Khronika tekushchikh sobytii,* 24:9.

[85]*Ukrains'kyi visnyk 6* (Smoloskyp, 1972), p. 11.

[86]Franko's recantation is in *Radians'ka Ukraina,* March 2, 1972; Seleznenko's appears in *Rabitnycha hazeta,* July 8, 1972.

[87]Undoubtedly in return for his freedom. He was later deported. For
the text of the press conference, see "Ukrains'kie burzhuaznye natsio-
nalisty - naemniki imperialisticheskikh razvedok. Press konferentsiia
v Kieve," *Pravda Ukrainy,* June 3, 1972. The text is reprinted in
Khronika tekushchikh sobytii, 26:17-19, along with commentary on the
case.

affair had been fabricated, and comparing the trials of 1972
to those of the 1930s.[88]

Whether or not fabricated, the Dobosh affair illustrates
the key role of the myth of hostile Western predators,
willing to seduce or purchase any Soviet citizen who for a
moment wavers from ideological vigilance, and use him to
propagandize against the Soviet Union, with the ultimate
object of tearing the Ukraine away and restoring capitalism,
with all the unimaginable terrors that may be associated
with in the popular mind. This myth is closely related to,
and exploited in conjunction with, the very potent "condensation" symbol of Ukrainian bourgeois nationalism.

2. Ukrainian Bourgeois Nationalism

Ukrainian bourgeois nationalism is the prime symbol employed
by the Soviet regime to discourage nationalist dissidence
and criticism of Soviet nationalities policies. However,
it is crucial to observe that the concept of nationalism,
as it is presented by the regime, is itself a mythical
construct: the regime does not address the cultural pluralists on their own grounds, arguing the merits or demerits
of cultural and political autonomy. Ukrainian bourgeois
nationalism is made into an all-encompassing "condensation"
symbol, embodying all the sometimes chimeric and sometimes
real bogeymen of recent Soviet history. It is in the use
of Ukrainian bourgeois nationalism to describe any effort
at preservation of Ukrainian culture and language that we
find the best examples of "metaphoric transfer": the transfer of the evils associated in the popular mind with
"nationalism" by association to individuals or activities
the regime wishes to discourage or discredit.

The word "nationalism" in the Soviet media nearly always
means "integral nationalism" - the exclusivist ideology of

---

[88]Vasylyi Stus, "Ia obvyniaiu" (1972), AS 2307.

nationalism that is historically associated with fascism.
For this reason, Ukrainian dissenters frequently object to
being described as Ukrainian "nationalists," many preferring
instead the term "patriots," so as to escape the ingrained
pejorative connotation of the word in the Soviet usage.

The source for the symbolic content of Ukrainian bourgeois nationalism is the activity of the Organization of
Ukrainian Nationalists (OUN) and the Ukrainian Insurrectionary Army (UPA) during and after World War II, when
these groups, espousing an integral nationalist ideology
and sometimes actively collaborating with the German armies,
resisted by force of arms the incorporation of the West
Ukraine into the Soviet Union.[89]

The victory over the Nazi invaders and the liberation of
the Ukraine are among the more potent symbols that legitimate Soviet rule today; the memory of the devastating war
against the fascists is deliberately kept alive for that
reason. A second connotation of the term Ukrainian bourgeois nationalism is, therefore, its association with
fascism. Numerous books and pamphlets are published to
reinforce this association.[90] Works and articles such as
these never fail to mention the collaboration of the OUN
with the Nazis, and rarely fail to describe in detail the
crimes which members of the organization are alleged to
have committed against Soviet citizens during and after the
war.[91] Radio broadcasts and television documentaries also
periodically remind the citizen of the OUN's alleged atroc-
ities.

The effect of this is accentuated and made immediate by

[89]John A. Armstrong, *Ukrainian Nationalism, 1939-1945*, 2nd Edition
(New York: Columbia University Press, 1963), *passim*.

[90]See, e.g., V. Iu. Evdokymenko, *Krytyka ideinykh osnov Ukrains'koho
burzhuazhnoho natsionalizmu* (Kiev: "Naukova dumka," 1967), and Vitalyi
Maslovs'kyi, *Zhovto-blakytna mafiia* (L'viv: "Kameniar," n.d.).

[91]See, e.g., *Ikhne sprazhne oblichchia* (Kiev: Tovaristvo "Ukraina,"
1975).

the continuous trials of individuals periodically "uncov-
ered" as having been connected in one way or another with
the OUN, or guilty of crimes during the war that can plau-
sibly be attributed to OUN connections or sympathies.
These trials receive conspicuous publicity and, unlike the
trials of dissidents, are always open to the public.
Unlike dissident activities, these are crimes of violence,
usually murders or mutilations. Our sample of the Soviet
press includes reports of twelve separate trials of individuals or groups for crimes committed during the war, and
directly attributed to the OUN connections of the accused.[92]

Second only to its efforts to link nationalism to
fascism, the Soviet official press attempts to tie bourgeois
nationalism to the West. In this sense, the analytically
distinct symbols - Ukrainian bourgeois nationalism and the
hostile West - are linked. Ukrainian bourgeois nationalism
as a symbol can be made to evoke not only suspicion and
distrust through the association with fascism, but through
xenophobia as well. This theme is so ubiquitous that extensive quotation will serve no purpose; a single example
will suffice. A review of a book published in L'viv on the
occasion of the 40th anniversary of the revolution defines
the purpose of the book as follows:

> The material in this book unmasks
> Ukrainian bourgeois nationalists as
> disgusting traitors, agents of foreign
> imperialism, and condemned enemies of
> the Ukrainian people.[93]

---

[92]*Pravda Ukrainy*, October 29, 1957; *Vil'na Ukraina*, June 1, 1958;
Radians'ka Ukraina, March 8, 1959 and *Molod Ukrainy*, March 8, 1959 (the
same trial); *Vil'na Ukraina*, July 17, 21-23, 1959; *Rabitnycha hazeta*,
No. 925(1959); *Trud*, December 11, 1959; February 4, 1960, and February
19, 1960 (separate trials); *Radians'ka Ukraina*, February 2, 1967;
Vil'ne zhyttia, July 3, 1968. Trials were also reported in *Visti z
Ukrainy*, March 12, 1967. In *samvydav*, such trials are reported in
Ukrains'kyi visnyk 3 (Smoloskyp, 1971), and *Khronika tekushchikh
sobytii*, Nos. 5,6 and 8. In the Western press, see *Le Monde*, December
6, 1959, and *The Ukrainian Review*, XIII, No. 3(1966), p. 80.

[93]*Literaturna hazeta*, May 24, 1957.

The language is this quote is typical and instructive.
Enemies of the people are always "unmasked;" their tactics
are contemptuous in the parlance of propaganda. They do
not openly proclaim their hostility but rather, having been
rejected and beaten in open battle, "lurk" behind their
moneyed protectors, the imperialists, and seek to undermine
the Soviet order by devious means. This further evokes unknown fears: a "lurking" enemy is doubly dangerous, for he
can appear in any guise; it is only the Party to whom the
unsuspecting people can turn for protection.

The third element with which Ukrainian nationalists as a
symbol are often associated is the Uniate Church. Count-
less articles, pamphlets, films and radio programs detail
the alleged activities of Metropolitan Sheptyts'kyi, the
head of the West Ukrainian Church during the war.[94] Sheptyts'kyi is portrayed in the worst possible light: as an
Austrian spy, as a fascist, a plunderer of Ukrainian cultural relics, and as committed to Polonization and German-
ization of the Ukraine, and as "probably" one of those
responsible for the arrest of Lenin at Poronino.[95]

Beginning in the 1970s, the long propaganda battle
against Zionism was also linked to Ukrainian bourgeois
nationalism The negative connotations inherent in popular
anti-Semitism can be transferred to the nationalists, and
no doubt, vice-versa. The link here is again the alliance
of anti-communist forces under imperialist protection. In
Shelest's words:

---

[94]Klym Dmytruk, *Bezbatchynky* (L'viv: n.p., n.d.), and *Pid chornymy
sutanamy* (Kiev: Tovaristvo "Ukraina," 1975). According to *samvydav*
sources, "Klym Dmytruk" is the *nom de plume* of KGB Major Klimentyi
Evhenovych Hals'kyi, a Russified Pole from Zhytomyr, now living in
L'viv, and a specialist on Ukrainian bourgeois nationalism. Aged about
fifty, he is reputed to have been active in the Soviet security forces
during and after World War II. His writings are characterized by
gruesome details of alleged OUN crimes, and nearly hysterical condem-
nation of the Uniate Church. *Ukrains'kyi visnyk 6* (Smoloskyp, 1975),
p. 164.

[95]*Vitchyzna*, No. 7(1964). On recent persecutions of the Church, see
Ukrains'kyi visnyk 1 (Smoloskyp, 1970), pp. 45-62, and 7-8, pp. 140-47.

>The imperialist ideologists place
their main wager on anti-Sovietism....
On these positions all forces of reaction
have joined hands, beginning with aggressive American imperialism and rabid
Zionism, and ending with the White Guard
remnants, the bourgeois nationalist
riff-raff, and all sorts of opportunists
and traitors.[96]

Jews are accused of "spreading insinuations regarding the intensification of the nationalities question in the Ukraine," of providing money to emigre Ukrainian nationalist organizations, and of racism and fascism.[97] In a polemical discussion of the Judenrat, Zionists are accused of having been collaborators with the Nazis in the invasion of the Ukraine.[98] Jews who had served in the Petlura government are prominently ridiculed.[99]

Finally, beginning with the Ussuri River crisis of 1969, Ukrainian nationalism is portrayed as hand-in-glove with revisionist Maoism. During the fiftieth anniversary celebrations, Radio Peking apparently began broadcasting in Ukrainian to Soviet troops in the Far East, detailing the faults of Soviet nationalities policy, and informing its listeners that the "lion's share" of the inmates in Soviet prison camps are Ukrainians.[100] *Literaturna Ukraina* published on March 12, 1969, a photograph of a plaque erected at the graves of Soviet soldiers who fell in the Ussuri

[96]*Radians'ka Ukraina*, April 1, 1971.

[97]*Radians'ka Ukraina*, January 6, 1971; *Rabitnycha hazeta*, December 1, 1965; *Radians'ka Ukraina*, September 30, 1971.

[98]*Ibid.*

[99]For example, Professor Sholom Goldman, now in Israel; *Pravda Ukrainy*, September 29, 1971. On the "unmasking" of Zionism, see the openly anti-Semitic *Ostorozhno! Sionizm!* (Moscow: "Politizdat," 1972). Anti-Zionism (a euphemistic anti-Semitism) is probably a powerful symbol with regard to the Russian and Ukrainian masses.

[100]Roman Rakhmanny, "Peking raises Ukrainian problem in war with Moscow enemies," *The Montreal Star*, May 10, 1969.

204

River clashes, in which about 50% of the names were Ukrainian; presumably the intent was to demonstrate that Ukrainians had died in defense of a Soviet cause. The Peking
boradcasts continued, and increased in hostility over the
next several years; the Chinese beamed broadcasts to
Ukrainians in the Soviet Army in the Khabarovsk region,
advocating separation of the Ukraine from the USSR and the
formation of a "Ukrainian Socialist People's Republic."[101]

Presumably in retaliation, the Soviet press began to
carry harsh criticisms of Chinese nationalities policy,
accusing the Chinese of Sinofication (*kitaizatsiia*) of
languages, colonization of national territories, destruction
of the autonomy of national minorities, etc.[102]

From 1972, the "alliance of the bankrupt with the bankrupt" of Ukrainian nationalists abroad and both Nationalist
China and the Maoists of the People's Republic of China has
received wide coverage in the Soviet press. As with the
supposed collusion of Ukrainian nationalists with other
ideological enemies, the purpose is represented as fundamentally anti-Soviet: the goal of the collusion is to
destroy Soviet power in the Ukraine.[103]

As with most such symbols, there is a grain of truth
underlying it. The emigre Ukrainian press has, as the
Soviet press accuses, discussed the relationship of the
Sino-Soviet split to the Ukrainian problem, although not in
the hysterical manner that the Soviet press alleges.[104]
There is also a historical basis for the concern with

[101] *Neue Zuricher Zeitung*, July 14, 1971.

[102] See, e.g., *Pravda Ukrainy*, June 17, 1973.

[103] *Rabitnycha hazeta*, February 27, 1972; *Radians'ka Ukraina*, February
26, 1972; *Literaturna Ukraina*, June 13, 1972.

[104] See, e.g., M. Prokop, "Rosiia, Kytai, i Ukraina," *Suchasnist'*,
No. 12(1971); Anatol Kaminsky, "Za suchasnu kontseptsiiu Ukrains'koi
revoliutsii," *Suchasnist'*, No. 2(1970).

Chinese-Ukrainian relations. Ukrainian nationalists in
1917 adopted a resolution to strive to incorporate heavily
Ukrainian populated areas in the Far East - the former
Ussuri, Amur, Transbaikal and Primorskaia *oblasts*, and
other territories along the Trans-Siberian railway[105] -
into the Ukrainian National Republic, although this had
no relation to "collusion" with the Chinese. Similarly,
the OUN sent some troops to Khabarovsk and elsewhere in the
Far East after the invasion of Manchuria by the Kwangtung
Army. Historical incidents such as these serve to strengthen the regime image that Ukrainian nationalists, whatever
their demands, are fundamentally anti-Soviet, and are hire-
lings of the regime's most viciously despised enemies.

The effect of Soviet manipulation of the symbol of
Ukrainian bourgeois nationalism in its various incar-
nations is to make it into a very potent "condensation
symbol." Non-dissident informants relate that it is the
worst label that can be applied to someone, and that
individuals living outside the Ukrainian SSR will avoid the
use of Ukrainian and report their nationality as Russian
out of fear of being branded with the label. The availability of such a potent symbol makes it possible for the
regime to discourage activities much less threatening than
Ukrainian nationalism, such as concern over Russification,
idealization of the national past, and enthusiasm for
elements of Ukrainian culture such as folk art or music.
Even simple nepotism, should an enterprise manager hire a
Ukrainian in preference to a local Russian who wants the
job, for example, can be labelled "Ukrainian bourgeois
nationalism," according to our informants.

---

[105]The so-called *Zelenyy* and *Siryy Klyn*.

CONCLUSIONS

We have argued in this chapter that symbolic action has
been the dominant mode of interaction between the Soviet
regime and its critics on nationalities policy. Nationalist dissidents have been obliged to resort to symbolic
action because of the lack of open channels for the voicing
of their demands, and because the substantive content of
their demands evokes severe sanctions. The regime has
resorted to symbolic action partly because of unwillingness
openly to discuss the problems of Soviet nationalites
policy, and partly to shape the thinking of people to
accept the official myth of proletarian internationalism,
and not to give serious consideration to the grievances
and demands of the nationalist intelligentsia.

For the short term, it appears that the regime has been
successful in quashing nationalist dissent through coercion
and symbolic action; it cannot, of course, be judged what
success it has enjoyed in terms of mass resocialization.

Although, as we have emphasized, we do not have the data
to make a definitive judgment, the information we do have
suggests that it may well have been the intercession of
Shelest that hindered the regime in moving against the
Ukrainian dissenters, especially before the dismissal of
Nikitchenko. The trimming of Shelest's *khvost* ("tail," or
following, or proteges), and the fall of Shelest himself,
followed closely upon the dismissal of Nikitchenko. In
subsequent years, Moscow severely curtailed the autonomy
of the Ukrainian *apparat*.

The dissent movement has been muffled, although not
silenced. The regime has not, however, moved to alleviate
the conditions that gave rise to it, hoping, perhaps, for
the sake of stability in the present, to pass the problem
on to a future generation of leaders.

VI

SUMMARY AND CONCLUSIONS

By way of summary and conclusion, we may now assay to
answer the five broad questions which we set forth in
Chapter One.

1. What is the substantive content of the competing myths
and meaning-sets associated with nationalism and proletarian internationalism in the Ukrainian and Soviet context?

The officially articulated content of the myth of proletarian internationalism is that the citizens of the
Soviet Union identify with the proletarian *class* as an
increasingly relevant reference group, and that identification with the nation, while it may persist for some time,
will decline in salience as the society approaches the
stage of communism. National languages and cultural peculiarities are to be tolerated among the non-elite, but
are not to be encouraged. Bilingualism is to be encouraged, and the role of the Russian language as a *lingua
franca* - a rational medium to facilitate inter-republican
scientific and administrative communications - is also to
be encouraged.
We have seen, however, that the myth of proletarian
internationalism is informed, and interpreted through the
lens of, an unarticulated myth of Russian primacy - the
belief that, for reasons largely to be found in historical
experience, the Soviet Union is a *Russian* enterprise, and
that the prerogative of rule belongs to Russians and to
national elites that are unambiguously Russified. All-Union

208

economic and foreign policy interests clearly take prece-
dence over the parochial interests of any republic, but the
primary value that is protected by the myth of Russian
primacy is the integrity of the Soviet Union as a political
entity, centrally governed from Moscow. Our findings support the conclusion that this is the first and most important (although not necessarily the only) criterion applied
to any policy proposal - whatever the substantive content -
originating with non-Russian national cultural and political elites.

The myth of national moral patrimony holds that particu-
laristic national cultural and linguistic heritages are
worth preserving for their own sake. So stated, the myth
of national moral patrimony is not totally inconsistent
with the proletarian internationalist myth as the latter is
embodied in Leninist nationality policy, as is amply illustrated by the arguments of dissidents such as Ivan Dzyuba,
who have criticized the Russification of Ukrainian language
and culture from a strictly Marxist-Leninist viewpoint.
Challenges to the official political myth such as Dzyuba's
are "reformist" challenges: they maintain that proletarian
internationalism has been corrupted by the myth of Russian
primacy. To restore legitimacy and to serve the ends of
justice, the myth must be restored to its original pristine
purity. Dzyuba thus represents a "Mykola Skrypnyk" tradition: the full development of the national potential of
the Ukraine, but fully within the Soviet federation, according to the original vision of Lenin, as the reformists
interpret it. There is impressionistic evidence, although
we have not assayed in this work to evaluate it, that this
is a popular position among the Ukrainian political elite.

A second version of the myth of national moral patrimony
holds that not only is the nation at the present stage of
historical development the only repository of human spirituality, but that in order to preserve this spiritual
inheritance, a nation must be governed only by itself.
This is a "revolutionary" challenge to the proletarian

internationalist myth, because it rejects not only the myth
of Russian primacy, but the principle of the political integrity of the Union as well. This position appears to be
an incarnation, however, not of the integral nationalism
of the OUN, but of the principle of "national self-determination" prevalent in the world today. We have examined
the philosophy of Valentyn Moroz in detail as the foremost
exponent of this ideology of modern Ukrainian nationalism.
This is a highly demotic form of ethnic nationalism, which
does not set the nation up as superior to all others, nor
necessarily destined by history to fulfill some mystic
mission, but rather as an entity necessary to the spiritual
health of its people, and deserving an equal place among
the other nations of the world.

2. How have the proponents of each major myth attempted to
inject elements of these respective myths into the official
ideology, so as to legitimate policies favorable to their
interests, and how successful have these efforts been?

Cultural pluralists and assimilationists who have attempted to articulate their demands through ideological
discourse have tried to demonstrate that the policies they
prefer - either expanded cultural expression or aggressive
de-nationalization - follow logically from tenets of the
ideology that have become enshrined in official policy, as
represented by the resolutions of Party Congresses. They
have attempted to extrapolate from official policy stances
to policy recommendations that may or may not have been
envisioned by the original spokesmen of the ideological
line.
Statements by top Party spokesmen are watched closely,
and seemingly innocuous terms such as *edinstvo* (unity), or
splochennost' (solidarity) are frequently raised to ideological status. They thus become symbols, because they
come to evoke one or another of the major myths we have
discussed, and become an indicator - whether intended or

not, and whether accurate or not - of the policy predispo-
sitions of the individuals employing such terms. Often,
their mythic content is ambiguous, and efforts are made to
interpret them in one way or another, as in the effort of
cultural pluralists to interpret "unity" in class terms,
rather than ethnic (and thus assimilationist) terms. The
dramatic recent example of such disputation over ambiguous
concepts, which we have discussed at length, is the widespread discussion of the "Soviet *narod*" as a "new historic
community of people."

The extended controversy over the new Constitution, and
the fact that the 1977 Constitution makes no alterations in
USSR federal arrangements - as many, the author included,
expected it would - seems to indicate that for the time
being, at least, the cultural pluralists have been more
successful than the assimilationists in translating their
demands into concrete policy. Likewise, the insistence of
Brezhnev that *both* elements of the dialectic of national
relations - "flowering" and "drawing together" - are
operative, strongly suggests that the Party leadership is
eager *not* to come to terms with the nationality problem at
present, either in the hope that it will go away or, more
likely, as a calculated decision to defer a seemingly in-
soluble problem to a future generation of leaders. It is
understandable that Brezhnev, who has articulated his
desire to retire with honor, may be unwilling to climax his
tenure by unleashing the full fury of nationalistic hos-
tilities and resentments.

3. How have symbols of the national and the proletarian
internationalist myth been employed in Soviet cultural and
linguistic policy to legitimate the expansion or contraction
of the expression of national distinctiveness?

We have examined the ways in which symbols of the continuity of Ukrainian history and culture have been employed
in order to accentuate the *authenticity* of the Ukrainian

national moral patrimony. Particularly important in this
regard have been emphasis on the independent origins of
Ukrainian culture, as a form of resistance to the officially
approved thesis that all national cultures developed under
the tutelage of the Russians, and emphasis on the heritage
of great men who are at least nominally also praised by the
regime: foremost among these has been Taras Shevchenko.

Symbols of entrenched Ukrainian distinctiveness, however,
such as monuments of antiquity and folk choral societies,
have been singled out by the regime for particularly severe
repression.

We have argued that the vitality of the Ukrainian language among both the rural and urban populations of the
Republic does not appear to be as direly threatened as
Ukrainian dissidents argue that it is; there is significant
linguistic Russification of the Ukrainian population only
in a half dozen or so of the historically most Russianized
cities and *oblasts* of the East Ukraine. All other areas
have shown, if anything, gains in adherence to the Ukrainian
language. There does appear to be, however, some deterior-
ation of the quality of the culture of the Ukrainian language in urban areas due to the adoption of *calques* and
Russicisms, and that at least in the areas of science and
technology, this trend is actively encouraged by the regime.
The status, or prestige, of the Ukrainian language is also
low; in addition, there is evidence of discrimination
against the language in broadcasting and publishing.
Ukrainian intellectuals concerned with the purity of the
Ukrainian language appear implicitly to base their concerns
on the symbolic function that language serves of ethnic
differentiation.

4. How have Ukrainian nationalist dissenters employed symbolic action to circumvent closed communications channels
and the proscription of the articulation of nationalist
demands in the Soviet Union, and what symbolic devices has
the regime at its disposal to counter the dissidents' appeal?

Both dissenters and the regime are forced to employ symbolic action and symbolic discourse in their dialogue, because the restricted communications system of the Soviet Union discourages open discussion of many substantive policy areas.

Ukrainian nationalist dissenters have attempted to exhaust all legal means of redress before resorting to symbolic action. The types of strategies that they have pursued which fall into this category have included petitioning for the realization of rights that are constitutionally guaranteed, but known to be punishable; this type of activity graphically confronts officials with the discrepancies between officially articulated policies and the more dismal reality, pointing up the illegitimacy of the government's actions by the government's own standards. Whether the officials or the masses actually see the discrepancies or civil disobedience remains a lonely exercise in irony remains undetermined.

A second strategy has been the opening of alternative channels of communications, or *samvydav* (*samizdat* in Russian), in order to circumvent the structurally imposed *maximization of redundancy* in Soviet political communications. Ukrainian *samvydav* has operated under more severe restraints than has the underground movement in Russia, because Kiev is more isolated from constraining influences such as international press correspondents, and because the KGB appears to be given greater rein at the periphery than at the center.

We have discussed the inchoate structure of the Ukrainian dissident movement, and the failure of the Ukrainian nationalist dissenters to form a common front with civil rights dissenters in Moscow, and with Jews in the Ukraine agitating for the right to emigrate. Although this is in part because the regime has gone to extra lengths to prevent just such a coalescence of dissident movements, it is also because all of these groups fear the submergence of their concerns under the concerns of the others.

The principle weapon that the regime has employed against
the nationalist dissenters in recent years has been the
judicial system. Dissenters are tried and convicted as
criminals (and some are treated as mentally ill), detracting
from the appeal of their arguments in the popular mind, and
no doubt deterring the growth of the movement because of
fear. In addition, the regime is able to discredit the
demands of nationalist dissenters by associating these demands with symbols which evoke fear or xenophobia in the
popular mind, based on previous socialization or on historical experience. The regime thus makes every effort to
associate the nationalist dissenters with the OUN, with
fascism, with Western imperialism, and even with improbable
symbols such as Zionism and Maoism. We have identified the
operative symbolic mechanism here as "metaphoric transfer."

5. What are the political uses of the mythology and symbolism of nationalism and internationalism in the struggle
for political mobility and power of elites, and can conflict
with its source in nationalism *per se* be separated from
conflict arising out of federalism and regionalism, i.e.,
the natural desire of republican elites to further their
regions' interests, and to protect their decisional autonomy
from encroachments from the center?

While Petro Shelest was certainly not a Ukrainian
"nationalist," he was an "autonomist." In his efforts,
however, to protect his decisional autonomy from encroachments from Moscow, he built a power base in the Ukraine
that included large numbers of people who can be considered
to have leaned in the direction of Ukrainian nationalism.
He thus made himself vulnerable to charges of nationalism,
and indeed, the attack on Shelest opened with a criticism
of his book *Ukraino nasha radians'ka (O Ukraine, Our Soviet
Land*, Kiev, 1970). The book, a light-weight, travelogue-
type popular celebration of the Ukraine (and probably
largely ghost-written), was attacked on the grounds of its

emphasis on the Ukraine out of the context of the general
development of the USSR as a whole, and for idealization of
certain aspects of Ukrainian history.[1]   .

While Shelest may have - without, perhaps, intending to
do so - placed himself in a position of "tolerating bourgeois nationalism," and while there was certainly a desire
on the part of Moscow to limit Ukrainian autonomism, both
these considerations are probably secondary to considerations of power politics: Shelest was removed because he
lost a power struggle with Shcherbitsky. Shcherbitsky's
rise was facilitated not only because of his association
with the Brezhnev patron-client network (the so-called
"Dnipropetrovs'k mafia"), but also because Shcherbitsky
was able to bring to bear against Shelest the full force of
the mythology and symbolism of nationalism and proletarian
internationalism. In short, Shelest fell victim to a power
struggle, and the principal weapon used against him was the
polemics of the proletarian internationalist myth.

Shelest was not ignorant of ideology, nor of the myths
that inform it. Our surmise, rather, is that he invoked
elements of the myth of national moral patrimony, adding to
his power-base the nationalist intelligentsia, in order to
strengthen his position *in the Ukraine*, taking the calculated risk that the strategy would not back-fire in Moscow.

A corollary of this interpretation is that the Ukrainian
nationalist dissent movement in the late 1960s and early
1970s went as far as it did only because of this unique
constellation of factors in the Ukraine during this period.
Fragmentary evidence regarding Shelest's personal relation-
ships, both with the former Ukrainian KGB head Nikitchenko,
and with the Ukrainian intelligentsia - particularly through
his son Vitalyi and the chemist *qua* ideological secretary
Ovcharenko - lends credence to the tantalizing thesis that

---

[1]"Pro seriozny nedoliky ta pomylky odniiei knyhy," *Komunist Ukrainy*,
No. 4(April, 1973), pp. 77-82. Translation in *Digest of the Soviet
Ukrainian Press*, Vol. 1973, No. 5, pp. 1-6. Shcherbitsky himself may
have written the article.

there was indeed some protection of outspoken dissidents from above. This hypothesis is strengthened by the fact of the rapidity with which the nationalist dissenters were oppressed after Shelest's fall.

On the other hand, some of our informants, most notably Plyushch and Nekrasov, scoffed upon being apprised of this hypothesis, arguing that Shelest was little more than a political opportunist, and more emphatically that the Ukrainian nationalist dissent movement was an independent force in its own right, dependent least of all on Shelest and the KGB. If this is correct, it suggests that the post-1972 dissidents have themselves co-opted Shelest as a symbol - the latter is described in *Ukrains'kyi visnyk 7-8* as a nationalist sympathizer - in order to give the illusion that sympathy with their concerns reaches higher into the Ukrainian Party than in fact it does.

Whether Shelest, in a search for political support, in fact purposely included the Kiev intelligentsia as part of his power base, or whether he has been co-opted as a symbol by the dissidents, the phenomenon of Shelest deserves considerably more research. This should include the degree of his dependence, if any, on the Kiev intellectuals, and their dependence, if any, on him; the extent of his interests in and contacts with foreign communist parties; and the relationship between the demise of Shelest and factional struggles among the Dnipropetrovs'k, Donets'k, and other patronage groups. Unfortunately, our own research experience convinced us early that the data for such an investigation is still too scanty to be rewarding.

If our preferred interpretation of Shelest's personal influence on developments in the Ukraine is correct, however, it implies that the personalistic power of individual elites in the Soviet system - particularly that of Republican First Secretaries - is still very great. Furthermore, if Shelest was indeed largely responsible for the success, however short-lived, of the nationalist dissent movement, that is cause for optimism it would imply that individuals can make a difference in the Soviet system, and that on the eve of a generational change in the leadership, the direction of systemic change is not a foregone conclusion.

Further research should also be done - and innovative methods sought to accomplish it - on the problem of meaning and the transmission and persistence of entrenched meanings. This will involve research in socialization and primary education, as well as in ideological polemics. It has often been noted, for example, that the care of small children in the Ukraine, as in Russia, is frequently entrusted to *babushkas*, which may go far to reinforce symbols of the national patrimony (or even of the pre-Soviet patrimony) in children's attitudes long before they enter the school system. There are implications here, obviously, of the biologically-mandated gradual disappearance of *babushkas*, and of increasing state responsibility for the pre-school care of children. We urge research into the problem of meanings in culture and language in other Union Republics, comparison of Union Republics at various levels of development, and comparison with the experience of national minorities in other communists states, and outside the communist sub-system.

It is fitting to conclude as we began, by emphasizing that the nationalities problem in the Soviet Union has not been solved. Ukrainian nationalism has a respectably long history, and it is a contemporary and ongoing problem. Grand conclusions and confident predictions, therefore, are inappropriate, beyond noting that it is unlikely that the issue has been finally decided.

BIBLIOGRAPHY

I. PRIMARY SOURCES

A. *Marxist-Leninist Classics*

ENGELS, FRIEDRICH. *The Origins of the Family, Private Property, and the State*. Moscow: Foreign Languages Publishing House, 1948.

LENIN, V.I. "Critical Remarks on the National Question." *National Liberation, Socialism and Imperialism: Selected Writings of V.I. Lenin*. New York: International Publishers, 1968. P. 12-44.

___ "On the Question of Nationalities, or 'Autonomization.'" *Ibid.*, pp. 165-171.

MARX, KARL and FRIEDRICH ENGELS. *The Manifesto of the Communist Party*. New York: International Publishers, n.d.

STALIN, J.V. *Marxism and Linguistics*. New York: International Publishers, 1951.

___ *Marxism and the National and Colonial Question*. Moscow: Foreign Languages Publishing House, 1940.

___ *The National Question and Leninism: A Reply to Comrades Meshkov, Kovalchuk, and Others*. Moscow: Foreign Languages Publishing House, 1950.

V.I. Lenin, KPSS o bor'be s natsionalizmom. Moscow: Izdatel'stvo "Politicheskoi literatury," 1974.

B. *Official Documents*

BREZHNEV, L.I. "O piatidesiatiletii sovetskikh sotsialisticheskikh respublikh. Doklad General'nogo Sekretara KPSS." *Kommunist*, 18(1972), 3-42.

___ "Otchetnyi doklad Tsentral'nogo Komiteta KPSS." *XXIII s'ezd Kommunisticheskoi Partii Sovetskogo soiuza: stenograficheskii otchet*. VI. Moscow: Izdatel'stvo "Politicheskoi literatury," 1966.

Itogi vsesoiuznoi perepisi naseleniia 1959 goda. Ukrainskaia SSR. Moscow: "Gosstatizdat," 1963.

Itogi vsesoiuznoi perepisi naseleniia 1970 goda. IV. Moscow: "Statistika," 1973.

218

KHRUSHCHEV, N.S. "On the Program of the Communist Party of the Soviet
Union." *Current Soviet Policies IV*. Edited by Charlotte Saikowski
and Leo Gruliow. New York and London: Columbia University Press,
1962. Pp. 83-116..

___ "Secret Speech on the 'Cult of the Individual' delivered at the 20th
Congress of the CPSU, February 25, 1956." *The New Communist Manifesto
and Related Documents*. 3rd Edition. Edited by Dan N. Jacobs. New
York: Harper and Row, 1965. Pp. 115-67.

"K piatidesiatiletiiu Velikoi Oktiabrskoi Revoliutsii: Tezisy Tsentral'-
nogo Komiteta KPSS." *Partinaia zhizn'*, 12(June, 1967), 21-25.

*KPRS v rezoliutsiiakh i rishenniiakh z'izdiv, konferentsiy i plenumiv
TsK*. III. Kiev, 1954.

"The Program of the Communist Party of the Soviet Union." *Current Soviet
Policies IV*. Edited by Charlotte Saikowski and Leo Gruliow. New York
and London: Columbia University Press, 1962. Pp. 1-33.

Resolution of the CC CPSU: "O podgotovke k piatidesiatiletiiu obrazovaniia SSSR." *Partinaia zhizn'*, 5(March, 1972), 3-13.

"Resolution of the 20th Party Congress on the Report of the Central
Committee, Adopted Unanimously February 20, 1956." *Current Soviet
Policies II*. Edited by Leo Gruliow. New York: Praeger, 1957. Pp.
189-95.

"Theses on the 300th Anniversary of the Reunification of Ukraine and
Rùssia (1654-1954), Approved by the Central Committee of the Communist Party of the Soviet Union." *Pravda* and *Izvestiia*, January 12,
1954, pp. 2-3. *Current Digest of the Soviet Press*, V, 51:3.

Visti vseukrains'koho Tsentral'noho Vykonavs'koho Komiteta. Kiev:
January 17, 1933.

C. Soviet Books and Articles

ALEKSANDROV, G. "O razvitii konstitutsii SSSR v svete reshenii XXI
s'ezda KPSS." *Sovetskoe gosudarstvo i pravo*, 9(1959), 113-15.

ANANCHENKO, N.P. "Ot natsii k internatsional'noi obshchnosti liudei."
Voprosy istorii, 3(March, 1967), 82-96.

ANTONENKO-DAVYDOVYCH, BORYS. *Iak my hovorymo*. Kiev: "Radians'kyi
pysmennyk," 1970.

AZIZIAN, A.K. *Leninskaia natsional'naia politika v razvitii i deistvii*.
Moscow: "Nauka," 1972.

BILODID, A.K. "Flowering of Language in the Ukrainian Soviet Nation."
Ukrains'ka mova i literatura v shkoli, 12(December, 1967), 5-11.
Digest of the Soviet Ukrainian Press, XI, 4:20-21.

___ "The Role of Native Language in the Development of Education and
Culture of a People." *Ukrains'ka mova i literatura v shkoli*, 6(June,
1967), 1-8. *Digest of the Soviet Ukrainian Press*, X, 9:18-20.

BILODID, I.K. *Rosiys'ka mova - mova mizhnatsional'noho spilkuvannia narodiv SRSR.* Kiev: "Radian'skyi pys'mennyk," 1962.

BOGINA, Sh. "Review of Glazer and Moynihan's *Beyond the Melting Pot.*" *Sovetskaia etnografiia,* 1(1966), 184-87. *Soviet Sociology,* (Summer, 1967), 56-60.

BURMISTROVA, T. Iu. "Nekotorie voprosy teorii natsii." *Voprosy istorii,* 12(December, 1966), 100-110.

DESHERIEV, Iu. and M. MELIKIIAN. "Development and Mutual Enrichment of the Languages of the Nations of the USSR." *Ukrains'ka mova i literatura v shkoli,* 12(December, 1965), 3-13. *Digest of the Soviet Ukrainian Press,* IX, 2:23-25.

DMYTRUK, KLYM (K.E. Hals'kyi). *Bezbatchynky.* L'viv: n.p., n.d.

___ *Pid chornymy sutanamy.* Kiev: Tovarystvo "Ukraina," 1975.

DUBINA, K.K. "Rastsvet Sovetskoi Ukrainy v bratskoi sem'e narodov SSSR." *Vestnik obshchestvennikh nauk,* 8(1967), 81-94.

DZYUBA, IVAN. *Grani krystala.* Kiev: Tovarystvo "Ukraina," 1976.

EMELIANENKO, H. "Lenins'ky pryntsypy proletars'koho internatsionalizmu," *Kommunist Ukrainy,* 11(1971), 81-98.

EVDOKYMENKO, V. Iu. *Krytyka ideinykh osnov Ukrains'koho burzhuaznoho natsionalizmu.* Kiev: "Naukova dumka," 1967.

GAFUROV, B. "Uspekhi natsional'noi politiki KPSS i nekotorie voprosy internatsional'nogo vospitaniia." *Kommunist,* 11(August, 1958), 10-24.

HOLOBUTS'KYI, V.A. *Zaporozhskoe kozachestvo.* Kiev: Radians'kyi pysmen- nyk," 1957.

HONCHAREVA, V.M. "Radians'kyi narod - nova istorychna spil'nist' liudei," *Filosofs'ka dumka,* 2(March-April, 1972), 36-45.

HUMETS'KA, L.L. "Fifty Years of Linguistics in the Ukraine," *Ukrains'ka mova i literatura v shkoli,* 5(May, 1968), 85-87. *Digest of the Soviet Ukrainian Press,* XI, 7:23-24.

HUSLYSTYI, KOST'. "On Bourgeois Nationalist Distortions in the Study of the Ethnogeny of the Ukrainian People." *Narodna tvorchist' ta etno- hrafiia,* 1(January-February, 1971), 41-51. *Digest of the Soviet Ukrainian Press,* XV, 10:12-17.

IGNAT, A.M. "Zdisnennia lenins'koi polityki v shkolakh Zakarpattiia." *Radians'ka shkola,* 6(1970), 43-45.

KHANDROS, B. "Chtoby sreda ne zaela." *Uchitels'kaia gazeta,* February 21, 1967.

KONDRATIUK, A.A. "From the Experience of Teaching the Ukrainian Lan- guage in Crimean Schools." *Ukrains'ka mova v shkoli,* 2(March-April, 1961), 50-56. *Digest of the Soviet Ukrainian Press,* V, 8:24.

KOZLOV, V.I. *Dinamika chislennosti narodov: metodologiia, issledovaniia i osnovnye faktory.* Moscow: "Nauka," 1969.

___ "Nekotorie problemy teorii natsii," *Voprosy istorii,* 1(1967), 88-99.

KYRYLIUK, E.P. "The Ideological Struggle Surrounding the Works of Shevchenko." *Radians'ke literaturoznavs'tvo*, 3(March, 1972), 62-72. *Digest of the Soviet Ukrainian Press*, XIV, 10:6-8.

LOMIDZE, G. *Edinstvo i mnogoobrazovanie*. Moscow: "Sovetskii pisatel'," 1957.

"Luchshe uchit' russkomu iazyku vo vsekh shkolakh strany." *Narodnoe obrazovanie*, 7(1970), 125-27.

M., A. "About Admission Examinations in the Ukrainian Language and Literature at the T.H. Shevchenko Kiev State University." *Ukrains'ka mova v shkoli*, 6(November-December, 1958), 91-93. *Digest of the Soviet Ukrainian Press*, IV, 12:23.

MALANCHUK, V.E. "Fal'sifikatorskie izmyshleniia burzhuazhnykh 'ukrainovedov.'" *Voprosy istorii KPSS*, 8(1971), 38-48.

MANELIS, B.L. "Sootnoshenie konstitutsionnogo zakonodatel'stva Soiuza SSR i soiuznykh respublikh." *Obshchestvennye nauki v Uzbekistane*, 1(1965), 24-26.

MASLOVS'KYI, VITALII. *Zhovto-blakytna mafiia*. L'viv: "Kameniar," n.d.

OVCHAROV, H. "On the Occasion of Light Shed on the Problem of Borot'bism." *Komunist Ukrainy*, 2(February, 1958), 36-47. *Digest of the Soviet Ukrainian Press*, I, 7:1-5.

RAUKOV, V. "Sreda zaela." *Uchitel'skaia gazeta*, December 24, 1966.

ROGACHEV, P.M. and M.A. SVERDLOV. "SSSR - otechestvo mnogonatsional'nogo sovetskogo naroda." *Filosofskie nauki*, 2(1973), 2-15.

SHCHERBITSKY, V. "Mezhdunarodnoe znachenie opyta natsional'nykh otnoshenii v SSSR." *Kommunist*, 17(1974), 14-25.

SHELEST, P. Iu. *Ukraino nasha radians'ka*. Kiev: Izdatel'stvo "Politichnoi literatury Ukrainy," 1970.

SHERSTIUK, P. Iu. "Exposure and Rout of the Nationalist Deviation by the CPU in 1926-1928." *Ukrains'kyi istorychnyi zhurnal*, 3(May-June, 1958), 73-83. *Digest of the Soviet Ukrainian Press*, II, 12:1-3.

TAVAKALIAN, M.A. "Nekotorie voprosy poniatiia 'natsiia.'" *Voprosy istorii*, 2(1967), 115-123.

"Torzhestvo Leninskoi natsional'noi politiki." *Kommunist*, 13(1969), 4-12.

Torzhestvo Lenins'kykh pryntsypiv proletars'koho internatsionalizmu. L'viv: "Kameniar," 1971.

TSAMERIAN, I.P. *Teoreticheskie problemy obrazovaniia sovetskogo mnogonatsional'nogo gosudarstva*. Moscow: "Nauka," 1973.

UDOVYCHENKO, P.P. "Rastsvet narodnogo obrazovaniia, nauki i kul'tury." *Sovetskaia pedagogika*, 10(1967), 38-48.

ZLATOPOL'SKII, D.L. "Sovetskaia federatsiia na novom etape razvitii natsional'nykh vzaimootnoshenii." *Vestnikh Moskovskogo Universiteta*, 2(1962), 21-22.

D. *Samvydav: Collections and Anthologies*

BROWNE, MICHAEL, Editor. *Ferment in the Ukraine: Documents by V. Chornovil, I. Kandyba, L. Lukyanenko, V. Moroz and others.* New York: MacMillan, 1971.

Dokumenty po delu Leonida Plyushcha. Frankfurt: Posev, 1974.

Khronika tekushchikh sobytii. Nos. 1-27. SDS Vols. 10A and 10B. Munich: Radio Liberty Research Department, n.d. Nos. 28-31. New York: "Khronika" Press, 1974.

MOROZ, VALENTYN. *Valentyn Moroz: esei, lysty i dokumenty.* Munich: Suchasnist', 1975.

REDDAWAY, PETER, Editor. *Uncensored Russia: Annotated Text of "Chronicle of Current Events" Nos. 1-11.* London: Jonathan Cape, 1972.

SAUNDERS, GEORGE, Editor. *Samizdat: Voices of the Soviet Opposition.* New York: Monad Press, 1974.

Sobranie dokumentov samizdata. (SDS). Vol. XVIII: "Ukrainskii samizdat." Munich: Radio Liberty Research Department, n.d.

Ukrains'ka inteligentsiia pid sudom KGB: materialy z protsesiv V. Chornovila, M. Masiutka, M. Ozernoho ta in. Munich: Suchasnist', 1970.

Ukrains'ki iurysty pid sudom KGB: vstupne slovo Ivana Maistrenka. Munich: Suchasnist', 1968.

E. *Samvydav: Individual Documents*

Note: Citation of individual *samvydav* documents follows Radio Liberty's classification system. Individual documents are assigned an AS *(Arkhiv Samizdata)* number; where documents have been gathered into volumes, the volume is designated by an SDS *(Sobranie Dokumentov Samizdata)* number.

"Anonimnoe soobshchenie iz Kieva ob arestakh na Ukraine." (March, 1972). AS 1088, SDS Vol. XXII.

"Anonimnoe soobshchenie 'Lukianenko Lev Grigorevich.'" AS 2301.

BERDYLO, STEPAN. "Do narodiv v'soho svitu." (Autumn, 1969). AS 979, SDS Vol. XVIII.

BRAICHEVS'KYI, M.Iu. "Prisoedinenie ili vossoedinenie? Kriticheskie zamechaniia po porodu odnoi kontseptsii." *Natsional'nyi vopros v SSSR: sbornik dokumentov.* Edited by Roman Kupchinsky. Munich: Suchasnist', 1975. Pp. 62-125.

BUKOVSKYI, VLADIMIR. "Eshche raz o natsionalizme i russifikatsii." AS 2364.

_____ and S. GLUZMAN. "A Manual on Psychiatry for Dissidents." *Survey,* XXI, 1-2(Winter-Spring, 1974-75), 180-99.

Chlen Spilky Pys'mennykiv Ukrainy. "Lyst do Olesa Honchara i sekretariv SPU pro kul'turni vidnosyny mizh Ukrainoiu i ChSSR." (1968). AS 970, SDS Vol. XVIII.

CHORNOVIL, VIACHESLAV. "Ia nichoho u vas ne proshu...." AS 941, SDS Vol. XVIII.

___ "My Trial." *Index on Censorship,* V, 1(Spring, 1976), 57-69.

___ *The Chornovil Papers.* New York: McGraw-Hill, 1968.

DZYUBA, IVAN. *Internationalism or Russification?* 3rd Edition. New York: Monad Press, 1974.

GORNOVOI, OSIP. "Nashe otnoshenie k russkomu narodu." *Natsional'nyi vopros v SSSR: sbornik dokumentov.* Edited by Roman Kupchinsky. Munich: Suchasnist', 1975. Pp. 11-25.

HONCHAR, OLES'. *Sobor.* New York and S. Bound Brook: Museum of the Ukrainian Orthodox Memorial Church, 1968.

Initsiatyvnyi komitet komunistiv Ukrainy. "Zvernennia do vsikh komunistiv narodno-demokratychnykh i kapitalistychnykh krain, do kerivnykh organiv komunistychnykh i robitnychykh partii svitu." (December, 1964). AS 912, SDS Vol. XVIII.

"K sobytiiam v Dneprodzerzhinske letom 1972 g." AS 1437.

KANDYBA, IVAN. "Za pravdu i spravedlivist': lyst pershomu sekretarevi TsK KPU Shelestovi P. Iu." (Autumn, 1967). AS 904, SDS Vol. XVIII.

KARAVANS'KYI, SVIATOSLAV. "Klopotannia do Pershoho Sekretaria TsK PORP V. Gomulky, pro stan radians'koi natsional'noi polityki, pro fakty bezpidstvanykh represii proty Ukrains'koi intelihentsii." (September, 1965). AS 919, SDS Vol. XVIII.

___ "Klopotannia prokurorovi URSR pro seriozni pomilky i progoloshennia rusyfikatsii ministrom vyshchoi ta serednoi osviti URSR Iu. M. Dadenkova." (February, 1964). AS 915, SDS Vol. XVIII.

___ "Po odnu politychnu pomylku." (September, 1965). AS 916, SDS Vol. XVIII.

___ "Sim klopotan na im'ia piznykh ofitsiinykh ustaniv, napysanykh z trudovoho taboru." (January-June, 1966). AS 942, SDS Vol. XVIII.

KHODOROVICH, TATIANA. "Ia bol'she ne vyderzhu!" AS 1676.

___ *Istoriia bolezni Leonida Plyushcha.* Amsterdam: Alexander Herzen Foundation, 1975.

"Lyst rosiyskkoho shovinista." AS 280, SDS Vol. IV.

"Lyst tvorchoi molodi Dnipropetrovs'koho." AS 974, SDS Vol. XVIII.

LOBKO, VASYL' ta 9 inshykh. "Nashi propozitsii." (February, 1964). AS 908, SDS Vol. XVIII.

LUKIANENKO, LEVKO. "Skarha general'nomu prokurorovi Soiuzu RSR pro nezakonnist' sudu, vidbuvshohosia nad nym i shist'oma inshymy." AS 906, SDS Vol. XVIII.

___ "Zaiava Holovi Prezydii Verkhovnoi Rady URSR D.S. Korotchenko pro represii hromadian, obvynuvachenykh v 'natsionalizmi." (May, 1967). AS 987, SDS Vol. XVIII.

LUTS'KIV, V. "Zaiava TsK KPU, vyiavliaiucha, shcho vsi pokazy, dani avtorom L'vivs'komu sudu v travni 1961 r., e nishcho inshe iak fabrykatsiia KGB." (October, 1965). AS 921, SDS Vol. XVIII.

MARCHENKO, ANATOLII. *Moi pokazaniia.* AS 106, SDS Vol. I.

MEDVEDEV, ROY. *Kniga o sotsialisticheskikh demokratii.* Amsterdam and Paris: Herzen Foundation and Editions Grasset et Fasquelle, 1972.

MOROZ, VALENTYN. "Khronika soprotivleniia." AS 411, SDS Vol. VI.

_____ "Moisei i Datan'." (Analiz statti). AS 980, SDS Vol. XVIII.

_____ "Otryvki iz pis'ma sem'e." AS 2083.

_____ "Reportazh iz zapovidnykha imeni Berii." (April, 1967). AS 957, SDS Vol. XVIII.

_____ "Sredi snegov." AS 596, SDS Vol. VIII.

"Obrashchenie 3-kh Ukrainskikh politzakliuchennikh v kommyssiiu po pravam cheloveka pri OON." AS 261, SDS Vol. IV.

"Pis'mo 139 s Ukrainy protiv zakrytikh politicheskikh sudov." (April, 1968). AS 46, SDS Vol. I.

"Programma demokratov Rossii, Ukrainy i Pribaltiki." AS 340. SDS Vol. V.

"Protest 64 hromadian L.I. Brezhnevu, P. Iu. Shelestu, i I. Kh. Holovchenko proty dii militsii 22 chervnia 1967 r., v den shchorichnoho shanuvannia pam'iati Tarasa Hryhorovycha Shevchenka bilia iovo monumenta u Kyivi." (June, 1967). AS 961, SDS Vol. XVIII.

"Z pryvodu protsesu nad Pohruzhal's'kym." AS 911, SDS Vol. XVIII.

SHAFAREVICH, IGOR. "Separation or Reconcialiation? The Nationalities Question in the USSR." *From under the Rubble.* Edited by Aleksandr Solzhenitsyn. Boston: Little, Brown and Co., 1975.

SKOCHAK, P.V., V. CHORNOVIL and L. SHEREMET'EVA. "Lyst do redaktsii *Pertsia* proty napadiv zhurnalu na I. Dzyuba." (September, 1966). AS 945, SDS Vol. XVIII.

STENCHUK, BOHDAN. *Shcho i iak obstoiue I. Dzyuba?* Kiev: Tovarystvo "Ukraina," 1969.

STUS', VASYL'. "Vidkrytyi lyst do presydii Spiĺky Pys'mennykiv Ukrainy na zakhyst V. Chornovila." AS 973, SDS Vol. XVIII.

SVERSTIUK, IEVHEN. "Ivan Kotliarevs'kyi smietsia." AS 981, SDS Vol. XVIII.

_____ *Sobor u ryshtovanni.* Baltimore: Smoloskyp, 1971.

"Tovaryshi bat'ky shkoliarev." AS 909, SDS Vol. XVIII.

Ukrains'kyi visnyk 1. Paris and Baltimore: P.I.U.F. and Smoloskyp, 1970.

Ukrains'kyi visnyk 2. Paris and Baltimore: P.I.U.F. and Smoloskyp, 1970.

Ukrains'kyi visnyk 3. Paris and Baltimore: P.I.U.F. and Smoloskyp, 1971.

Ukrains'kyi visnyk 4. Paris and Baltimore: P.I.U.F. and Smoloskyp, 1971. English translation: *Ukrainian Herald IV.* Munich: ABN Press Bureau, 1972.

Ukrains'kyi visnyk 6. Paris and Baltimore: P.I.U.F. and Smoloskyp, 1972. English translation: *Dissent in Ukraine: Ukrainian Herald, Issue 6.* Introduction by Yaroslav Bilinsky. Translated and edited by Lesya Jones and Bohdan Yasen. Baltimore-Paris-Toronto: Smoloskyp, 1977.

Ukrains'kyi visnyk 7-8. Paris and Baltimore: P.I.U.F. and Smoloskyp, 1975. English translation: *Ethnocide of Ukrainians in the U.S.S.R. Ukrainian Herald, Issue 7-8.* Introduction by Robert Conquest. Translated and edited by Olena Saciuk and Bohdan Yasen. Baltimore-Paris-Toronto: Smoloskyp, 1976.

"Usilenie natsionalisticheskikh techenii i tendentsii na Ukraine." *Politicheskii dnevnik,* No. 9 (June, 1965). AS 1002, SDS Vol. XX.

"Vyrok L'vivs'koho sudu po spravi Ivana Helia i Iaroslavy Menkush." (March, 1966). AS 933, SDS Vol. XVIII.

"Zaiava hromadian s. Kosmach prokuroru Ivano-Frankivs'koi oblasti pro vypadok na tserkovnyi terytorii." AS 990, SDS Vol. XVIII.

II. SECONDARY SOURCES

A. Myths, Symbols and Communications Theory

ARMSTRONG, JOHN A. "Mobilized and Proletarian Diasporas." *American Political Science Review.* LXX, 2(June, 1976), 393-408.

CASSIRER, ERNST. *The Myth of the State.* New Haven: Yale University Press, 1968.

DEUTSCH, KARL W. "Social Mobilization and Political Development." *American Political Science Review.* LV, 3(September, 1961), 493-514.

EDELMAN, MURRAY. "The Political Language of the Helping Professions." *Politics and Society.* IV, 3(1974), 295-310.

___ *Politics as Symbolic Action.* Chicago: Markham Publishing Co., 1971.

___ *The Symbolic Uses of Politics.* Urbana: University of Illinois Press, 1967.

FAGEN, RICHARD R. *Politics and Communication: An Analytic Study.* Boston: Little, Brown and Co., 1966.

FISHMAN, JOSHUA A. *Language and Nationalism: Two Integrative Essays.* Rowley, Mass: Newbury House Publishers, 1973.

___ "National Languages and Languages of Wider Communication in the Developing Nations." *Anthropological Linguistics.* 11(1969), 111-35.

___ "A Systematization of the Whorfian Hypothesis." *Behavioral Science.* 5(1960), 323-29.

GEERTZ, CLIFFORD. "Ideology as a Cultural System." *Ideology and Discontent.* Edited by David E. Apter. London: Free Press of Glencoe, 1964. Pp. 47-76.

GEORGE, ALEXANDER L. *Propaganda Analysis: A Study of Inferences made from Nazi Propaganda in World War II.* Evanston, Ill: Row, Peterson, 1959.

GOLOMSHTOK, IGOR. "The Language of Art under Totalitarianism." Radio Liberty Special Report 404/76. September 8, 1976.

GOODMAN, NELSON. *Languages of Art: An Approach to a Theory of Symbols.* Indianapolis: Hackett Publishing Co., 1976.

GRIFFITH, WILLIAM E. "Communist Esoteric Communication: Explication de Texte." *Handbook of Communications.* Edited by Ithiel de Sola Pool and others. Chicago: Rand McNally College Publishing Co., 1973. Pp. 512-20.

GUSFIELD, JOSEPH R. *Symbolic Crusade: Status Politics and the American Temperance Movement.* Urbana: University of Illinois Press, 1963.

HOLLANDER, GAYLE DURHAM. "Political Communication and Dissent in the Soviet Union." *Dissent in the USSR: Politics, Ideology and People.* Edited by Rudolf Tökes. Baltimore and London: Johns Hopkins University Press, 1975. Pp. 233-75.

___ *Soviet Political Indoctrination: Developments in Mass Media and Propaganda since Stalin.* New York: Praeger, 1972.

LANGER, SUZANNE K. *Philosophy in a New Key.* Cambridge: Harvard University Press, 1974.

LASSWELL, HAROLD D. *Language of Politics.* Cambridge: Massachussetts Institute of Technology Press, 1949, 1965.

McDONALD, LEE C. "Myths, Politics and Political Science." *Western Political Quarterly.* XXII, 1(March, 1969).

MORRIS, CHARLES. *Signs, Language and Behavior.* Englewood Cliffs, N.J: Prentice-Hall, 1946.

MOSSE, GEORGE L. *The Nationalization of the Masses: Political Symbolism and Mass Movements in Germany from the Napoleonic Wars through the Third Reich.* New York: Howard Fertig, 1975.

MUELLER, CLAUS. *The Politics of Communication.* London, Oxford, New York: Oxford University Press, 1973.

POOL, ITHIEL DE SOLA. "Communications in Totalitarian Societies." *Handbook of Communication.* Edited by Ithiel de Sola Pool and others. Chicago: Rand McNally College Publishing Co., 1973. Pp. 462-511.

ROSE, ARNOLD M. "A Systematic Summary of Symbolic Interaction Theory." *Human Behavior and Social Processes: An Interactionist Approach.* Edited by Arnold M. Rose. London: Rutledge and Kegan Paul, 1962.

SAPIR, EDWARD. "Language." *Encyclopedia of the Social Sciences.* New York, 1933.

___ "Symbols." *Encyclopedia of the Social Sciences.* New York, 1934.

TURBAYNE, COLIN MURRAY. *The Myth of Metaphor.* Revised Edition. Columbia: University of South Carolina Press, 1970.

B. Nationalism and Ethnic Politics

BRETON, RAYMOND. "Institutional Completeness of Ethnic Communities and the Personal Relations of Immigrants." *American Journal of Sociology.* 70(1964), 193-205.

CONNOR, WALKER. "Nation-Building or Nation-Destroying?" *World Politics.* XXIV, 31(April, 1972), 319-45.

DEUTSCH, KARL W. *Nationalism and Social Communication: An Inquiry into the Foundations of Nationality.* Cambridge: Massachussetts Institute of Technology Press, 1953.

DOOB, LEONARD W. *Patriotism and Nationalism: Their Psychological Foundations.* New Haven and London: Yale University Press, 1964.

ENLOE, CYNTHIA H. *Ethnic Conflict and Political Development.* Boston: Little, Brown and Co., 1973.

GEERTZ, CLIFFORD. "After the Revolution: The Fate of Nationalism in the New States." *The Interpretation of Cultures: Selected Writings by Clifford Geertz.* New York: Basic Books, 1973. Pp. 234-54.

GLAZER, DANIEL. "Dynamics of Ethnic Identification." *American Sociological Review.* XXIII (February, 1958).

GLAZER, NATHAN and DANIEL P. MOYNIHAN. *Beyond the Melting Pot: The Negroes, Puerto Ricans, Jews, Italians and Irish of New York City.* Second Edition. Cambridge: Massachussetts Institute of Technology Press, 1970.

GORDON, MILTON M. *Assimilation in American Life: The Role of Race, Religion, and National Origins.* New York: Oxford University Press, 1964.

NAHIRNY, VLADIMIR C. and JOSHUA A. FISHMAN. "American Immigrant Groups: Ethnic Identification and the Problem of Generations." *The Sociological Review.* XIII (November, 1965), 311-26.

PARENTI, MICHAEL. "Ethnic Politics and the Persistance of Ethnic Identification." *American Political Science Review.* LXI (September, 1967), 717-26.

ROSENTHAL, ERICH. "Acculturation without Assimilation: The Jewish Community of Chicago, Illinois." *American Journal of Sociology.* LXVI (November, 1960).

SHIBUTANI, TAMOTSU and KIAN M. KWAN. *Ethnic Stratification: A Comparative Approach.* New York: MacMillan, 1965.

SNYDER, LOUIS L. *The New Nationalism.* Ithaca: Cornell University Press, 1968.

SYMMONS-SYMONOLEWICZ, KONSTANTIN. *Nationalist Movements: A Comparative View.* Meadville, Pa: Maplewood Press, 1970.

C. *Soviet Nationality Problems: General*

ALLWORTH, EDWARD. "Restating the Soviet Nationalities Question." *Soviet Nationality Problems.* Edited by Edward Allworth. New York: Columbia University Press, 1971. Pp. 1-21.

ARMSTRONG, JOHN A. "The Ethnic Scene in the Soviet Union: The View of the Dictatorship." *Ethnic Minorities in the Soviet Union.* Edited by Erich Goldhagen. New York: Praeger, 1968.

___ "Societal Manipulation in a Multiethnic Polity." *World Politics.* XXVIII, 3(April, 1976), 440-49.

ASPATURIAN, VERNON V. "Nationality Inputs in Soviet Foreign Policy: The USSR as an Arrested Universal State." *Process and Power in Soviet Foreign Policy.* Edited by Vernon V. Aspaturian. Boston: Little, Brown and Co., 1971. P. 429-51.

AZRAEL, JEREMY R., Editor. *Soviet Nationality Policies and Practices.* New York: Praeger, 1978.

BILINSKY, YAROSLAV. "Education of the Non-Russian Peoples of the USSR." *Slavic Review.* 27(September, 1968), 411-37.

___ "The Soviet Education Laws of 1958-59 and Soviet Nationality Policy." *Soviet Studies.* XIV (October, 1962), 138-57.

BLOEMBERGEN, S. "The Union Republics: How Much Autonomy?" *Problems of Communism.* XVI, 5(September-October, 1967), 27-35.

CONQUEST, ROBERT. *Soviet Nationalities Policy in Practice.* London: The Bodley Head, Ltd., 1967.

DUEVEL, CHRISTIAN. "Accelerated or Gradual Convergence?" Radio Liberty Research Special Report 15/73, January 9, 1973.

___ "Brezhnev at Odds with Podgorny: Socialist Democracy vs. Secret Police Oppression." Radio Liberty Research Paper CRD 231/70, June 22, 1970.

D'ENCAUSSE, HÉLÈNE CARRERE. *Decline of an Empire: The Soviet Socialist Republics in Revolt.* Translated by Martin Sokolinsky and Henry A. LaFarge. New York: Newsweek Books, 1979.

GOLDHAGEN, ERICH. *Ethnic Minorities in the Soviet Union.* New York: Praeger, 1968.

HODNETT, GREY. "The Debate over Soviet Federalism." *Soviet Studies.* XVIII, 4(April, 1967), 458-81.

___ *Leadership in the Soviet National Republics: A Quantitative Study of Recruitment Policy.* Oakville, Ontario: Mosaic Press, 1978.

___ "What's in a Nation?" *Problems of Communism.* XVI, 5(September-October, 1967), 2-16.

JANOS, ANDREW C. "Ethnicity, Communism and Political Change in Eastern Europe." *World Politics.* XXIII, 3(1971), 493-521.

KAMENETSKY, IHOR, Editor. *Nationalism and Human Rights: Processes of Modernization in the USSR.* Littleton, Colo: Libraries Unlimited, 1977.

KATZ, ZEV, ROSEMARIE ROGERS and FREDERIC HARNED. *Handbook of Major Soviet Nationalities*. New York: The Free Press, 1975.

KOHN, HANS. "Soviet Communism and Nationalism: Three Stages of a Historical Development." *Soviet Nationality Problems*. Edited by Edward Allworth. New York: Columbia University Press, 1971. Pp. 42-71.

KUCERA, JINDRICH. "Soviet Nationality Policy: The Linguistic Controversy." *Problems of Communism*. III, 2(March-April, 1954),.24-29.

LEWYTZKYJ, BORYS. *Die Sowjetische Nationalitaten Politik nach Stalins Tod*. Munich: Ukrainische Freie Universitat, 1970.

LIPSET, HARRY. "The Status of National Minority Languages in Soviet Education." *Soviet Studies*. XIX, 2(October, 1967), 181-89.

PIPES, RICHARD. "Introduction: The Nationality Problem." *Handbook of Major Soviet Nationalities*. Edited by Zev Katz, Rosemarie Rogers, and Frederic Harned. New York: The Free Press, 1975. Pp. 1-5.

___ "'Solving' the Nationality Problem." *Problems of Communism*. XVI, 5(September-October, 1967), 125-31.

POOL, JONATHAN. "Developing the Soviet Turkic Tongues: The Language of the Politics of Language." *Slavic Review*. XXXV, No. 3(September, 1976).

POSPIELEVSKY, DMITRIY. "The Resurgence of Russian Nationalism in Samizdat." *Survey*. XIX, 1(Winter, 1973), 51-74.

RAKOWSKA-HARMSTONE, TERESA. "The Dialectics of Nationalism in the USSR." *Problems of Communism*. XXIII, 3(May-June, 1974), 1-22.

___ "The Dilemma of Nationalism in the Soviet Union." *The Soviet Union under Brezhnev and Kosygin: The Transition Years*. Edited by John W. Strong. New York: Van Nostrand, 1971. Pp. 115-34.

___ *Russia and Nationalism in Central Asia: The Case of Tadzhikistan*. Baltimore: Johns Hopkins University Press, 1970.

SHEREKH, Iu. "Prysmerk Marryzmu." *Novy dni* (Toronto). 6(June, 1950), 8-12.

SILVER, BRIAN D. *Ethnic Identity Change among Soviet Nationalities*. PhD Thesis. Department of Political Science. University of Wisconsin-Madison. 1972.

___ "Bilingualism and the Maintenance of the Mother Tongue in Soviet Central Asia." *Slavic Review*. XXXV, 3(September, 1976).

___ "Social Mobilization and the Russification of Soviet Nationalities." *American Political Science Review*. LXVIII, 1(March, 1974), 45-66.

SIMMONDS, GEORGE W., Editor. *Nationalism in the USSR and Eastern Europe in the Era of Brezhnev and Kosygin*. Detroit: University of Detroit Press, 1977.

SZPORLUK, ROMAN, Editor. *The Influence of East Europe and the Soviet West on the USSR*. New York: Praeger, 1976.

___ "The Nations of the USSR in 1970." *Survey*. XVII, 4(Autumn, 1971), 67-100.

TAAGEPERA, REIN. "National Differences within Soviet Demographic Trends." *Soviet Studies*. XX, 4(April, 1969), 478-89.

___ "The 1970 Census: Fusion or Crystallization of Nationalities?" *Soviet Studies*. XXIII, 2(October, 1971), 216-21.

TILLETT, LOWELL. *The Great Friendship: Soviet Historians on the Non-Russian Nationalities*. Chapel Hill: University of North Carolina Press, 1969.

D. The Ukraine

ARMSTRONG, JOHN A. "New Prospects for Analyzing the Evolution of Ukrainian Society." *Ukrainian Quarterly*. XXIX, 1(Spring, 1973), 349-57.

___ *The Soviet Bureaucratic Elite: A Case Study of the Ukrainian Apparatus*. New York: Praeger, 1959.

___ "The Soviet Intellectuals: Observations from Two Journeys." *Studies on the Soviet Union*. 1(1961), 30-33.

___ *Ukrainian Nationalism, 1939-1945*. Second Edition. New York: Columbia University Press, 1963.

BILINSKY, YAROSLAV. "Assimilation and Ethnic Assertiveness among Ukrainians of the Soviet Union." *Ethnic Minorities in the Soviet Union*. Edited by Erich Goldhagen. New York: Praeger, 1968. Pp. 147-84.

___ "The Incorporation of Western Ukraine and its Impact on Politics and Society in Soviet Ukraine." *The Influence of East Europe and the Soviet West on the USSR*. Edited by Roman Szporluk. New York: Praeger, 1976. Pp. 180-228.

___ "Mykola Skrypnyk and Petro Shelest: An Essay on the Persistance and Limits of Ukrainian National Communism." *Soviet Nationality Policies and Practices*. Edited by Jeremy R. Azrael. New York: Praeger, 1978. Pp. 105-43.

___ "Politics, Purge and Dissent in the Ukraine since the Fall of Shelest." *Nationalism and Human Rights: Processes of Modernization in the USSR*. Edited by Ihor Kamenetsky. Littleton, Colo: Libraries Unlimited, 1977. Pp. 168-85.

___ *The Second Soviet Republic: The Ukraine since World War II*. New Brunswick: Rutgers University Press, 1964.

"The Birth of Ukrainian Opposition Prose." Radio Liberty Daily Information Bulletin, August 24, 1962.

BOCIURKIW, BOHDAN R. "The Orthodox Church and the Soviet Regime in the Ukraine." *Canadian Slavonic Papers*. XIV (1972), 191-211.

___ "The Uniate Church in the Soviet Ukraine: A Case Study in Soviet Church Relations." *Canadian Slavonic Papers*. Vii (1965), 89-113.

BORYSENKO, V. "Ukrainian Opposition to the Soviet Regime." *Problems of the Peoples of the USSR*. 6(1960), 37-42.

CYZEVS'KYJ, DMYTRO. *A History of Ukrainian Literature*. Littleton, Colo: Ukrainian Academic Press, 1975.

DE VINCENZ, A. "Recent Ukrainian Writing." *Survey*. 46(January, 1963), 143-50.

DUEVEL, CHRISTIAN. "A Brezhnev Protege as Chief Editor of *Komunist Ukrainy*?" Radio Liberty Research Paper 343/72, November 29, 1972.

GITELMAN, ZVI. "The Social and Political Role of the Jews in Ukraine." *Ukraine in the Seventies*. Edited by Peter J. Potichnyj. Oakville, Ontario: Mosaic Press, 1975. Pp. 167-86.

HODNETT, GREY and PETER J. POTICHNYJ. *The Ukraine and the Czechoslovak Crisis*. Canberra: Australian National University, 1970.

HORAK, STEPHAN M. "Problems of Periodization and Terminology in Soviet Ukrainian Historiography." *Nationalities Papers*. III, 2(Fall, 1975), 5-24.

_____ "Soviet Historiography and the New Nationalities Policy, a Case Study: Belorussia and Ukraine." *Change and Adaptation in Soviet and East European Politics*. Edited by Jane P. Shapiro and Peter J. Potichnyj. New York: Praeger, 1976.

JONES, LESYA and LUBA PENDZEY. "Dissent in Ukraine: Bibliography." *Nationalities Papers*. Vi, 1(Spring, 1978), 64-70.

KHODOROVICH, TATIANA, Editor. *The Case of Leonid Pliushch*. Boulder, Colo: Westview Press, 1976.

KOLASKY, JOHN. *Education in Soviet Ukraine: A Study in Discrimination and Russification*. Toronto: Peter Martin Associates, Ltd., 1968.

_____ *Two Years in Soviet Ukraine*. Toronto: Peter Martin Associates, Ltd., 1970.

KOSHELIVETS, IVAN. "Khronika ukrainskogo soprotivleniia." *Kontinent*. 5(1975), 173-99.

_____ *Ukraina: 1956-1968*. Paris: Instytut Literacki, 1969.

LEWYTZKYJ, BORYS. *Die Sowjetukraine, 1944-1963*. Cologne and Berlin: Kiepenheuer und Witsch, 1964.

LUCKYJ, GEORGE S.N. "Polarity in Ukrainian Intellectual Dissent." *Canadian Slavonic Papers*. XIV (1972), 269-79.

_____ "The Ukrainian Literary Scene Today." *Slavic Review*. XXXI, 4(1972), 863-69.

LIBER, GEORGE and ANNA MOSTOVYCH. *Non-Conformity and Dissent in the Ukrainian SSR, 1955-1975: An Annotated Bibliography*. Cambridge, Mass: Harvard Ukrainian Research Institute, 1978.

NEKRASOV, VIKTOR. "V dome Turbinov." *Novyi mir*. 8(1967), 132-42.

PELENSKI, JAROSLAW. "Recent Ukrainian Writing." *Survey*. 59(April, 1966), 102-112.

_____ "Shelest and his Period in Soviet Ukraine (1963-1972): A Revival of Controlled Ukrainian Autonomism." *Ukraine in the Seventies*. Edited by Peter J. Potichnyj. Oakville, Ontario: Mosaic Press, 1975. Pp. 283-99.

PLYUSHCH, LEONID. *History's Carnival: A Dissident's Autobiography.* Edited, translated and with an Introduction by Marco Carynnyk. New York: Harcourt, Brace Jovanovich, 1979.

POSSONY, STEFAN T. "The Ukrainian-Jewish Problem: A Historical Retrospective." *Ukrainian Quarterly.* XXXI, 2(Summer, 1975), 139-51.

"Report of Delegation to Ukraine." *Viewpoint* (Organ of the Central Committee of the Communist Party of Canada). 1(January, 1968), 1-13.

RESHETAR, JOHN S. JR. "The Significance of the Soviet Tercentenary of the Pereyaslav Treaty." *Annals of the Ukrainian Academy of Arts and Sciences in the U.S.* IV, 3(Winter-Spring, 1955), 981-94.

___ *The Ukrainian Revolution, 1917-1920.* Princeton: Princeton University Press, 1952.

RUDNYCKYJ, JAROSLAW B. "The Ems Ukase of 1873 and the Problem of Linguicide." *Nationalities Papers.* IV, 2(Fall, 1976), 153-56.

RUDNYTSKY, IVAN L. "The Role of the Ukraine in Modern History." *Slavic Review.* XXII, 2(June, 1963), 199-216.

___ "The Role of the Ukraine in Modern Society." *The Development of the USSR: An Exchange of Views.* Edited by Donald W. Treadgold. Seattle: University of Washington Press, 1964. Pp. 211-28.

___ "The Soviet Ukraine in Historical Perspective." *Canadian Slavonic Papers.* XIV, 2(Summer, 1972), 235-50.

"Russification and Socialist Legality in the Dnepropetrovsk Area." Radio Free Europe Research Bulletin, March 10, 1969.

SAWCZUK, KONSTANTYN. *The Ukraine in the United Nations Organization: A Study in Soviet Foreign Policy, 1944-1950.* New York and London: Columbia University Press for East European Quarterly, 1975.

___ "Valentyn Moroz: A Voice of the Ukrainian National Renaissance." *Nationalities Papers.* I, 2(Summer, 1973), 1-9.

SZPORLUK, ROMAN. "The Ukraine and the Ukrainians." *Handbook of Major Soviet Nationalities.* Edited by Zev Katz, Rosemarie Rogers, and Frederic Harned. New York: The Free Press, 1975. Pp. 21-48.

"The State of Soviet Basic Sciences: An Unusual Criticism by Ukrainian Academicians." Radio Liberty Research Paper CRD 335/70, September 16, 1970.

SULLIVANT, ROBERT S. *Soviet Politics and the Ukraine, 1917-1957.* New York and London: Columbia University Press, 1962.

___ "The Ukrainians." *Problems of Communism.* XVI, 5(September-October, 1967), 46-54.

SZAMUELY, TIBOR. "The Resurgence of Ukrainian Nationalism." *The Reporter,* May 30, 1968, 16-17.

TILLETT, LOWELL. "Ukrainian Nationalism and the Fall of Shelest." *Slavic Review.* XXXIV, 4(December, 1975), 752-68.

"Ukrainian KGB Boss in Politburo." Radio Free Europe Research Paper No. 1900, October 8, 1973.

"Ukrainian Novel Raises a Storm." Radio Free Europe Research Bulletin, July 1, 1968.

232

"Ukrainian Writers Protest." Radio Free Europe Research Paper F-100, February 19, 1975.

"Vitaliy Shelest: Soviet Science on a Reform Course?" Radio Free Europe Research Paper 0749, n.d.

"Writers' Congress in the Ukraine." Radio Free Europe Research Paper 1043, June 16, 1971.

WYNAR, LUBOMYR T. "The Present State of Ukrainian Historiography: A Brief Overview." *Nationalities Papers.* VII, 1(Spring, 1979), 1-23.

E. *Other*

ALMOND, GABRIEL A. *The Appeals of Communism.* Princeton: Princeton University Press, 1954.

ARMSTRONG, JOHN A. *The European Administrative Elite.* Princeton: Princeton University Press, 1973.

BORKENAU, FRANZ. "Getting at the Facts behind the Soviet Facade." *Commentary.* 17(April, 1954), 393-400.

CONQUEST, ROBERT. *Power and Policy in the USSR: The Struggle for Stalin's Succession.* New York: Harper and Row, 1961.

DEWITT, NICHOLAS. *Education and Professional Employment in the USSR.* Washington, D.C: National Science Foundation, 1961.

FELDBRUGGE, F.J.M. *Samizdat and Political Dissent in the Soviet Union.* Leyden: A.W. Sijthoff, 1975.

MANN, GEORG. "Abuses of Soviet Psychiatry." *Dissent.* Winter, 1975, 90-92, 102.

MANN, THOMAS C. "Theories, Dogmas and Semantics of Communism." *Department of State Bulletin.* March 26, 1962, 500-509.

MEDVEDEV, ROY and ZHORES. *A Question of Madness.* New York and London: W.W. Norton, 1979.

PETROVICH, MICHAEL BORO. *The Emergence of Russian Panslavism, 1856-1870.* New York: Columbia University Press, 1956.

PLOSS, SIDNEY L. *Conflict and Decision Making in Soviet Russia: A Case Study of Agricultural Policy 1953-1963.* Princeton: Princeton University Press, 1965.

PYE, LUCIAN W. *Aspects of Political Development.* Boston: Little, Brown and Co., 1966.

___ "Identity and Political Culture." *Crises and Sequences in Political Development.* Edited by Leonard Binder and others. Princeton: Princeton University Press, 1971.

___ *Politics, Personality and Nation-Building.* New Haven: Yale University Press, 1962.

Reestr osuzhdennykh ili zaderzhannykh v bor'b'e za prava cheloveka v SSSR. Radio Liberty Research Handbook No. 78, February, 1971.

233

RIASANOVSKY, NICHOLAS. *Nicholas I and Official Nationality in Russia, 1825-1855*. Berkeley: University of California Press, 1969.

RUSH, MYRON. *The Rise of Khrushchev*. Washington, D.C: Public Affairs Press, 1956.

SKILLING, H. GORDON and FRANKLYN GRIFFITHS. *Interest Groups in Soviet Politics*. Princeton: Princeton University Press, 1971.

VAN DEN BERGHE, PIERRE L. "Dialectic and Functionalism: Toward a Theoretical Synthesis." *American Sociological Review*. XXVIII (October, 1963).

WING, J.K. "Psychiatry in the USSR." *British Medical Journal*. I, 5905 (Saturday, March 9, 1974), 433-36.

INDEX

240

147; and modernization, 12; and
Plyushch, 168-169; and prole-
tarian internationalism, 89; pro-
tests against, 114,146-147,188;
resistance to, 7; statistical
analysis by B. Silver, 14-15;
Ukrainians and Belorussians
scheduled for, 11; West Ukrain-
ians spared before WW II, 5
Rusyn, Ivan, 187
Ruthenia, 5n
Ryls'kyi, Maksym, 81,83,96,144
Sadoul, Georges, 84n
Sakharov, Andrei, 162
Samizdat, 24,53. *See also* Samvydav
Samvydav, 6,34,93,95,96,103,112,113,
115,116,138,139,140,146,150,154,
156-158,162,162,165,170,172,185-
187,194-196,212
Sapir, Edward, 29n
Sarcasm, 33
Savchenko, V.V., 158-159
Schools, 134-139
Science (and language), 149-151
Secessionists, 154-155,159-160,
177,186,188
Seleznenko, Leonid, 198
Self-immolation, 187-188
Semantic space, 29,31,33
Semykina, Liudmyla, 111
Separatists: *See* Secessionists
Serbenchuk, Rostislav, 157
Sevruk, Halyna, 111
Shapiro, Jane P., 91n
Shcherban, Hanna, 193-194
Shcherbitsky, Volodymyr, 1n,139,214
Shelest, Petro: and Dadenkov, 142,
143; protection of dissidents,
206,214-215; and intellectuals,
147,197; and Nikitchenko, 189;
purge of, 75,197,206,213-216
Shelest, Vitalii P., 150n
Sheptyts'kyi, Metropolitan, 202
Shestydesiatnyki, 99,100,113
Shevchenko, Taras: opposed to anti-
Semitism, 165n; birthday cele-
brations, 113; May 22 celebrations,
113-114; removal of monuments to,
116; said to owe debt to Russians,
86; stained glass window incident,
111-112; as a symbol, 4,110-116;
Symonenko compared to, 100;
Washington, D.C. monument to, 112
Shovkovoi, Ia.V., 160
Shums'kyi, Oleksandr, 41

Shumuk, Danylo, 198
Shumylo, Mykyta, 144
Sign (in communications), 28
Silver, Brian, 7n,14-17,131,132
Siniavsky, Andrei, 193,195
Siryy klyn, 205
Skaba, A.D., 93,99,147
Skilling, H. Gordon, 21n
Skoropadsky, Paul, 4
Skrypnyk, Mykola, 94,170
Smolych, Iu., 196
Sobor, 158
Socialist Realism, 79,80,85
Socialization, 32,216
Social mobilization, 11-15,184
Sokul's'kyi, Ivan, 158-159
Solzhenitsyn, Aleksandr, 45
Sorel, Georges, 26
Sorenko, V.F., 71n
Soroka, Mykhaylo, 157n
Sosiura, Volodymyr, 81,105,106
Stalin, Josef: Art in era of,
80; criticized, 47-48; def-
inition of nation, 56-57,67;
on language, 124-125; on the
nation, 39,56-57,67; purges of
Ukrainian intellectuals, 82;
preference for Russification,
41; toast to Russian people,
43
Stalinism, revival of, 159
Status (function of symbols),
123,132,133-134,143
Stenchuk, Bohdan, 167,196
Strokata, Nina, 166n,169,170
Stus, Vasylyi, 198,199
Sullivant, Robert S., 47n
Sumy *oblast*, 128,129,177,179
"Surzhyk" (hodgepodge), 140
Suslov, Mikhail, 3n
Sverdlin, M.A., 68,72
Sverstiuk, Ievhen, 80,97,101,
108-109,117,198
Svitlychnyi, Ivan, 80n,81,97,
101,193-195,198
Symbolic action, 153,173,185,
190,212
Symbols: ambiguity of, 95; and
arts, 78-79; and communication
theory, 28,29; condensation
and referential, 29; and
education, 133; and language,
122,149; and metaphoric trans-
fer, 31,32; of national identity, 109; and nationalities

Made in the USA
Las Vegas, NV
07 November 2024

11121529R20142